695
495

IMPERIAL DEMOCRACY

*the text of this book is printed
on 100% recycled paper*

IMPERIAL DEMOCRACY

THE EMERGENCE
OF AMERICA
AS A GREAT POWER

Ernest R. May

HARPER TORCHBOOKS

Harper & Row, Publishers

New York, Hagerstown, San Francisco, London

For John and LaRee Caughey

CONTENTS

CONTENTS

IMPERIAL DEMOCRACY

PART ONE

TUMULT IN THE WEST

"If one takes this point of view, it follows that . . . the status of a great power . . . is conceivable only under a monarchical form of government. . . . In this connection neither the North American union nor France serves as an example. The former, while certainly a republic, is not a great power; the latter is a great power but not a republic."

> *Phillip Zorn, "Zur Frage von der 'besten Staatsform,' "* Deutsche Revue, *II (May, 1878)*

In 1835, when the United States had just under fifteen million people and the least of the European powers had nearly thirty million, the French traveler and political analyst, Alexis de Tocqueville, wrote of America and Russia: "Their starting-point is different, and their courses are not the same; yet each of them seems marked out by the will of Heaven to sway the destinies of half the globe." Just before the Civil War, when America's population equalled that of the greater European states, a German philosopher asserted that in the long run only three political combinations were conceivable—"Russia and Europe against North America, North America and Europe against Russia, or Russia with North America against Europe." Just after that conflict, a French writer warned that if Europe did not unite, "the continent will fall under the yoke of an Asiatic despotism; England will disappear, smothered between Russia and America, and there will be but two powers on earth and it will be partitioned into light and darkness."[1]

But these were the words of prophets, not practical men. Until the late 1880's the United States was dealt with as a second-rate power. When in 1880 the Sultan of Turkey decided to pare expenses, he closed his diplomatic missions in Sweden, Belgium, the Netherlands, and the United States. Legations in these minor countries were expendable. A German envoy in the United States volunteered to take a cut in pay if he could be transferred to Madrid. The Russian legation in Washington had no minister at all for nearly two years.[2]

In 1881 when the British government named a new envoy to the United States, it chose Sir Lionel Sackville-West. He was the son of an earl and the brother-in-law of both the Duke of Bedford and the Conservative statesman, Lord Derby. Otherwise his sole distinction came from having been the constant lover of a celebrated Spanish dancer and the father of her six illegitimate children. In posting him to Washington, the government evidently felt that it was putting him where he could cause the least embarrassment and do the least harm.

It would be less wounding to American pride if this undervaluation could be blamed on European nearsightedness, perhaps a residual suspicion that the world really did end just beyond the Azores. This was not the case.

Two decades before, European governments had shown marked awareness of America's existence. During the Civil War, statesmen in all major capitals debated whether advantage could be pried from intervention. Afterward, the Russian government thought of possibly making a friend of the United States. They were concerned about the Turkish straits, where British diplomacy denied Russia access to the sea, and reasoned that if they could make Britain believe that an attack by the United States on Canada would coincide with an assault on the Turkish straits, the British government might become more willing to negotiate a compromise. Consequently, an American official who visited Russia in 1866 was welcomed with such fanfare as nowadays greets rulers of wavering neutralist states. Semiofficial Russian newspapers predicted that Russia and the United States would eventually partition Turkey. The Tsar's court endeavored to give the impression that the two nations had or would soon have a secret alliance.

At about the same time, the Prussian prime minister, Count Bismarck, was contemplating (to use no stronger term) a war with France, and sought to prevent Britain's meddling. It occurred to him as to the Tsar that the English might be made to worry about Canada. He instructed Prussian diplomats, "We must lay the greatest stress on excellent relations with Washington." He did not deny a rumor that Prussia was seeking a naval alliance with the United States.

English statesmen themselves soon recognized that the United States could prove an annoyance. Luckily, they saw a way of neutralizing it—they had only to make concessions at the expense of Canada. Many Englishmen expected Canada to become independent in any case. A formidable number of "Little Englanders" believed the homeland would be better off without it. The government, reconciling itself readily to a sacrifice of Canadian interests, offered to arbitrate outstanding issues. In 1871 a bargain was struck. Russia meanwhile obtained a new straits convention and Prussia won her war. Britain had made it harder for them to use America as a diplomatic lever a second time.[3]

Partly as a result, European interest in the United States afterward flagged. Statesmen thought of it again occasionally as a possible chess piece in the game of world politics. They were never oblivious to its existence. But neither did they conceive of it, any more than of the Netherlands or Sweden, as a nation that might become a player of power in its own right.

Before long, all this changed. When Sackville-West in 1888 blundered into endorsing an American Presidential candidate and was recalled, the British government did not replace him with another remittance man. Instead, it sent over Sir Julian Pauncefote, the Permanent Under-Secretary in the Foreign Office. In 1892 all the powers except Austria-Hungary raised their legations in Washington to embassies. In 1898 the Russian government appointed as its ambassador Count Arturo Cassini, who had just distinguished himself in a critical negotiation with China. The French sent Jules Cambon, previously Governor General of Morocco and concededly one of the three or four ablest men in the diplomatic service. In 1902 Austria-Hungary at last joined the other powers in making its envoy an ambassador.

By the early twentieth century, some European statesmen looked upon America as a very formidable power indeed. A German diplomat in America concluded that his country would have to struggle "even to achieve . . . coexistence." Another in Vienna wrote Berlin that he feared a "war for survival," and on the margin of his dispatch, Kaiser Wilhelm II noted that he entirely shared this foreboding. After a meeting between the Kaiser and Tsar Nicholas II in 1903, the Tsar's chief of staff wrote, "England disturbs [the Kaiser] and America even more. The Tsar observed that America alarms him too." For the President of the French Republic the United States was not only the chief but the sole menace to the peace and prosperity of Europe. A former foreign minister of France asked, "Are we to be confronted by an American peril . . . before which the Old World is to go down to irretrievable defeat?"[4] The words "American peril" often appeared in German parliamentary and press debates. They cropped up in Austrian and Italian and, less frequently, in Russian writings. W. T. Stead, an English journalist very partial to the United States, declared in his book *The Americanization of the World* that Britons had only two options: to federate with the United States or be "reduced to the status of an English-speaking Belgium." In 1905 a distinguished and judicious French historian, Henri Hauser, wrote, "One hears nothing spoken of in the press, at meetings, in parliament, except the American peril."[5]

In the early 1880's diplomats and writers rarely spoke of the United States in the same breath with the six recognized great powers— Britain, France, Germany, Austria-Hungary, Russia, and Italy. By the beginning of the twentieth century they included it almost invariably.

This was more than a change in form, for the substance and the appearance of power are not separate things. Between wars judgments are entirely subjective; war is the only objective test. Except when war provides proof, no nation enjoys respect and prestige as a great power except insofar as it is recognized as such by others. And since a nation ordinarily defends its interests with its prestige rather than its arms, the United States, in a very real sense, became a great power when it came to be thought one.

The change occurred partly because of America's sheer physical growth. It covered a larger area than any European state except Russia. It had developed the most extensive network of roads and railroads in the world, and its population had increased at a startling rate—it had fewer people in the 1850's than either France or England; by the 1880's it led every industrialized nation but Russia. American farm and factory output had grown and by the 1880's the United States led the world in production of wheat. A decade later it led or almost led in coal, iron, and steel. The total of capital and deposits in banks exceeded that in any other state, and the total value of American manufactures equaled that of any two competitors. Michael G. Mulhall's ponderous *Dictionary of Statistics* of 1892 showed the United States overtaking or surpassing Europe by nearly every measurable standard.

But it was more than economic growth that foreign observers saw. Though the Jefferson administration had made a display of strength against the Barbary pirates, neither in the war of 1812 nor later had America added to its reputation. In the Civil War it did prove that it could raise and officer armies of millions and that it could create a formidable fleet. But afterward, not only had it demobilized the army but, more important, scrapped well over half its warships and allowed the rest to rot. The government made no effort to keep abreast of other nations in construction of ironclad steam vessels. "Never was such a hapless, broken-down, tattered, forlorn apology for a navy as that possessed by the United States,"[6] said an English naval publication in 1876. Even the merchant fleet declined and deteriorated. The United States could threaten a land invasion of Canada to be sure. But even that menace remained unreal so long as it lacked means of preventing Britain from retaliating by destroying American ocean commerce and bombarding American ports. Statistics on resources and production remained irrelevant until the United States possessed some evident capacity to assert that it had interests beyond its shores and that it was prepared to protect them.

Beginning in the early 1880's Congress authorized new coast fortifications and the construction of big-gun steel warships. By 1890 the projected fleet consisted of fifteen cruisers and six battleships—three of them designed to be the most heavily armored and gunned vessels in the world; their completion was expected to bring the United States' navy abreast of Germany's and ahead of Austria-Hungary's and Italy's.

With this rising might grew an ebullient, almost reckless mood. Little about it was new. Since winning independence, Americans had periodically become aggressive and quarrelsome. In the 1840's they had gone to war with Mexico and threatened war with England on the curiously amoral ground that it was the country's "manifest destiny" to hold the Pacific coast. Some had then talked of robbing Spain of Cuba, others of intervening in Europe to support republican revolutions in Hungary and elsewhere. Responsible members of the Senate asserted that the United States could defeat any coalition of European powers. When the Civil War was about to break out, Secretary of State Seward urged President Lincoln to avert it by provoking a conflict with Europe. The Union-Confederate struggle and subsequent problems of reconstruction merely brought a lull in this chauvinism.

The mid-1880's merely saw numerous Americans talking again of "manifest destiny." John Fiske, a leading popularizer of Darwinian biology, spoke on "manifest destiny" in more than thirty American cities and towns. The Anglo-Saxon race was increasing and enriching itself so rapidly that other nations would ultimately be forced to imitate America's example, he said; he spoke of the United States "stretching from pole to pole," but he did not plead for new conquests. On the contrary, he envisioned "the whole of mankind . . . [constituting] politically one huge federation,—each little group managing its local affairs in entire independence, but relegating all questions of international interest to the decision of one central tribunal supported by the public opinion of the entire human race."

The Reverend Josiah Strong, a Congregationalist minister in Cincinnati, a leader in the American Home Missionary Society and the American Evangelical Alliance, declared that America was taking from England the scepter for the Anglo-Saxon race. Americans would have to recognize, he said, that "the Anglo-Saxon is divinely commissioned to be, in a peculiar sense, his brother's keeper" and that the race had "an instinct or genius for colonizing." "This race of unequaled energy . . . , having developed peculiarly aggressive traits calculated to impress its institutions upon mankind, will spread itself over the earth . . . down upon Mexico, down upon Central and South America, out upon the islands of the sea, over upon Africa and beyond."

Neither Fiske nor Strong was much heard or read outside the United States. The American who did reach a large foreign audience was by European standards more conventional and realistic. He was Captain Alfred Thayer Mahan, president of the Naval War College; his *Influence of Sea Power on History, 1660–1783,* published in 1890, was an immediate success in England. After the German Kaiser read it, he had it translated and placed in all German naval libraries. Before long, Mahan's name was as well known in Europe as in the United States.[7]

The captain had analyzed the concept of national power using

England as a model and concluding that the basic elements of power were trade—including open markets and protected markets like colonies—the ships to carry trade, and military and naval strength to protect shipping and trade in time of war. Those abroad who read Mahan's writings could reasonably infer that his government might soon use its resources and its growing fleet in open competition with the older powers of Europe.

At the time, American businessmen were pushing aggressively into foreign markets. The Standard Oil Company organized itself to battle French, Russian, and Dutch interests in the Near East and Asia, and in these regions it employed the same ruthless tactics that had given it a virtual monopoly at home. American copper interests sometimes fought, sometimes combined with the powerful French copper syndicate. American steelmakers competed with English, German, and French concerns in the world market and even in Europe itself. Business associations in the United States increasingly discussed and passed resolutions in favor of expanded foreign commerce. Consuls spoke up more and more vigorously in behalf of American firms, and even the most staid and respectable of American business journals, the *Commercial and Financial Chronicle,* declared (as the Marxists also did) that American industry produced too much and had to find foreign markets if the country were to escape economic collapse.[8]

The behavior of the American government had become increasingly bellicose. Despite the arbitrations of 1871, irritation persisted in American-Canadian relations. Fishermen from New England and Nova Scotia got in one another's way. Incidents occurred. Each time, newspapers and members of Congress indulged in more and more violent talk. When the British government helped to arrange a new treaty composing these and other issues, a Republican-controlled Senate not only rejected the agreement but condemned it as dishonorable. The Democratic President responded by asking Congress, as an alternative, to declare economic war against Canada. Congress did not do so, and the administration reached a *modus vivendi* with the dominion and Britain.

Less than a year later, in 1889, Americans inveighed just as fiercely against another great power—Germany. The United States, along with Britain and Germany, possessed certain ill-defined rights in the far-off Samoan islands, and the Germans seemed ready to oust the other two. Congressmen came to their feet immediately and one declared for many others that America would maintain its rights "even if we have to do it at the cannon's mouth." Editors called upon the government to stand firm. The crisis passed only when the German government declared that it had no intention of displacing the others. The German minister in Washington concluded regretfully that America was becoming "overconfident . . . and yielding to the temptation to measure its exuberant strength against a European enemy." Bismarck himself said in a letter to his minister to Washington that America might soon become a menace.[9]

In the winter of 1891–1892 the American government almost precipitated a war with Chile, a nation believed to have indistinct but close ties with Britain. The only issue was a point of honor. Chile had been slow to apologize for the deaths of some American seamen in a riot. War was averted only by a hasty and humble Chilean plea for forgiveness and an offer of reparation, and the American press and Congress applauded President Benjamin Harrison for his bellicose punctilio. Said Senator Shoup of Iowa, "The American Republic will stand no more nonsense from any power, big or little."

Neither population and production statistics nor the naval building program nor writings such as Fiske's, Strong's, and Mahan's nor the government's threats of war against Britain, Germany, and Chile served in themselves to convince the world that America had become a great power. They merely alerted some foreign observers to future possibilities.

If the United States followed Fiske, Strong, and their like, who preached a form of Gladstonism, it would concern itself with moral causes. If it followed Mahan, on the other hand, who advocated doctrines much like those of contemporary European imperialists, it would enter into rivalry with other states for markets, coaling stations, and colonies. The editors and politicians who agitated issues with Canada seemed to argue for yet another alternative—a resumption of the century-old contest with England and the conquest of new territory on the North American continent. And both in the press

and in Congress many still contended that the best course for the
United States remained isolationism—deliberate avoidance of any
crusade, competition, or conflict.

It was by no means clear that the American government and public
were really interested in foreign affairs. Press reports in Europe made
it clear that the 1888 crisis over Canadian fisheries was incidental,
and not unconnected with that year's Presidential campaign—by re-
jecting the treaty, Republicans in the Senate hoped to win Irish votes
away from the Democrats; by proposing an economic war, the President expected to win them back. The Presidential message did not
in the least alarm the London *Times,* which observed calmly that the
message "dished the Republican party."

And in the naval building program itself, some representatives and
senators admitted that their primary concern was the prosperity of
naval yards and shipbuilding and ship-repairing firms in their states
or districts. Others were mainly interested in disposing of surplus
revenue—protective tariffs brought in far more money than the government could use and if new ways of spending it were not devised,
tariffs would have to be lowered, and to a majority in both parties
that was unthinkable. Naval building would also help to sustain and
stabilize the important and volatile steel industry. More than one
congressman called attention to the fact that armaments expenditures
in Europe gave European steel firms competitive advantages.

In April, 1892, the Naval Affairs Committee recommended that
the House authorize one additional battleship. Its cost would be just
enough to absorb the coming year's anticipated surplus. A representative from coastal Maine introduced an amendment to enlarge
this program and the amendment lost, 135–62. The minority consisted almost exclusively of members from districts with navy yards,
iron mines, steel mills, or a section of the Pennsylvania Railroad
system, a line whose profits and losses varied directly with the prosperity of the steel industry.

With regard to the Samoan crisis, European observers felt less
certain. Bismarck concluded that it had all been gotten up by "chauvinistic adventurers, unscrupulous speculators, and fanatics." He and
other Europeans were not altogether sure that it did not augur future

trouble, but they suspected that its origins might have been in American domestic politics and that it gave no sure indication of the nation's future foreign policy.[10]

Whether or not real convictions about foreign policy would emerge remained to be seen. In the nation could be heard eloquent voices attempting to stir up a crusading spirit, or an imperialist movement, or a revival of aggressive Anglophobia. Others appealed for the maintenance of isolationism. The choice among them was yet to be made.

On January 28, 1893, Americans read in their evening newspapers a bulletin from Honolulu, Hawaii. Two weeks earlier, said the news report, a group of American residents had overthrown a young native queen and formed a provisional government. Marines from the U.S.S. *Boston* had landed at the request of the American minister in order to protect lives and property. Violence had ended quickly. The rebels were in full control and were said to have enthusiastic support from the populace. Most noteworthy of all, they had announced the intention of asking the United States to annex the islands.

The proposal was not so startling as it might have seemed. Most of the large landowners in the islands were Americans or the children of Americans. So were the men who grew, refined, and shipped the sugar that was Hawaii's principal export. So were many of the kingdom's Protestant clergymen, lawyers, bankers, factors, and other leading citizens. Though numbering only two thousand in a total population of around ninety thousand, these Americans had already given the islands an appearance of a colony. As far back as 1854 they had almost persuaded a native monarch to request annexation by the United States. Subsequently they had seen to it that the dynasty secured tariff reciprocity and ceded a naval station, and they had awakened enough interest in the United States so that Presidents from Tyler on periodically warned European powers to keep hands off Hawaii. Thus the new proposal was that the United States annex a state that seemed already Americanized and virtually a protectorate.

Even so, the proposition came unexpectedly, and neither politicians nor journalists knew quite what to make of it. Editorials and comments from Capitol Hill were at first noncommittal. The molders of public opinion seemed waiting to learn what mold the public wanted.

San Francisco's leading Republican and Democratic dailies, the *Chronicle* and *Examiner,* declared that Hawaii should certainly be taken and the *Chronicle* on January 29 reported a poll of local businessmen overwhelmingly of this view. Some businessmen expected

profit. Claus Spreckels, for example, who owned Hawaii's largest
sugar plantation, could hope to obtain the two-cent-a-pound bounty
that the United States government paid domestic sugar producers.
He could also anticipate more freight for his Oceanic Steamship line
and more and cheaper raw sugar for his California Sugar Refinery
Company.[1]

But most of the San Francisco businessmen were probably not reacting to the scent of profit. The fight against the Southern Pacific Railroad and its subsidiary, the Pacific Mail Steamship Company, was
a matter of principle to them. They genuinely believed that the annexation of Hawaii would increase Pacific Ocean trade, benefit the
city and region, and, above all, help undermine the power of this
monopoly. The Chamber of Commerce, the Board of Trade, the
Produce Exchange, and the Manufacturers Association all produced
resolutions calling for annexation as a patriotic duty. The business
community of San Francisco thus became the first identifiable imperialist group in the country.[2]

Businessmen elsewhere on the Pacific coast followed their lead.
San Diego was virtually the property of the Spreckels family; at least
a few merchants, bankers, warehouse owners, real estate dealers,
and contractors in Los Angeles, Fresno, and San Jose were allies in
the battle against the railroad; and the Chambers of Commerce of
Portland and Seattle had long co-operated with that of San Francisco
in pressing for national policies advantageous to the West. It was not
long before businessmen all along the coast were reported as favoring annexation.[3]

Nor was the growing movement confined to members of exchanges
and commercial clubs. Protestant clergymen delivered sermons pointing out that some of the Hawaiian revolutionaries were sons of missionaries, contending that the revolution symbolized aspirations for
freedom and good government that had grown out of the teachings
of missionaries, and saying that American annexation would enlarge
the empire of Christianity. Writers in newspaper Sunday supplements
extolled the resources and beauties of the islands. Individuals who
had traveled there spoke to their friends. Ed Dekum of Portland, for
one, carried about his collection of Honolulu souvenirs, hoping that

the sudden surge of public interest might create a market for them.

There was some dissent. Newspapers which were thought to speak for the Southern Pacific urged caution. The editor of San Francisco's best known magazine, the *Overland Monthly,* raised a moral objection. "It may be all right about Hawaii; but the look of the thing is questionable. . . . The record of our country . . . has never been creditable in its dealings with any weaker people—Indians, Negroes, Chinese, or Spanish-Americans,—and it would be an inexplicable pity to add another stain. There could be no gain that could compensate for it." Nevertheless, the California state assembly and the Oregon senate passed proannexation resolutions by voice votes, and the Oregon lower house approved one 48–8. The San Francisco *Examiner* declared, "California wants Hawaii annexed," and writers in eastern journals seemed justified in saying that the west coast as a whole favored taking the islands.

Reports from San Francisco and other Pacific coast cities emboldened men in other parts of the country. Army and navy officers in Washington spoke out on the strategic advantages of annexation. So did the editor of *The Army and Navy Journal.* Eastern sponsors of the projected Nicaragua canal added their voices, as did others like Representative Charles S. Randall of Massachusetts, who saw profit for the East as well; he was quoted in the Boston *Herald* of February 1 as saying, "We have vast business interests in our commerce with Hawaii, and much of it is done from my own city of New Bedford."

Especially zealous were foreign mission enthusiasts. The nondenominational New York *Independent* boasted that the Hawaiian islands had been "taken possession of and annexed religiously . . . two generations ago" by the American Board of Commissioners for Foreign Missions, formerly a joint Congregationalist-Presbyterian organization and now exclusively Congregationalist. Former missionaries wrote to Washington and to New York newspapers advocating immediate annexation. Religious weeklies followed suit, almost before any secular journals did. Some of their editorials were remarkably materialistic. The *Independent* said: "The ripe apple falls into our hands, and we should be very foolish to throw it away. . . . The possession of Hawaii gives perfect control of the ocean route across the Pacific. . . . We need its tropical products, and we need its harbors. . . . This will give us a dominating influence among all the islands of Oceanica [*sic*]."

But no national movement was developing. No chamber of commerce or board of trade except on the west coast took up the cause. The Pennsylvania legislature passed a resolution, as the California and Oregon assemblies had, but to the state's newspapers it was a casual affair. Monday morning accounts of Sunday sermons in Boston, New York, Philadelphia, Chicago, and St. Louis suggested that the topic came up only in pulpits occupied by former missionaries or ministers with friends or relatives in the islands.

Yet judges of public opinion came to believe that the people would approve of annexation. At first newspaper editors who came out for it felt obliged to allege that England would seize the islands if the United States did not. But by the end of February, *Public Opinion* could cite many editorials that spoke of positive advantage to America, of prospective commercial and strategic benefits. Even in Louisiana, where sugar interests feared Hawaiian competition, the New Orleans *Times-Democrat* conceded that nine-tenths of the people probably wanted the islands.

Not everyone greeted the idea of annexation with enthusiasm. A few editors suspected a "sugar conspiracy," in which Spreckels and the eastern sugar trust were co-operating. Some were put off by the threat of trouble with Britain—the Minneapolis *Times* warned of "a war with England over our right to confer citizenship upon the leprous descendants of the Sandwich Island cannibals." Others were disturbed, as was the Boston *Herald,* by the thought that Hawaiians belonged to an inferior and unassimilable race. The prim New York *Evening Post* and many other mugwump journals worried lest colonies require additions to the civil list and hence cancel out hard-won victories for civil service reform. Carl Schurz, the recognized elder statesman among German-American Republicans, announced that he opposed annexation, and German-American papers across the country generally followed his lead. Except for the New York *Herald,* which had a special correspondent sending in regular reports from Honolulu, newspapers opposing annexation were little more zealous

than those favoring it. The editor of the Chicago *Herald* explained to
one of the Hawaiian commissioners that he dared not be too vehe-
ment because he knew a majority of his readers favored annexation.
Practically no newspaper took up anti-imperialism as a cause.[4] The
relative absence of fire tended to confirm the impression that the government, if it chose, could make Hawaii a colony. All at once, it was
revealed to politicians and other would-be opinion leaders that at
least a segment of the public might be ready to embrace imperialism.

James G. Blaine, who had been Secretary of State between 1889
and 1892, may have anticipated the possible public reaction and
been prepared to capitalize on it. He was warned of the approaching
revolution in Hawaii and the likelihood that a revolutionary government would appeal for annexation. It occurred to him even then that
annexation could be represented as necessary to prevent English conquest and that Hawaii might be treated as belonging to an "American
system." He wrote to President Benjamin Harrison in 1891, "I think
there are only three places that are of value enough to be taken, that
are not continental. One is Hawaii and the others are Cuba and
Porto Rico."[5] Though he was too canny to put himself on record
as favoring either assistance to the revolutionaries or acceptance of
their proposal when and if it came, he did anticipate that the American minister in Honolulu would promote the revolution, and he made
no attempt to restrain or discourage him. But ill-health had forced
him out of the State Department, and he died in 1893 almost at the
moment when the Hawaiian revolution occurred.

President Harrison, who had been a hard-working and successful
Indiana lawyer, had gone to the Senate and thence to the White
House without being distracted by any national issues except tariff
and currency. He had assumed the Presidency without preconceptions about foreign policy. Blaine seemed to him untrustworthy and
exasperatingly unsystematic, so he looked for advice to a fellow lawyer, Secretary of the Navy Benjamin F. Tracy. Ultimately, the advice he sought probably came from the president of the Naval War
College, Captain Mahan. As a result, Harrison had been inspired to
investigate possible coaling stations in the Caribbean and off the
coasts of South America and had become convinced of "the necessity

of maintaining and increasing our hold and influence in the Sandwich Islands." But, as he wrote Blaine in September, 1891, "just how far we can go and what action we can take . . . I do not yet see."[6]

In 1892, defeated for re-election and, at sixty, unlikely ever to be renominated, Harrison may have decided to gamble on the public's reaction. Newspaper stories of November and December, 1892, that seemed officially inspired, foretold a Hawaiian revolution. An officer newly appointed to command the Pacific squadron testified that before leaving Washington in December, 1892, he was told, "the wishes of the Government have changed. They will be very glad to annex Hawaii."[7] It may be that the President intended to act, hoping for public acquiescence.

In any case, it was the public's response that enabled him to proceed. During the first few days after news came of the proposal for annexation, he remained silent. Not even the best informed correspondents, those of the New York *Tribune* and the Washington *Post,* knew his attitude. Three days had passed before they could even report rumors that some members of the cabinet favored annexation and that the President probably did. Not until February 2, following a conference between Harrison and a delegation of congressmen, did they know that the administration would send an annexation treaty to the Senate. Perhaps the President actually did not even make up his mind until February 7. One of the Hawaiian commissioners was told that the decisive cabinet meeting took place on that day.[8] Only after the public had shown where it was willing to go did the executive branch step forth to lead.

Congressmen seemed to sense popular opinion more quickly, but the same delay occurred on Capitol Hill. Two to seven days elapsed before senators or representatives committed themselves. It was January 31 before the Boston *Journal* could report that Massachusetts' new senator, Henry Cabot Lodge, favored annexation. The sharp-voiced little "scholar in politics" had told a *Journal* reporter that the time had come for "decisive action"; Hawaii stood like "a Gibraltar in the pathway of American commerce," and the United States needed the islands to secure naval control of the Pacific. He spoke as an imperialist.

So did Senator Frye. A small, fragile man with heavy-lidded eyes, trailing mustaches, and a fiery tongue, he had devoted himself to the interests of Maine shipbuilders and declaimed often and loudly on the need for naval expansion and enlarged ocean commerce. But it was still a new departure for him to say, as he did on January 31, that the United States should take Hawaii for the sake of commercial and naval supremacy in the Pacific.

It was slightly less of a departure for the senior Democrat on the Foreign Relations Committee. John Tyler Morgan of Alabama was nearly seventy, old enough to have been an elector in 1860 and to have cast his vote proudly for the proslavery ticket of Breckinridge and Lane, been a brigadier general in the Confederate army, and his state's senator ever since the compromises of 1876; old enough, too, perhaps to have vivid memories of pre-Civil War southern expansionism. He had made himself a leading spokesman for the Nicaragua canal, and his enthusiasm had thrown him into contact with naval officers who were promoters of and stockholders in the canal company and probably believers in the doctrines of Mahan. He had advocated naval building and bolder foreign policies as auxiliary to the great enterprise with which he had identified himself. Since Hawaii or other colonies in the Pacific seemed likely to improve prospects for a canal, he found it easy to conclude that they were desirable. Newspapers soon reported that he, rather than any Republican, would be the chief advocate of the administration's projected treaty.[9]

Others adopted the Hawaiian cause with almost equal alacrity. Some, like the shrewd and cantankerous William E. Chandler of New Hampshire, had been ardent navalists. Before coming to the Senate, Chandler had been Secretary of the Navy under President Arthur; he was senior Republican on the Naval Affairs Committee; and he had probably been in touch with more of Mahan's disciples than any other member of Congress. Others, like Senator Orville H. Platt of Connecticut, had no such background but became converts to imperialism just as easily. Platt told a Boston *Herald* reporter, "A policy of isolation did well enough when we were an embryo nation, but today things are different. . . . We are sixty-five million of people, the most advanced and powerful on earth, and regard to our future welfare demands an abandonment of the doctrines of isolation." According to journalists covering Capitol Hill, a clear majority in both houses had come to favor annexation.

Some Democrats, sensing the public's apparent mood, may have been reluctant to see annexation accomplished by Republicans. But about the first of February, Don M. Dickinson of Michigan, who had been Postmaster General in the previous Democratic cabinet, came to Washington and declared that Grover Cleveland, the incoming President, wanted Hawaii and also wanted Canada and the West Indies. Thomas F. Bayard, who had been Secretary of State in Cleveland's earlier government, said Hawaii should become America's. Some members of the party remained suspicious, but as the administration prepared to send a treaty to the Senate, reporters judged that it would be ratified by more than the necessary two-thirds vote.

Cleveland himself then intervened. John G. Carlisle, the Treasury Secretary-designate, brought to Washington an apparently authentic message in which the incoming President asked that the Senate defer action and give him time to study the matter. Since Cleveland did not even intimate that he would oppose annexation and since he would soon have patronage with which to reward the co-operative, both Democrats and Republicans acquiesced.

The new President decided that scrutiny of the question would require some time. He was no doubt aware that some of his more important newspaper supporters, such as the New York *Evening Post, Herald,* and *World,* the Boston *Herald,* and the Chicago *Herald,* were among those who opposed annexation. He was fully conscious that Schurz and mugwump German-Americans, who had also backed him, held a similar view, for Schurz wrote him long letters on the subject. Perhaps, as a cautious politician, he wished to discover whether annexationism or anti-annexationism would prove the more enduring and intense. Perhaps he was troubled by reports that the revolutionary government in Honolulu lacked popular support, that it had come to power only because assisted by the American minister and United States marines, and that annexation was not desired by the natives. Perhaps, however, his mind, like his body, was simply ponderous and slow.

He withdrew the treaty and sent a commissioner to Hawaii to survey opinion among the native population. After a time, he proclaimed an end to the provisional protectorate which the Harrison administration had established. Cleveland's acts troubled some of the more zealous annexationists. Many thought, with the *Independent,* "it is well to make plain . . . to the most skeptical that annexation is desired by the people of Hawaii." It was still possible, furthermore, that Cleveland would eventually call for approval of the treaty. He had written Schurz that he did not think "annexation in all circumstances and at any time unwise," and well-informed journalists continued to report that he simply remained undecided.[10]

Eventually, Cleveland did make up his mind. The agent whom he had sent to Hawaii was James H. Blount, a Georgian and former chairman of the Foreign Affairs Committee, just defeated for reelection after twenty years' service in the House. Since Blount had openly opposed annexation while still in Congress, a favorable report from him would have carried great weight both with the administration and with anti-annexationists outside. But Blount did not report favorably. On the contrary, he charged Harrison's minister and the revolutionaries with conspiracy, and he produced much evidence showing the native population opposed to the revolutionary government and to annexation.

Cleveland's new Secretary of State, Walter Q. Gresham, found the facts in this report shocking. Though something of a poseur, who greeted visiting diplomats in shirtsleeves and galluses and entertained them with his marksmanship on the spittoon, he had been a distinguished judge and had been considered for Presidential nomination by three parties, the Republican, and, after his refusal to support Blaine, the Populist and Democratic; he had profound belief in American goodness and the soundness of American traditions. After reading Blount's report, he drafted a Presidential statement declaring not only that annexation should be renounced but that justice called for redressing the wrong and restoring the deposed Queen.[11]

Cleveland felt compelled to accept at least the first of Gresham's recommendations. The second was discussed among the cabinet.

The Attorney General, Richard Olney, remarked that justice, as the Secretary of State defined it, might require the use of force and that the President could hardly ask Congress for permission to overthrow an Anglo-Saxon republic and put in its place a Polynesian monarchy. Cleveland settled for a mere apology to the Queen, accompanied by a quiet effort to persuade the revolutionaries that they should restore her.[12]

A severe economic depression had settled over the country. Price declines, unemployment, lockouts, strikes, business failures, and bankruptcies had become the currency of conversation. On the west coast, Spreckels concluded that Hawaiian annexation would not be beneficial after all. By increasing the supply, it would drive sugar prices still farther down. Some religious leaders also showed second thought. "Stealing an island from a poor old colored woman is not a great national achievement; it belongs to the cheat-your-washer-woman style of diplomacy," said the editor of the *Christian Enquirer*.

In late November, after most odd-year state and municipal elections had taken place, newspapers learned of Gresham's recommendation that the Queen be restored. Instead of denying this report or explaining it away, the President allowed Gresham's memorandum to be published. He thus offered hostile congressmen and newspaper editors a perfect target. "To attempt to overthrow a righteously organized republic, and put in its place a discredited monarchy, is an outrage beyond words to describe," sputtered the Blaine-oriented *Independent*.

The President serenely announced that he would give out additional information later. On November 20, after newspaper editors and other commentators had girded themselves to support or oppose a recommendation for restoring Queen Liliuokalani, Cleveland published Blount's report. On the one hand, the former Republican minister to Hawaii denied its charges; representatives of the Hawaiian provisional government condemned it as biased and ill-informed; missionaries in Honolulu defended the innocence and good intentions of the islands' new rulers. On the other hand, as Cleveland may have anticipated, Blount's evidence unsettled many who had earlier thought annexation unquestionably the right policy. Even the New York *Tribune,* which prided itself on being the authentic voice of Republicanism, admitted on November 23 that the facts reported by Blount might preclude annexation. The *Tribune's* editorials continued to harp on the contemplated restoration of the Queen.

The blossoming imperialist movement temporarily lost its force. From the beginning, it had been moralistic as well as imperialist. While leaders like Lodge, Frye, and Morgan spoke of security, advantage, and gain, many editors and most clergymen used words like "duty," "destiny," and "mission." Albert Shaw, a snappish young journalist editing the recently founded and immensely popular *American Review of Reviews,* exemplified this dualism. He wrote in 1893 of America's past failure to seek colonies as "a policy more selfish and timid than it was broad and enlightened." After annexation had come to seem unlikely, he described the great powers as "watching . . . with a somewhat puzzled and bewildered but also a very alert and fixed attention" and urged Congress to exhibit a "sense of the national dignity and the national destiny."

Like Shaw, many Americans could not decide whether to think of issues in foreign relations as matters of business or of conscience. When Cleveland raised moral questions, conviction faltered among those who judged by conceptions of right and wrong. In a special message delivered four weeks after publication of the Blount report, the President did not call for restoring the Queen or even for renouncing annexation. He merely invited Congress to submit "any legislative plan . . . which is consistent with American honor, integrity, and morality." But senators who tried to revive sentiment for annexation failed. By February, 1894, Secretary Gresham wrote with relief, "The sentiment in favor of annexation . . . [is] obviously on the wane." The project was as dead as Grant's Santo Domingo scheme, the Buffalo *Courier* said.[13]

In fact, it was only quiescent, and in a few years was to be pulsing more vigorously than ever. An imperialist movement had come into being and was not to be demolished by one setback. Its leaders had discerned that public opinion could be captured for an imperialist cause, if only that cause could be clothed in the rhetoric of piety. They were stubborn, willful men, whose one common characteristic was self-esteem beyond that ordinarily found even in the upper house of Congress. They would not relent without further effort to win the nation to their new faith.

III · THE HEATHEN'S KEEPER

During 1894 and 1895 European powers combined to exert their influence both in Asia and the Near East, after war broke out between China and Japan and massacres erupted in the Armenian provinces of Turkey. Many Americans wondered if the United States, too, should not exhibit concern over these faraway happenings.

Americans had been interested in the Orient ever since ships sailed to China from Boston in the 1780's. Things Eastern had enjoyed great vogue in America in the early nineteenth century, and though the fad died out when the trade dwindled and Christian missions sent back dispiriting reports, sinophilism lingered on, as in New England's determined opposition to far western demands for exclusion of Chinese immigrants. In the 1880's industrialists had begun again to think of Asia's millions as potential customers. Japan, forcing the pace of her industrial revolution, imported more and more from America. Missionaries, too, reported encouraging new progress; some even voiced hope that Japan and China might become Christian nations.

During the Sino-Japanese war American newspapers gave the conflict front-page coverage and several journals sent special correspondents abroad. Yet President Cleveland's offer of mediation was turned down by the Japanese and was criticized by Republican newspapers as gratuitous meddling. To Democratic journals the gesture symbolized America's impartiality and disinterestedness. When Russia, France, and Germany demanded that Japan abate her territorial demands, virtually no editor cried alarm. Though the British press thundered about possible perils to trade, Americans seemed detached and untroubled on the whole.

But American concern grew after the war, when antiforeign riots broke out in central China; and when American mission property was looted and burned, probably with encouragement from the Chinese government, enraged newspapers demanded China's punishment. The clamor was short-lived, however, for the Chinese government presently yielded, demoted the offending provincial viceroy, and executed some of the rioters.

Now a committee of the Congregationalist American Board of Commissioners for Foreign Missions described China as "the field for our next great forward movement." "It is the opinion of many who are endowed with the Christian clairvoyant vision that the opportunity in China is the supreme one of missions." A pastoral letter from the Episcopal bishops of the United States termed the antiforeign riots "a crisis in missionary work" and declared, "the moral of this calamity is more, not less, men in the field and larger offerings by the Church to sustain them."[1] The potential Chinese market seemed as tantalizing to American businessmen as the ground for conversion to the missionaries. After China's defeat, hopes rose and the New York banking houses of J. P. Morgan and Co. and Charles R. Flint and Co. sought, though unsuccessfully, the contract for China's war indemnity loan, and an American China Development Company was formed to obtain railroad concessions. The Massachusetts Board of Trade began to think of sending a commission to investigate the Chinese market, and the New York *Journal of Commerce*'s editorials speculated on the vast opportunities in China.

Interest in investment in China grew. The China Development Company had been formed by some of the nation's richest bankers and industrialists, but its original capital was only one million dollars. Gradually, its sponsors became more optimistic. By the end of 1895 its agents were proposing vast schemes for railway and mining development in Manchuria. When frustrated in this effort, they opened negotiations for a railroad concession in southern China. Representatives of other companies, like the Baldwin Locomotive Works, appeared in Peking to seek contracts. All of these endeavors indicated that some businessmen had become willing to bet on China's future.[2]

When reports arrived on a treaty in which China had granted Russia extraordinary economic privileges, Americans joined the British in grave warnings that Britain could not tolerate such an upset in the Asian balance of power, and a few endorsed the suggestion of an alliance among Britain, Japan, and the United States. Now the conservative and pacific Boston *Herald* declared, "we are justified in going, if need be, quite a way in defence of our international trade."[3]

In another corner of the world, further events aroused the American people about troubles beyond their own shores. In the autumn of 1894, some ten thousand Armenians had been massacred without intervention or condemnation from England, Russia, or Russia's ally, France. The Ottoman government, after long delay, permitted an international committee "to inquire into the criminal conduct of Armenian brigands," and late in the spring of 1895 the Porte endorsed some innocuous reforms for the Armenian provinces. In the meantime the toll of dead rose to at least thirty-seven thousand.

In England, an Anglo-Armenian Committee and the Evangelical Alliance denounced the British government's inaction and sought to rekindle the passions that Gladstone had fired at the time of the Bulgarian massacres eighteen years earlier. These bodies had counterparts. The Armenian Hentchak Revolutionary Federation already had branches in the United States. After the massacres, other Armenian-Americans became aroused. In Boston an Armenian-American committee of five hundred was formed. Public meetings were held in Malden, Andover, and other Massachusetts towns, and resolutions were forwarded to Congress.[4]

In Boston, M. H. Gulesian and Hagop Bogigian, two well-to-do rug dealers, persuaded Julia Ward Howe to add Armenia to the long list of her causes. It was not long before other habitual humanitarians, like Robert Treat Paine and William Lloyd Garrison, Jr., had been enlisted. Their United Friends of Armenia began to collect donations. Meetings and rallies were held in New York, in Hartford and Chicago, and later in many other cities of the northern United States.[5]

Congregationalists with more than a hundred missionaries in the Ottoman Empire ministering to seventy thousand proselytes and pupils and holding six million dollars' worth of property, began to speak out in their magazines, sermons, and lectures on "the unspeakable Turk" and the sufferings of Armenians. When the church's National Council met in October, a special committee on the Armenian massacres accused the Turks of "inhuman atrocities" and called for United States "moral support" to any combination of the powers. Still another committee, including dignitaries like Governor Nelson Dingley of Maine and the Reverend Dr. Washington Gladden, dealt with "the Duty of Our Government to Protect Missionaries in Foreign Lands." The Reverend Dr. Cyrus Hamlin, former President of Roberts College in Constantinople, who knew the Hentchaks to be at least as much at fault as the Turks, served as a restraining influence in the American Board and presumably in the National Council as well, but tempers were high and one board committee declared support for "any action . . . looking to sympathy with the sufferers, and especially towards the protection by the forces at command of our own government of American citizens engaged in missionary work abroad."⁶

By midsummer, violence was edging toward Syria, where Presbyterian missions centered, and the church's journals grew more attentive to the Near East and more emphatic in denunciation of the Turk. In mid-November mission stations and schools at Harput and Marash were looted and burned. The destruction was far worse than that in central China earlier in the year; the evidence of official complicity was at least as grave. Episcopalian ministers joined Congregationalists and Presbyterians in excitement and alarm, and in New York, Boston, and Chicago, churchmen and business leaders co-operated with the Armenians and others to organize rallies, which were often as full of fervor as an evangelical Protestant revival meeting. The audience responded to appeals with heartfelt amens. The Baptist Pastors Association of New York City urged that the United States join others in teaching Turkey a lesson. The Evangelical Alliance said the American government should act "promptly and effectively," and a Baptist clergyman in Chicago declared, "Columbia . . . has a voice that can be heard across the sea, and loud as apocalyptic thunders let it be heard again." The "Christian general," the deeply pious Oliver Otis Howard, demanded that the navy be sent at once to the Mediterranean.⁷

As massacres continued and Europe still failed to act, religious journals like the *Independent,* the *Congregationalist,* the Baptist Philadelphia *Commonwealth,* and even the Methodist *Western Christian Advocate* began to say Turkish rule would have to be overthrown by force. When it was rumored that the Sultan meant to expel American missionaries, Abbott's *Outlook* declared it the duty of the United States to protect them "and, if necessary, to spend its last dollar and call out its last soldier for that purpose." The Constantinople riots of August, in which five to six thousand Armenians were slain, brought denominational demands that the navy be sent at once to punish the Turk.

In the gubernatorial campaign of 1895 in Massachusetts Republicans assailed the Cleveland administration for its failure to act in Armenia. Representative Elijah A. Morse from Canton said guns should fire if one American citizen were hurt. Republicans in Congress, immediately after the elections, were reported ready to resolve in favor of naval action, and Senator George Frisbie Hoar introduced a resolution calling upon the President to protect missionaries. Both houses of Congress passed resolutions urging the executive to act.

As clergymen and editors of religious journals became more bellicose, however, support fell away. Mrs. Howe noted a decline in relief contributions. The Congressional resolutions drew criticism from scholars, from some business organs, and from conservative newspapers like the New York *Herald* and the Indianapolis *Journal*. Though clamor continued, Armenia came increasingly to seem nothing but the hobby of a few ministers and editors.[8] Little more was heard of it on the hustings.

The episode had nevertheless showed that Americans could become aroused over events far from home. That clergymen, laymen, and politicians could talk even momentarily of action in the eastern Mediterranean—as they did of action in China—indicated how far consciousness of America's new might had spread.

Some of those who joined most ardently in the Armenian agitation, like Hoar and Robert Treat Paine, were subsequently to become anti-imperialists. Yet in 1895 they and others were ready even for a foreign alliance if it would advance the cause of Christianity. The Hawaiian episode had indicated that popular support might be rallied for imperialism. The furor over Armenia demonstrated that public opinion could be mobilized also for a moral crusade.

PART TWO

LISTEN, COUSIN!

"*It has been stated . . . that Mr. Canning was the author of what is known as the Monroe Doctrine. The Monroe Doctrine is as old as humanity. God was the author of the Monroe Doctrine.*"

> *Roger Q. Mills (Democrat of Texas) in the United States Senate, March 24, 1896*

"*My doctrine is briefly this, that you cannot build up in any desirable form an influence or popularity among the governing classes of another country. . . . The benefits of today are forgotten tomorrow. The popularity of today disappears. . . . 'Influence' disappears; territory remains.*"

> *The Marquis of Salisbury to Sir Henry Drummond Wolff, July 17, 1899 (Salisbury Papers)*

Still, in America of 1895, stronger than either the Hawaiian imperialist movement or the Gladstonism excited by the disturbances in China and Armenia seemed to be the traditional hostility toward England. At the beginning of that year, the Nicaraguan government arrested a British consul and Britain retaliated by seizing the customs house at Corinto. The Nicaragua canal lobby cried alarums and the San Francisco Chamber of Commerce called on the government to act. Britain promptly withdrew the landing party, and the tempest might have subsided, if it had not been for the American Presidential nominating conventions, only a year away. Some Republicans and many Democrats called for free coinage of silver and identified England with the gold standard. President Cleveland himself staunchly supported the gold standard and so silver agitators also seized gleefully on the Nicaragua episode. Several Democratic state conventions assailed Cleveland's "pro-British" foreign policies. In Massachusetts, Republicans condemned the administration's inaction on the Corinto seizure. In New York a Republican-dominated state assembly called for resolute and effective opposition to Britain in Nicaragua by an overwhelming vote. The New York Democratic convention voted a platform with even stronger language, to the applause of Manhattan's leading German-American paper, the *Staatszeitung,* ordinarily an opponent of any kind of chauvinism.[1]

Politicians all over the country took note of these signs. On June 1, 1895, the New York *Tribune* quoted the chairman of the Republican National Committee as saying that the chief issue in state and local elections should be the administration's weak foreign policy. In Ohio the Democratic gubernatorial nominee called for intervention in a boundary dispute between Britain's Guiana colony and the republic of Venezuela, and one of his managers wrote Cleveland's Secretary of State pleading for "a little 'Jingo' " to help him out. Another, from Texas, advised the President: "Turn this Venezuela question up or down, North, South, East or West, and it is a 'winner.' "[2]

President Cleveland believed devoutly in the gold standard, but he was alarmed to find that so many southern and western Democrats had come out for free silver, while newspaper straw polls showed sentiment veering toward this view even in Boston and Chicago. During his previous Presidency, when Republicans charged him with weakness in the fisheries dispute, he had counterattacked by calling on Congress to declare economic war against the British Empire—a gesture which Blaine, his opponent, as well as the European press, had judged a play for Irish votes. But in the Corinto affair, his hands had been tied. He had been warned in advance of Britain's intention to seize the customs house, and advised her against it. London agreed, but said it could not get orders to the expedition's commander in time.[3] In the circumstances, Cleveland could not protest; he could only wait for the English force to withdraw. He could, however, raise another issue, and it may well have occurred to him that by precipitating a crisis with Britain he might outflank his domestic enemies.

Britain and Venezuela were at odds over the ill-defined Venezuelan-Guianan boundary, and there were potent arguments for American intervention—the disputed zone had produced the largest nugget of gold ever discovered (509 ounces), and by helping Venezuela confirm her title, the United States might obtain enough new gold to ease the shortage of specie that had given rise to demands for silver coinage. More important, by courting trouble now, the United States might escape worse trouble later. Newspapers and diplomatic pouches were full of warnings that European powers eyed Latin America covetously. Britain had seemed obliging enough in the Corinto affair, but Cleveland may have suspected that all was not as she said. His Secretary of State thought Lord Kimberley, the British Foreign Secretary and the most inoffensive of men, "jingoistic." Both Venezuela and Brazil accused the English of refusing to settle territorial disputes, and Brazil laid the same charge against France. There were quotations in the *Literary Digest* from French colonialist journals advocating settlement by force, and from German imperialist periodicals marking out potential colonies in the Western Hemisphere.[4] Cleveland could have seen merit in reminding Europe that the United States would not be indifferent to territorial changes in the Western Hemisphere.

Enthusiasts in America, England, and France were pressing their governments for treaties that would substitute arbitration for war. Congress, the English House of Commons, and the French Assembly had all endorsed such treaties in principle. But Assistant Secretary of State Alvey A. Adee warned that arbitration could be dangerous if the European signatories had not first acknowledged America's special position in the Western Hemisphere—the United States might find itself forced to arbitrate about British or French seizure of a new colony.[5]

If Cleveland had been Blaine or even Harrison, any one of these considerations might have decided him. But he was of a different type. In the first place, he did not have their imagination. In his rise from sheriff and mayor of Buffalo to the governorship of New York and the Presidency, Cleveland showed many admirable traits: courage, loyalty, stubbornness, good humor, and diligence. In the White House his lights burned late at night, and hardly a post office candidate or pension applicant received his deserts until after careful, personal study of the case by the President. But by 1895 Cleveland had passed through nearly two administrations and eleven years of party leadership without ever inventing anything. He had not initiated a single new departure in national or Democratic policy. He had distinguished himself by battling against the protective tariff, bimetallism, and other social and economic heresies, and in foreign policy he had been, on the whole, cautious, conservative, and strikingly unimaginative.

In the second place, Cleveland lacked the cynicism of Blaine and Harrison. His maneuver in 1888 had not been as Blaine judged it. Cleveland had called for an economic war only after the Senate rejected a treaty that would have composed American-Canadian differences. His real demand was that Republican senators fish or cut bait, and he knew they would back down. While the message served electioneering purposes, it also rebuked irresponsible partisans for playing politics with national interests. Early in 1895, he wrote one of his closest friends, "Do you know . . . that I have never been so sure that there is a high and unseen Power that guides and sustains the weak efforts of man? I feel it all the time and somehow I have come to expect that I shall find the path of duty and right, if I honestly and patriotically go on my way. I would be afraid to allow a bad, low motive to find lodgment in my mind, for I know I should then stumble and go astray."[6] Even if the thought occurred to him, it is hard to believe that he would in any circumstances have trumped up a war scare.

As the Venezuelan-British Guianan dispute was presented to him, however, it seemed more than a mere opportunity for display of cunning. His papers, his public messages, and his later book, *Presidential Problems,* show that he studied with some care the briefs and pleadings sent to him from Caracas.

The evidence he saw led him to believe that the British government had drawn its own boundary line without consulting the Venezuelans. When Britain acquired her part of Guiana from the Dutch, the northwestern frontier remained undefined. In the early 1840's, Sir Robert Schomburgk made a survey and suggested a boundary line. Though Venezuela insisted that she was entitled to much more, the British colonial government in Georgetown gradually extended jurisdiction up to and even beyond the Schomburgk line and, after the discovery of gold, issued deeds and began building roads out to the mining camps, all in seeming disregard of Venezuela's claims. Though Caracas proposed time and again that the question be referred to arbitration by a third party, the British government consistently refused.

No information reaching the President showed the inner history. After an envoy in Caracas had filed some years earlier a candid report, which had been accidentally published, forcing an American government apology to Venezuela, subsequent dispatches became, to say the least, circumspect. The most up-to-date reports available to Cleveland were those of President Harrison's minister, William Lindsay Scruggs, now Venezuela's lobbyist in Washington and author of a pamphlet, "British Aggressions in Venezuela or the Monroe Doctrine on Trial."

Cleveland did not know that the regime in Caracas demanded arbitration not because its sense of justice was outraged but because it could do nothing else. He was unaware that the long, corrupt rule of Antonio Guzmán Blanco had left Venezuela in such straits that her roads had disintegrated, her schools had been closed, and her administration had resorted to selling postage stamps at a discount. For a decade her government had refused even to resume diplomatic relations with Britain, largely because of unpaid debts to British nationals about which Venezuela could not afford to negotiate. The only bargaining counter she possessed was her boundary claim. And statesmen in Caracas could not afford to trade that away, for the eastern provinces were nearly in rebellion and would certainly revolt if deprived of all hope for Guiana gold. The Venezuelan government could only give up the claim, if at all, upon the demand of an international tribunal. Cleveland did not realize that Venezuela asked for arbitration because she dared not negotiate directly with London, nor did he know that she insisted on arbitration only by the United States or Spain, believing that either would be biased in her favor and give a verdict yielding some undeserved profit.[7]

The President was almost equally ignorant of Britain's side. He knew only that London had rejected Venezuela's appeals and disregarded American advice in favor of arbitration. He could infer, quite rightly, that British statesmen viewed a quarrel involving their colony, a Latin American nation, and a boundary over a thousand miles from the Rio Grande as no business of Washington's. But he was not told of their feeling that it would be bad precedent to arbitrate one trumpery case lest every other neighbor of the Empire invent a claim and insist on taking it to court. Nor was he informed of the Foreign Office's fear that neither the United States nor Spain would be impartial in arbitrating. So far as the information put before him showed, Britain was simply ignoring the just claim of a poor, weak American state.

For all his native caution and inertia, Cleveland could be moved by such a case. His message against the annexation of Hawaii had not been a brief against imperialism so much as an indictment of the methods used, and some of its phrases suggested attitudes he brought to consideration of the Venezuelan case. He had spoken, for example, of "right and justice" as determinants of policy, referring to "the mission and character of our Government and the behavior which the conscience of our people demands of their public servants." He had declared at the time:

The law of nations is founded upon reason and justice, and the rules of conduct governing individual relations between citizens or subjects of a civilized state are equally applicable as between enlightened nations. The considerations that international law is without a court for its enforcement and that obedience to its commands practically depends upon good faith instead of upon the mandate of a superior tribunal only give additional sanction to the law itself and brand any deliberate infraction of it not merely as a wrong, but as a disgrace.

From his standpoint, these rigorous standards must have seemed at least as applicable to Britain in Guiana.

The President believed, moreover, that he had a right and duty to interest himself in the Guiana-Venezuela dispute. During his first administration he had written to London of the "responsibility that rests upon the United States in relation to the South American Republics." In an oblique reference to Monroe's pronouncement, he had said: "The doctrines we announced two generations ago . . . have lost none of their force or importance in the progress of time."[8]

Cleveland thought the Venezuelans were being robbed of their rightful lands. He felt strongly that international law should be observed by all nations, great and small. He believed himself entitled by the interests and traditional policy of the United States to speak up for judicial settlement of the dispute. Since he and his predecessors had recommended and urged arbitration without success he saw reason for speaking with fresh sharpness and force.

His Secretary of State in an 1894 letter to London merely repeated the recommendation of arbitration and urged Britain to renew diplomatic relations with Venezuela. The ambassador in London predicted early collapse for Lord Rosebery's Liberal government and advised postponing further representations until after an election. Cleveland asked Secretary Gresham to draw up a formal note, but Gresham fell ill with pneumonia and died before he could complete a draft. Gresham's widow says that the note on which her husband was working bore no resemblance to an ultimatum, but still there is evidence that Cleveland may already have made up his mind to press the issue to such a point.[9]

In his annual message for 1894, the President had urged Congress to interest itself in the Venezuela boundary question. Early in 1895 Representative Leonidas F. Livingston of Georgia introduced a resolution asking that "friendly arbitration be most earnestly recommended to both the parties in interest." His resolution was reported out by the Foreign Affairs Committee, on which friends of the President had a clear majority. On the floor it was pressed by the committee chairman, James B. McCreary of Kentucky, usually viewed as a Presidential spokesman. The only opposition came from Republicans. The implication is that Cleveland, who tended toward a narrow construction of Presidential power, welcomed this resolution as authority to go farther than he had in the past.

About the time when the resolution passed, the Secretary of State sent a new message to London, warning plainly that this authority might be used, and describing the British position on the boundary issue as "contradictory and palpably unjust." He added: "If Great Britain undertakes to maintain her present position on that question, we will be obliged, in view of the almost uniform attitude and policy of our government, to call a halt." These stern words were not Gresham's own, for in private letters he described himself as resisting Venezuelan entreaties and relying as much as possible on British good judgment and good faith.[10] The harsher language was probably the President's.

Late in April, 1895, Cleveland talked at the White House with a friend, and shortly thereafter his friend made a speech denouncing British imperialism, especially on the Venezuela frontier, words widely read as jingoistic, hostile to the pacific spirit of the administration, and probably irritating to Cleveland.[11] They may in fact have echoed the President's own thoughts.

Certainly, when Cleveland selected a successor for Gresham, he chose a man who could be counted on for boldness and aggressiveness —Attorney General Richard Olney. Olney was more than bold in his behavior—political as well as personal. During the Pullman strike in 1894, he had advised a court injunction and the calling out of troops to break the strike; at home in Boston Olney in a rage had banished his daughter from his house, refusing to see her again, a threat he kept though he lived in the same city with her for thirty years. By naming Olney Secretary of State, Cleveland virtually made ready to force a crisis with Great Britain.[12]

Olney went to work at once on the note Gresham had begun. He brooded over the relevant papers in his summer home at Falmouth, Massachusetts, and by early July had completed a draft. Some of it came as a surprise to the President, as suggested by the tone of Cleveland's acknowledgment: "It's the best thing of the kind I have ever read and it leads to a conclusion that one cannot escape if he tries—that is if there is anything of the Monroe Doctrine at all. You show there is a great deal of that and place it I think on better and more defensible ground than any of your predecessors—or mine." The President said he had "a little more softened verbiage" to suggest, but it is impossible to tell from the surviving drafts what his changes were.[13]

The final note opened with a bold restatement of the Monroe doctrine. It proclaimed the doctrine part of American public law and went on to say: "That distance and three thousand miles of intervening ocean make any permanent political union between an European and an American state unnatural and inexpedient will hardly be denied. . . . To-day the United States is practically sovereign on this continent, and its fiat is law upon the subjects to which it confines its interposition." Addressed to Britain, the mistress of Canada, these unnecessarily offensive words probably came from Olney's tactless pen. But the principle thus aggressively stated was no more than what Cleveland had said eight years before—that the Monroe doctrine entitled the United States to intervene between Britain and Venezuela.

The critical element in the note was not its reassertion and elaboration of this principle, but its demand that Britain submit the whole dispute to arbitration. The key sentences were:

It seems . . . quite impossible that this position of Great Britain should be assented to by the United States, or that, if such position be adhered to with the result of enlarging the bounds of British Guiana, it should not be regarded as amounting, in substance, to an invasion and conquest of Venezuelan territory.

In these circumstances, the duty of the President appears to him unmistakable and imperative. . . . [N]ot to protest and give warning that the transaction will be regarded as injurious to the interests of the people of the United States as well as oppressive in itself would be to ignore an established policy with which the honor and welfare of this country are closely identified.

If Britain refused arbitration, the question would be submitted to Congress, where the constitutional power to declare war lay. Though the phrases may have been Olney's, it was the President who had decided what Britain should be told.

Both Cleveland and Olney undoubtedly recognized the seriousness of the step they had taken. Their note was written for eventual publication. Indeed, its own text made it plain that the President hoped to submit it to Congress along with Britain's reply when he delivered his annual message in December, 1895. At that time there would be only two alternatives. If Britain had given in, the President could announce the fact and, however restrainedly, crow over America's triumph. If not, he would have to say so and carry out or at least intensify the threat he had made. The note demanded that Britain either humiliate herself or prepare for war.

Both Cleveland and Olney seem to have felt confident that Britain would back down. Whenever either made reference to the note, it was with an insouciance that would have been impossible otherwise. The President observed calmly to a friend about Venezuela: "In due time it will be found that the Administration has not been asleep." When Britain seemed likely not to reply in time for the opening of Congress, Olney cabled London, asking the American ambassador to urge the government, "in the interests of the good relations of the two countries," to avoid an apparent discourtesy. He could hardly have been troubled by such a matter of etiquette if he anticipated a defiant note from London.[14] Neither expected the British reply to be what it was— a categorical denial that the Monroe doctrine applied to the case and a refusal of unconditional arbitration.

The President seemed more ready than his Secretary of State to accept the implicit British challenge. Olney prepared several drafts of a message to accompany the documents when they were presented to Congress. All stressed the narrow issue of the boundary rather than the applicability of the Monroe doctrine, and all contained loopholes for a diplomatic settlement. Cleveland accepted one broad suggestion made by his Secretary of State. Instead of a dramatic demand for Congressional action, he decided merely to announce that the United States would investigate and determine for itself what the Venezuelan-Guianan boundary should be. He rejected Olney's description of what was to follow this investigation. The Secretary's draft ran:

When such report is made and accepted it will then be incumbent upon the Government to communicate to Great Britain the boundary line thus ascertained and to give notice that any appropriation of territory or exercise of jurisdiction by Great Britain beyond said line (except with the consent of Venezuela) will be regarded by this Government as willful aggression upon rights and interests which this Government is bound to protect and defend and will be dealt with accordingly.

Cleveland's words were more curt and more threatening:

When such report is made and accepted it will in my opinion be the duty of the United States to resist by every means in its power as a willful aggression upon its rights and interests the appropriation by Great Britain of any lands or the exercise of any governmental jurisdiction over any territory which after investigation we have determined of right belongs to Venezuela.

In this, as in no other known case, the President sharpened rather than softened a text prepared by Olney.[15]

The message which Cleveland delivered to Congress on December 17, 1895, plainly a challenge to Britain, declared, in effect, that the Western Hemisphere was America's sphere of interest. It threatened Britain with war if she refused to acknowledge American supremacy there. In part an outgrowth of domestic politics, in larger part a product of Cleveland's conscience, the message was not meant to proclaim America's new might. But it was predicated on strength. By implication it warned Britain and the world of the emergence of a new power.

Once at a breakfast party Lord Salisbury had asked his host in a whisper the name of the man next to him, only to learn that it was a member of his cabinet. But absent-mindedness did not prevent him from also having acumen, discernment, and sagacity. He was probably the ablest diplomatist in public life anywhere in the world, and he headed the most talented government that England had had for a generation.

His shrew-tongued Colonial Secretary, Joseph Chamberlain, despite his monocle and the habitual orchid in his coat lapel, was a political tactician with few equals in imagination and energy. He knew the United States at first hand, had spent the summer of 1888 in Washington negotiating a fisheries treaty, had married an American, had made innumerable speeches referring to conditions in the United States, and on occasion had preached the importance of Anglo-American moral solidarity. Neither he nor Salisbury had any excuse for failing to see the implications of Olney's challenging note to Britain.

Yet Salisbury and Chamberlain went on, much as if that document had never reached them. To the American ambassador Salisbury "expressed regret, and surprise that it had been considered necessary to present so far reaching and important a principle and such wide and profound policies of international action, in relation to a subject so comparatively small." He said the result might be "a long and difficult discussion and much controversy." In due time he had the American note sent to the Colonial Office for Chamberlain's comments. When the summer recess was over and the crown's law officers returned to duty, he referred it to them, asking for an answer to Olney's contentions about the scope of the Monroe doctrine. When it was suggested that Britain might protest Venezuela's granting of concessions in the disputed zone, Salisbury ruled against doing so, commenting that such a protest might cause controversy with the United States. Otherwise he seemed wholly unaffected.

Meanwhile, officials in the Colonial Office dealt with Venezuelan issues as if they had no bearing on Anglo-American relations. Despite the State Department's repeated representations, Cleveland's explicit mention of the boundary dispute in his 1894 annual message, and the Congressional resolution that followed, they calmly discussed using force to drive the Venezuelans out. A police outpost had been set up on the Uruan River, at the limit of the British claim; Venezuelans had then raided it and taken some prisoners. In late August, several weeks after the arrival of Olney's note, the Colonial Office recommended an ultimatum, threatening military and naval action if the Venezuelans did not make prompt reparations for this incident. Putting the draft ultimatum on Salisbury's desk, the Foreign Office's Assistant Under Secretary remarked that Americans might view it as an indirect but impolite answer to themselves. Salisbury nevertheless approved it, suggesting only that another copy of the Olney note be sent to Chamberlain. He seemed to leave the entire subject of relations with Venezuela to the Colonial Minister.[1]

And Chamberlain appeared, if anything, more unmoved than his chief. Just before Salisbury sent him the first copy of the American note, he wrote the Prime Minister urging not only an ultimatum on the Uruan incident but also the forcible expulsion of any Venezuelans found beyond the Schomburgk line. It might be worthwhile, he said, to arbitrate about territory beyond that line, partly for the sake of securing Venezuela's admission that territory within it was indisputably British.

Conceiving Guiana to be potentially a new Transvaal, Chamberlain had already begun writing the governor of the colony, urging more vigorous efforts to develop its gold and other resources. He directed that roads be built into the disputed territory, partly to this end, partly to that of improving frontier policing. On the Olney note, his comments were caustic and pointed. On September 11, 1895, he sent Salisbury a memorandum on the frontier dispute and a summary of the British case:

In Mr. Chamberlain's opinion it is essential that the reply should emphatically repudiate this attempt to apply the Monroe doctrine to the question of the Venezuela boundary, and should place in strong relief the fact that Great Britain is an American Power with a territorial area greater than the United States themselves, and with a title acquired prior to the independence of the United States. Merely from the point of view of the Canadian Dominion, Mr. Chamberlain attaches the first importance to this repudiation.

Immediately after penning these haughty words, Chamberlain asked the Prime Minister's permission to order the forcible expulsion of Venezuelans found in the disputed zone, and soon was insisting successfully on the dispatch of an ultimatum with regard to the Uruan incident. He replaced the Governor General in Guiana with a man of more force and independence. He acted as if the opinions of the President of the United States were entitled to little or no consideration.

Chamberlain's views ruled the cabinet. In what appears to have been a brief if not perfunctory session that body approved two separate notes to the United States. One declared that the Monroe doctrine had no standing in British eyes and no application whatever to the dispute with Venezuela. The other, based on the Colonial Office memorandum, attacked the Venezuelan claims as baseless and rejected arbitration of them. When the Prime Minister reported to the Queen, he almost failed to mention that the cabinet had approved the documents. Neither he nor Chamberlain appeared to regard either as especially important, let alone as likely to bring on a crisis.[2]

More astonishing still, both ministers seemed less concerned with the United States than they had before. Barely two weeks later, Chamberlain made a proposal to Salisbury that, if carried out, would have contravened the Monroe doctrine no matter how narrowly it was interpreted. He suggested that Britain ask France to give up her fishing rights on the Newfoundland banks and give Britain Dahomey and its hinterland in Africa; in return England would cede her Dominica, a small island in the Caribbean, lying between Guadeloupe and Martinique. With assurance from the Admiralty that the island had no strategic value, Chamberlain pressed the suggestion until Salisbury accepted it.

The Prime Minister proposed this exchange to the French only two days after Cleveland's forceful message to Congress! France's ambassador remarked wryly that he thought values in the American real estate market were somewhat down, and the Prime Minister agreed to report to Chamberlain French disinterest in the proposal.[3] The whole episode displayed in startling relief how little attention the British government paid to the United States before the 1895 crisis.

That Chamberlain and Salisbury should have been so insouciant seems especially surprising in view of other facts: They had both heard their Liberal predecessors confess in the House of Commons that the navy was not adequate even for the burdens Britain already bore. Salisbury had been preoccupied with the Near East, where Britain needed all her composure and potential force to resist a threatened German-Austrian-Russian combination. He and Chamberlain were both aware that British interests were in grave danger in the Far East.

In the spring, when Russia, France, and Germany had formed a diplomatic combination against Japan, the Foreign Office had pointedly inquired what attitude Washington meant to take. In South Africa the Prime Minister and Colonial Secretary already anticipated not only a clash with the Boers but also perhaps with Germany. It should have been as obvious in the autumn of 1895 as it became in the winter of 1896 that Britain could not afford a serious conflict with the United States. Yet Salisbury and Chamberlain made no effort whatever to appease the American demands.

The explanation lies partly no doubt in their experience of American diplomacy. They could remember the *Alabama* agitation of the 1860's, when eminent and respectable United States senators called for the seizure of Canada. Salisbury had been Foreign Secretary and Chamberlain the British plenipotentiary in Washington when congressmen threatened war over the Newfoundland fisheries and Cleveland with tongue in cheek seconded their threat. Having had some experience since then of Blaine's meaningless bluster, both were accustomed to hearing Americans use words that Europeans would never speak without meaning war. Past events entitled them to discount in part the American note. The fact that Olney, its author, had but four weeks' experience as a diplomatist seemed to justify chalking it down still more.

All the advisers to the Prime Minister and the Colonial Secretary made light of the American stand. The British embassy in Washington ascribed the public agitation to speculators in Venezuelan concessions and dismissed the official note as a bid for Irish votes. The American ambassador in London, former Secretary of State Bayard, was wholly out of sympathy with Cleveland's policy, and probably added to the false impression that his government did not mean what it said.

But at the very root stood the fact that Salisbury, Chamberlain, and the majority of Englishmen had simply not been thinking of the United States as a potential factor in the balance of power. When they thought of it at all, it was rather as an example of the evils or benefits of democracy. Conservatives resented its success with egalitarianism and universal suffrage. When the North succeeded in restoring the union in 1865, Salisbury was so disappointed that his family for a time feared for his reason. Liberals of the Cobden and Bright school were correspondingly elated. This sharp division had, it is true, begun to blur. Seeing the great fortunes and the social snobbery that had risen in America after the Civil War, some Conservatives had begun to look upon the country with less hostility. *Blackwood's Magazine* still pictured it as a place where the natives went about armed and crime and licentiousness ran rampant, but other Tory journals carried articles praising some of its institutions and customs, among them one from the young Duke of Marlborough, who was soon to be Chairman of the Primrose League, and another from Lord Meath, who listed his occupation in *Who's Who* as owner of thirty thousand acres and a Rembrandt. Some Liberals had similarly begun to question their earlier faith. One, for example, wrote to an American acquaintance, "I am troubled and saddened . . . by the whole course of things in America. . . . I must confess I have had to take stock of my whole category of political beliefs and reverse my judgements."[4] Earlier Conservative and Liberal notions of America had grown hazy, and occasional writers even touched on such topics as a possible Anglo-American reunion. But up to the time of Cleveland's Venezuela message, America still remained for most Englishmen a metaphysical conception, like Thomas Arnold's Roman Republic or Stubbs's Anglo-Saxons. Only after that message did even such perceptive men as Salisbury and Chamberlain realize that the United States might have become a great power and might have to be treated as such.

As a result, the general reaction to Cleveland's warlike message was shock and dismay. "Many still living," wrote Chamberlain's biographer in 1934, "remember like yesterday with what stupefaction the Venezuelan ultimatum was received." Certain Liberal dailies that always viewed calamities abroad as results of villainy at home took it for granted in this case that the government probably had been stealing land from poor Venezuela. Even such an orthodox Liberal journal as the London *Daily News,* however, saw Olney's version of the Monroe doctrine as "an intolerable pretense," and Gladstone himself at first termed the American claims insupportable. Conservative and Unionist organs were much more outspoken. A rupture between the English-speaking peoples would be a calamity, said the *Times,* but the demands of the United States were too much for any self-respecting nation to concede.[5]

Members of the government, curiously enough, appeared less astonished than the public. Salisbury, recognizing the danger, wrote the Chancellor of the Exchequer, "war with the United States is a distinct possibility in the not distant future." On the other hand, he saw that Cleveland's ultimatum did not have an immediate fuse. He telegraphed the Queen, "My impression is that if we remain quiet this feeling will slowly disappear." He reassured the First Lord of the Admiralty that the whole affair would probably "fizzle out." And though Chamberlain exhibited less confidence, he too realized that if the day of battle were coming, it was still far off. He wrote his second in command:

The American affair cannot become serious for some time. First they have to get the assent of the Senate—then appoint a Commission—then make enquiry—and then? Suppose they decide that the line to the Essequibo is Venezuelan. Will they tell us to evacuate, and declare war if we do not?

As long as the Venezuelans do not attack us we shall not attack them. Altogether it must be months before there is a real crisis.

Salisbury declined to summon a meeting of the cabinet on the ground that it would only alarm the country, and put the meeting off until the second week in January.

In the interval the British government was informed that the public reaction in the United States was turning in their favor. As early as January 9, the Prime Minister felt able to assure the Queen that the United States wished to recede from its extreme position.[6]

In Britain a powerful demand arose for some conciliatory settlement, with Gladstone proclaiming that "common sense" should prevent a breach. The Liberal leader in the House of Commons, Sir William Vernon Harcourt, let it be known that he would make the Venezuelan question a leading issue in the approaching session of parliament, and other Liberals warned the government that they would be unable to restrain Harcourt if the cabinet did not take steps to settle the dispute.

Into the Foreign Office poured pleas for peace endorsed by various arbitration societies, Quaker meetings, Unitarian, Baptist, Methodist, Presbyterian, and other nonconformist churches, public rallies and assemblies. There was a petition from the Bradford Chamber of Commerce and another from the Bolton Vegetarian Society. Most of these groups were affiliated with the National Liberal Federation, which Chamberlain had created and from which he still drew support, even though he had left the Liberal party. They represented forces that the government might not respect but that it could not ignore.[7]

Nor was this sentimental Liberal reaction offset by Tory truculence. Few Conservative organs hardened their editorial lines, probably because they were unsure what their party's ministers meant to do. Some even bent toward the Liberal view. The usually hard-nosed *St. James Gazette,* for instance, said that it trusted the ultimate good sense of America's "shrewd, hard-headed, well-educated Anglo-Saxons and Anglo-Teutons."

Such disposition as there was to urge defiance of the United States dissipated when a crisis with Germany came hard on the heels of the one with America. When Cecil Rhodes's company police, commanded by Dr. Leander Jameson, invaded the Boer Republic, only to be humiliatingly defeated and forced to surrender, the German Kaiser sent a tactless though not unpremeditated telegram to the Boer President, Kruger, congratulating him on his success "in restoring peace and in maintaining the independence of the country against attacks from without." Since the British government did not acknowledge the complete independence of the Boer state, this message was read in England as a gratuitous insult. Reactions were so fierce that German shopkeepers and tourists became momentarily fearful for their lives, and intense hostility toward the German Empire lingered on for months. Conservative journals moved the Venezuelan question down to the bottom of their editorial columns. The result was that no demand for defiance of the United States materialized to offset the Liberal and nonconformist demand for conciliation.

The Jameson raid and the telegram to Kruger may themselves have affected the cabinet's attitude toward Cleveland's message. The Admiralty was certainly impressed by the fact that there were practically no ships to meet an American threat in the North Atlantic and the Caribbean, and that a special flying squadron had had to be formed to deal with possible German moves on the coast of Africa. The War Office had a warning from its Military Intelligence Division that Canada would be difficult if not impossible to defend.[8]

Salisbury had never refused unconditionally to arbitrate with Venezuela—he had only said that British title within the Schomburgk line should not be called into question. When the cabinet met on January 12, he declared himself willing to recede slightly from this position. Acknowledging that "the great majority—if not all—the Cabinet would be glad of any honourable settlement," he still said, according to Chamberlain's notes, "that if we were to yield unconditionally to American threats another Prime Minister would have to be found." He proposed merely to ask the United States if she would be satisfied with arbitration that covered territory on both sides of the Schomburgk line but that excepted all settled areas. In the end he agreed that the Americans be approached informally with a three-point program: (1) an international conference to adopt the Monroe doctrine as international law, (2) a subsequent arbitration to determine whether it applied to the Venezuela-Guiana dispute, and (3) a boundary commission or an arbitral tribunal to decide between British and Venezuelan claims to *unsettled* lands. If these terms were not satisfactory, the United States was to be asked for other suggestions that Britain could accept "without loss of honour."[9]

One gets the impression that cabinet members rushed from the meeting, each determined to negotiate some private settlement. Salisbury was in touch with the editor of the London *Times* and funneling the cabinet's proposals to Olney through George W. Smalley, the *Times* correspondent in America. The Lord Chief Justice, Lord Russell of Killowen, wrote to an eminent American lawyer friendly with Olney. Someone else, though perhaps not a member of the government, communicated with Henry Norman, the *Chronicle* correspondent in Washington. Chamberlain had thought of personally approaching the American ambassador, but at Salisbury's suggestion he asked Lord Playfair, a Liberal peer, to do it for him. A distinguished scientist, Playfair had an American wife, had visited the United States often, and was well known as an advocate of international arbitration. He made a hobby of studying lunatics and their treatment and may therefore have seemed especially well qualified to deal with Americans. Among all the unofficial envoys commissioned by members of the cabinet, Playfair had the most important role.

Both Playfair and the *Times* correspondent had to report that the cabinet's formula did not suit the American Secretary of State. Olney insisted that arbitration cover inhabited as well as uninhabited areas. Chamberlain offered through Playfair to ask exemption only for settlers with five years' tenure. Salisbury, through Smalley, raised it to ten. When Olney still refused, Chamberlain felt almost ready to break off negotiations. Salisbury instead shifted from unofficial to official channels. He wrote Pauncefote, whom he had theretofore kept in the dark, that various "amateur diplomatists" had been at work; "we certainly could not see our way to arbitrate districts that had been long settled. This point the U.S. have never been willing to concede. . . . We have a very scanty belief in the impartiality of national arbitrators in great international questions . . . but I do not doubt that we shall begin to move again shortly." He transferred all negotiations to Pauncefote, writing him that the investigating commission could proceed with its work, "and it may well be that when we have the facts before us . . . we shall see that in many respects they exclude the possibility of disagreement upon the main questions at issue."[10]

It was still many weary months before agreement was finally

reached. Olney continued to stick at excluding settled areas from arbitration. Chamberlain felt it worth while after the recess of parliament to take the final negotiations in his own hands. He traveled to the United States and there had several conferences with Olney. After a time, the Secretary of State offered to compromise by excluding settlements of more than sixty years' standing. A treaty was finally signed stipulating that the arbitrators would hold as absolutely valid any titles more than fifty years old and also take account of common law titles or any others acquired in good faith and held for a reasonable period of time. On this basis the two conflicting positions were reconciled, and face was saved on both sides.

In the meantime, however, the British government had decided to seek more than a mere settlement of this particular issue. It proposed to the United States a comprehensive arbitration treaty that would take care of all differences of opinion.

Chamberlain came up with this idea when searching for some means of distracting American attention from the Venezuelan issue. Salisbury eventually approved, probably with the same thought in mind. As soon as Olney agreed, a separate negotiation was begun. Draft after draft changed hands. A text was finally signed, providing for judicial settlement of nearly all disputes and for the acceptance of mediation in any case where judges failed.

Salisbury had once said, "like competitive examinations and sewage irrigation, arbitration is one of the famous nostrums of the age. Like them it will have its day and will pass away, and future ages will look with pity and contempt on those who could have believed in such an expedient for bridling the ferocity of human passions." Salisbury felt that Britain had not come out well in the few cases when governments had agreed to arbitrate; he must have recognized that an Anglo-American treaty would increase the pressure from Liberals and others for arbitration with other countries. Yet he devoted a good deal of time to negotiating the American treaty, and members of his cabinet, like Lord Russell and Sir Michael Hicks-Beach, who had little more use for the Gladstonian principle than he, approved the final document. The Conservative ministers had, in effect, gone against their principles in drawing up the treaty.[11]

The explanation lay in their heightened awareness of the trouble that American enmity could cause Britain. The treaty would not make the United States Britain's ally, but it would make it harder for the United States to become Britain's enemy. The potential gain from the British standpoint was reassurance against an American flank attack in case of trouble with other powers. Since the naval estimates for 1896–1897 had to break all records just to keep Britain abreast of her potential European enemies, this reassurance was evidently felt to be worth some stifling of conscience.

Olney had been as stubborn in negotiations over the draft arbitration treaty as in those over the Venezuelan boundary, and Salisbury had many opportunities to prevent the treaty's completion with only a minimum of soreness on either side. That he and the cabinet thought it worth while to complete the treaty suggested the impact upon them of Cleveland's declaration of strength.

There were more positive indications of the impression that Cleveland had made. Chamberlain now suggested to Salisbury that the United States be invited to co-operate with Britain in the Armenian question. He wrote to the Prime Minister:

Would it be possible to . . . appeal to them to join us in a Naval Demonstration to force the Sultan to stay the hand of his troops & to give the reforms he has promised . . . ? If the Americans were with us we need not fear any interference from France or Russia—they dare not provoke a combination of the two Anglo Saxon nations.

I think that such an appeal to the American people to join us in a work of charity & humanity would promote a great revolution of feeling. Here is the proper destiny of the two Nations—not to cut each others throats but to bring irresistible force to bear in defence of the weak & oppressed. . . . The mere fact of their alliance would settle the question & bring the Sultan to his knees. . . . In the stir created by such an alliance the Venezuela difficulty would be lost sight of & could not be revived in serious guise.

The more Chamberlain thought of the proposal, the more attractive it became to him. When Salisbury shelved the original suggestion, Chamberlain urged it a second time, remarking that in addition to everything else such an alliance could be "the greatest coup ever made in English politics." Though he had no evidence that Salisbury's mind was changed, Chamberlain proceeded to publicize the idea. Newspapers friendly to him picked it up. He himself advocated co-operation in humane enterprises in a public speech. When he visited Washington to tidy up loose strands in the Venezuelan negotiations, he raised the question with Olney and reported enthusiastically to Salisbury on the interest which Olney showed.[12] Nothing came of Chamberlain's inspiration, but that may have been partly because the Armenian question faded in importance after 1896.

Chamberlain returned to the idea of Anglo-American co-operation later when the continental powers began threatening partition of China, when Germany seized a strip of the Chinese coast late in 1897; and Russia seemed likely not only to take territory but to attempt to establish dominance over the court at Peking. To Arthur Balfour, who was acting as Foreign Secretary during Salisbury's illness, Chamberlain wrote urging that the United States be approached officially and be asked, "Will you stand in with us in our policy?" He suggested a similar question to Berlin. Balfour evidently approved the first proposal, for the proposition was put before the cabinet, and it was agreed to ask American co-operation before asking that of Germany. A secret message was sent to Washington. Only after the United States returned an evasive answer was a similar communication sent to Berlin.[13]

These gestures did not necessarily mirror a transformation in British attitudes toward America. Most Liberals saw the crisis of 1895–1896 as no more than a reassertion of America's moral strength, in which they had always believed. Some Tories, like the leader writers for the *St. James Gazette,* continued to speak as if Britain could give the Americans a drubbing any time she was so inclined. But others realized more or less suddenly that the population, resources, and potential strength of the United States could no longer be blinked away, indeed might have to be opposed. A self-styled "biologist" in an important series for the English *Saturday Review* concluded on social Darwinian grounds that Britain was doomed to fight first Germany and then the United States. Lord Dufferin, the ambassador in Paris, came to the same opinion from nonscientific premises.[14]

The government itself remained undecided about its future relationship with the United States. When the Spanish-American war loomed, the Queen and many others were ready to join Europe in giving moral support to Spain, and only after America's victory did Salisbury and other cautious statesmen finally reconcile themselves to the new power's coming-of-age. Only then did the idea of Anglo-American friendship really sweep through the British public. But the break with the past had begun with Cleveland's Venezuela message. Britain had been shocked into realization that the United States was a nation, not a myth.

VI · RAPPROCHEMENT

In the United States, Cleveland's special message had received roars of applause in the House and even in the Senate, where custom forbade applause. Old fire-eating papers like the Washington *Star,* the Baltimore *American,* the Chicago *Tribune,* and the San Francisco *Examiner* rejoiced, and even Republican journals found good words for the President. Civil War veterans eager for active service wrote to the War Department. One said, "I do hope war may come; first, for the selfish reason, that before I grow too old, I would once more like to 'swish' my sabre, for the glory of my country, and the honor of our flag; and second, because, for the Republic, it would open a glorious vista of conquest."[1] Employees of the Kansas City Board of Trade put on Revolutionary War costumes, and, singing patriotic airs and banging tin pans, marched up five flights of stairs to demand the surrender of the British consulate. All over the country, many treated Cleveland's declaration as occasion for a midwinter Fourth of July.

Even at the outset, however, there were unexpected responses to the President's message. Irish-Americans did not show quite their old zest. There was some tub-thumping to be sure. Patrick Ford's *Irish World,* though nominally Republican, praised the President to the skies, the St. Patrick Society of Boston offered to fête Olney, and Chicago Irish clubs volunteered to raise a regiment for service in war. But the overthrow and death of Parnell had fragmented the Irish party in the United States as in Ireland.[2]

Nor did other groups rally to the President quite as expected. Illinois' Governor John P. Altgeld charged that Cleveland would pack the boundary commission with his friends and that "there will be no interruption of those English influences which have been so potent with the present Federal administration." The Populist Chicago *Sentinel* accused the President of creating an artificial crisis so that he and his cronies might take profits in Wall Street. The southern agrarian leader, Benjamin R. Tillman, condemned Cleveland for acting at all and like the northern radical, Clarence Darrow, said that the President was merely trying to distract people from urgent domestic issues. Few radical Democrats were appeased by the administration's gesture.

Not even all jingoes supported the President. Joseph Pulitzer's usually chauvinistic New York *World* startled everyone by deploring the message and calling for a peaceful settlement. One reason was no doubt that Pulitzer disliked Olney intensely and had no wish to see him boosted toward the Presidency. Some other editors who had played along with the Irish in the past were shocked into sobriety by what seemed a real threat of war. Publisher Whitelaw Reid of the partisan New York *Tribune* confessed privately his dismay that Cleveland should have threatened "an awful calamity not only for our country, but for all Anglo-Saxon communities."[3] Other editors modified their praise once it occurred to them that Cleveland's prospects for a third term were improving.

Nor was it long before opposition rallied. Some immigrants from the United Kingdom and Canada remained loyal to their motherland. Scots in Chicago, for example, were reported solidly against the President. Episcopalians had been pro-British, even during the fisheries disputes, and so had other Protestants linked with English nonconformists. At the 1895 convention of the three-million-member Christian Endeavor Union, for example, there had been ceremonies under entwined British and American flags, and one speaker had referred to Queen Victoria as "that noble mother of us all."[4] German-Americans, though obviously little taken with Anglo-Saxonism, were traditionally opposed to chauvinism and especially to any variety of it that was applauded by Irish-Americans, and soon recovered from their original support of the President.

Chambers of commerce and boards of trade, especially in midwestern towns, had at first passed resolutions applauding Cleveland's message, but frightened English investors began unloading American securities on the day following Cleveland's speech. By Friday shares in Wall Street had fallen off alarmingly and financiers who had started their Christmas holidays scurried back to New York and wrote the President and Secretary of State pleading for moderation and restraint. Resolutions by chambers of commerce and boards of trade in Boston,

New York, Philadelphia, Baltimore, and elsewhere and editorials in the business press soon opposed the President.[5]

The Protestant clergy cooled off in much the same fashion. Just after the President's message, some ministers proclaimed their support of it, and early issues of some religious newspapers carried editorials praising his policy. On the first Sunday after the message, however, sermons preached in many big churches in Boston, New York, Philadelphia, Baltimore, and Washington appealed for compromise and reconciliation. A few weeks after the message, when the *Literary Digest* surveyed the religious press, it found only two important journals, the Philadelphia *Presbyterian* and the Cleveland *Evangelical Messenger,* still endorsing Cleveland's policy. A New Yorker who had earlier commented on the country's unity for war wrote on the day after Christmas: "The War appears to be over. The Churches have proven themselves [a] power again in demanding a peaceful settlement."

The jingo scholars in politics, Lodge and Roosevelt, applauded Cleveland, while Henry Adams wrote Olney that the message commanded his "strongest possible approval and support." But a number of eminent professors attacked Olney's version of the Monroe doctrine and Cleveland's interpretation of the boundary dispute, and faculty and students at many universities and colleges rallied in opposition to the President. Like businessmen and clergymen, they appealed for peace between the English-speaking peoples.[6] A small number of leading businessmen, clergymen, and academicians precipitated a popular reaction quite the contrary of what professional politicians had anticipated, as smaller cities followed the lead of the larger ones, and smaller colleges echoed the stand of their New England mentors.

In the past, Anglophobia had always seemed profitable and relatively safe. It was so no longer.

President Cleveland wrote a friend in Wall Street: "Nothing has ever hurt me so much as to know that these people who praised and flattered me . . . were ready to denounce and abuse me when my obligations to the country at large led me to do things which interrupted their schemes for money making." He and Olney both asserted

later that their policy had been popular and that the chief opposition
came from stock market speculators. At the time, however, James J.
Hill quoted the Secretary of State as saying the President's message
would not have been the same if it had been given two weeks later,
that Cleveland was sorry for what he had said, and that, for his own
part, "he never intended to threaten anyone."[7] And, as soon as possible, the administration edged its way back from the cliff's edge.

Olney discouraged the Senate Foreign Relations Committee from
putting forward a resolution endorsing his interpretation of the Monroe doctrine. Negotiating with Smalley, Norman, and then Pauncefote,
he appeared uncharacteristically flexible and inoffensive. He did
insist that arbitration extend to settled areas, and he rejected Salisbury's proposal of an international conference on the Monroe doctrine. Otherwise, however, he fell in with almost every British suggestion. Compelling the Venezuelans to make amends for the Uruan
incident, he showed that he was no longer merely an advocate for
Venezuela. He implied from the beginning that the arbitration could
be governed by ground rules that would protect all bona fide British
holdings, and when he found that the English simply would not accept
a tacit understanding, he gave way, finally agreeing to the application
of common law standards. Not once during the protracted negotiations did he even hint at breaking them off if Britain refused concessions. In his dealings with London in 1896, there was no echo of the
truculent tones of 1895.

There is evidence, indeed, that Olney changed the whole direction
of his thought after he saw the results of the President's message.
Among his contributions to the note of 1895 had been an eloquent
declaration of isolationist faith: "Europe, as Washington observed,
has a set of primary interests which are peculiar to herself. America
is not interested in them and ought not to be vexed or complicated
with them." For illustration, he added: "If all Europe were to suddenly fly to arms over the fate of Turkey, would it not be preposterous
that any American state should find itself inextricably involved in
the miseries and burdens of the contest? If it were, it would prove to
be a partnership in the cost and losses of the struggle but not in any
ensuing benefits."

Yet when Chamberlain broached the idea of Anglo-American co-operation in Armenia, Olney did not brush it aside. He knew that the President had told the American minister in Constantinople to keep the United States out of trouble but to protect American missionaries. He believed Cleveland would be willing to use force if missions were really in peril. He told the President of Chamberlain's overture and received authority to make some positive answer when Cleveland wrote, "It is hard to restrain oneself on this cursed Turkish question, but we must do so, I suppose. Of course you will not repel the idea he advances any more decidedly than necessary. . . . We don't want *him* to have any excuse for saying that we are in the least unmindful of the duty that rests upon us—even if his country is backward in doing hers."

The Secretary of State used this authorization to the full. He wrote the Colonial Secretary in terms that contrasted sharply with his dicta of the previous year:

Because of our inborn and instinctive English sympathies, proclivities, modes of thought and standards of right and wrong, nothing would more gratify the mass of the American people than to stand side by side and shoulder to shoulder with England in support of a great cause—in a necessary struggle for the defence of human rights and the advancement of Christian civilization. That a great cause of this sort is now presented by unhappy Armenia I cannot doubt. . . . If therefore England should now seriously set about putting the Armenian charnel-house in order there can be little doubt that the United States would consider the moment opportune for vigorous exertion on behalf of American citizens and interests in Turkey. . . . It would support . . . demands by all the physical force at its disposal—with the necessary result, I think, that its attitude would both morally and materially strengthen the hands of England.[8]

Olney worked for the projected arbitration treaty with even greater zeal. He made endless pettifogging changes in the drafts in order to make the treaty thoroughly practicable. When a Republican lawyer charged that it restricted the Monroe doctrine, he asked another eminent member of the bar to answer the accusation. He talked with members of the Senate and advised the treaty's managers on how to deal with recalcitrants. When it began to seem doubtful whether the necessary two-thirds could be mustered for ratification, he tried to stimulate public interest, especially in western cities and towns. At no time did he make use of any argument suggesting that he regarded the treaty as a step toward an alliance. On the other hand, he undoubtedly recognized that it would give England a guarantee of American neutrality. And shortly after leaving office he publicly called for abandonment of isolation and an entente with Britain. These thoughts may have been in his mind all the time.[9]

Cleveland certainly had no such hidden purpose. His attitude toward possible co-operation in Armenia was no more than acquiescent. Notes which he jotted concerning the projected treaty indicated that his sole interest lay in promoting arbitration. He may not even have perceived that the treaty would be tantamount to a pledge of neutrality. Nevertheless, he joined Olney in working for its success. The result was that an administration which began by experimenting with an anti-British foreign policy ended up promoting Anglo-American friendship.

Though public opinion had seemed decisively to reject the former policy, it did not appear immediately to endorse the latter. Pauncefote reported to London that the "better classes" were decidedly in favor of closer relations with England.[10] The opinions of the "better classes" obviously carried enough weight so that local leadership groups were afraid to endorse a policy they warned against. But inspiring positive support for some cause such as intervention in Armenia or an arbitration treaty was a different matter.

The idea of joint aid to the Armenians developed no appeal, despite the massacres in Constantinople in the late summer of 1896, which exceeded anything earlier. Congregational, Presbyterian, Episcopalian, and Baptist newspapers printed furious editorials, but nothing else happened. No mass meetings like those of 1895 were convened. No organizations except missionary boards resolved in favor of United States action. Pious businessmen seemed on the whole to have lost interest in the issue, and no strong sentiment ever appeared among writers and teachers. A number of Americans had shown that they were opposed to fighting England, but few of them warmed to the idea of joining forces with her to fight someone else.

The cause of Anglo-American arbitration was not an altogether new proposal. Long advocated by Quakers and members of peace societies, it had been endorsed also by the Methodist General Conference, the Presbyterian General Association, and the Women's Christian Temperance Union. In the aftermath of the Venezuela crisis, it was taken up by other churches and by the Y.M.C.A., the Epworth League, and the Christian Endeavor Union. A number of business groups joined in. The New York Chamber of Commerce formed a special committee on international arbitration. So did comparable bodies in Philadelphia and Chicago. Thirty-odd business organizations eventually addressed petitions to Congress. Anglo-American arbitration was called for publicly by the presidents of Harvard, Columbia, Pennsylvania, Northwestern, Michigan, and California and by faculty-student rallies at such widely separated institutions as Yale, the University of Tennessee, and the University of Puget Sound. The heavier monthlies and quarterlies brimmed over with learned articles in support of the treaty. The legal profession seemed absolutely captivated, though few lawyers had spoken either for or against Cleveland's Venezuela policy. The treaty won enthusiastic support from the President of the American Bar Association, Moorfield Storey, and from lawyers in Boston, New York, and elsewhere. Chief Justice Fuller summoned and presided over a Washington rally in support of the treaty, and it was attended by well-known lawyers from all over the country.[11]

When an English journalist interviewed members of the Foreign Relations and Foreign Affairs Committees early in 1896, he could not find one to say he opposed an arbitration treaty. In the New York state legislature in February, 1896, a German-American representative introduced a resolution in favor of Anglo-American arbitration as a substitute for the customary declaration in favor of larger coast defense appropriations. To nearly everyone's surprise, the assembly passed it. When it reached the senate, an Irish Democrat denounced it. The Republican floor leader took the precaution of saying that it was not his party's measure. Yet the chamber approved it, 27–7, with most of the Irish members abstaining rather than voting nay. At least some of the German-Americans in the body must have been doubtful, since British-German relations were at their worst. Nevertheless, only one German name appeared among the seven dissenters.[12] This episode, though trivial in itself, suggested the wariness which had grown upon politicians.

The real test only came, however, when the long negotiations ended and the draft treaty went to the U.S. Senate for ratification. It was obvious that there would be resistance. Apart from silverite objections to any pact with a gold standard power, many local interests seemed to be imperiled. The ability of one-third of the Senate to block a treaty protected New England's claims to Canadian fishing rights, the South's immunity from creditors of Confederate states, the Midwest's advantages over Canadian competitors, and the Far West's pretensions to coastlands south of Alaska. Under the Olney-Pauncefote treaty, arbitrators might rule on any of these matters. No minority in the Senate could stop them. The Senate itself would lose power and prestige. If two-thirds were to be won for ratification, Senators would have to become convinced that public opinion really demanded it.

The treaty's supporters did their utmost. The Merchant's Association of Boston and chambers of commerce in New York and Chicago passed appropriate resolutions. In Philadelphia a hundred prominent businessmen signed a petition to the two Pennsylvania senators. Local bar associations acted. An interdenominational conference of mission boards called on clergymen to preach sermons in behalf of the treaty, and a printed appeal to this effect went out to twenty thousand ministers over the signatures of leading Episcopalian, Methodist, Congregational, Presbyterian, Baptist, and Unitarian clergymen. There were mass meetings in Boston, New York, Philadelphia, Pittsburgh, Cincinnati, and other cities. Several state legislatures adopted resolutions endorsing the treaty. On the surface the movement seemed even stronger than that which had checked anti-British feeling after the Venezuela message.

Underneath, however, the movement lacked both fuel and fire. In New York, Cleveland's message had stirred men not ordinarily bothered by political issues that did not affect their own businesses. The chamber of commerce resolution then had reflected real feeling.

The resolution in favor of the treaty, on the other hand, was nothing but an accomplishment by two enthusiasts, William E. Dodge of the Phelps, Dodge, Co., and railroad promoter John J. McCook, who tried to interest the president of the chamber. In the end, he and Dodge had to round up votes themselves. Passage of the resolution demonstrated little except that other members did not oppose the treaty and that Dodge and McCook had friends willing to oblige them.

Sigourney Butler wrote Olney, his cousin, that it was he and Moorfield Storey who had set Boston groups "a-resolutin'." Support from the Maine and New Hampshire legislatures, Butler also reported, came as a favor from Olney's former client, President Lucius Tuttle of the powerful Boston and Maine Railroad. Tuttle had ordered the legislative resolves through his lobbyists in Concord and Augusta. In Chicago, a resolution by the local Bankers Club may well have been due to only one man, Lyman J. Gage, who took up spiritualism and theosophy as well as arbitrationism, but who was also president of the city's largest bank. In more than this one case a seeming display of enthusiasm for the treaty may have reflected no more than diligent effort by a handful of zealots.[13] When the Lord Chief Justice of England appeared before the American Bar Association, he was actually applauded most loudly when he warned that arbitration was no panacea and that treaties should be approached with caution and reserve. Despite surface appearances, the arbitration treaty simply did not excite the same feeling as the Venezuela crisis had.

After the treaty was published, resolutions denouncing it were introduced in the New York and Illinois state legislatures, and though the New York assembly rejected this motion, it also failed to pass a new resolution endorsing the treaty. In Boston, New York, Philadelphia, Pittsburgh, St. Louis, Chicago, Detroit, and San Francisco, Irish leaders organized rallies—one in New York with four governors and ten United States senators on the platform. Some prominent German-Americans participated and so, significantly, did numbers of local office-holders, candidates, and would-be candidates.[14]

When the treaty was first brought to the floor of the Senate, only twenty senators voted for early action; thirty others insisted on putting it over to some indefinite time in the future. The Foreign Relations Committee kept the document for months and finally reported it out with amendments stipulating among other things that no arbitration could be entered into without prior consent from two-thirds of the Senate. Other amendments were later attached. The treaty became so changed as to be hardly recognizable. Outright opponents conceded that it had become innocuous. Nevertheless, in a final vote on May 5, 1897, twenty-six out of sixty-nine senators cast ballots against it, and it thus lacked three votes of the two-thirds necessary for ratification. Members of the Senate had obviously reached the conclusion that there was no irresistible public demand for a closer tie with Britain.[15]

PART THREE

THE CUBAN TANGLE

"The South dearly loves a fighter, & if you will now show yourself strong and courageous in the defense of Cuba, you will have a solid South at your call. . . . Strengthen the Army and Navy of this country & in this way give employment to the thousands of idle men who need it."

> *Anonymous (Atlanta, Georgia) to Grover Cleveland, March 23, 1896 (Cleveland Papers)*

"This thing shames my man hood & my citizenship—as it does of every man with whom I have talked during the last six months."

> *Normond B. Harris (Houston, Virginia) to Grover Cleveland, June 10, 1896 (Cleveland Papers)*

"I believe it is not the fear of a war with impotent Spain that stays your hand from the execution of justice. It is your sympathy with tyranny."

> *T. J. Tanner (Kansas City, Kansas) to Grover Cleveland (Cleveland Papers)*

In early 1895 the Corinto affair had shared headlines with the new revolution in Cuba. At Baïre in February, the poet and essayist, José Martí, had proclaimed a war for independence and throughout the island small armed bands struck at Spanish garrisons and roads and railroad lines. The Spanish Governor General described the rebels as only a handful of brigands, but Madrid announced that fifty thousand fresh troops would be sent over to deal with them. It gradually became evident that there was a civil war in Cuba.

The United States reacted instinctively against Spain. A few weeks after the war opened, a New England railroad magnate wrote Senator Chandler, "Spain is and always has been an impudent, arrogant and barbarous nation. . . . Her history for centuries is a record of atrocities not parallelled by some of the Negro Kings in Africa. It is quite time she was boosted out of Cuba . . . and nine out of every ten of our citizens without regard to party will agree with me." It was said later that the Spanish legation hired a propagandist who finally quit because newspaper editors would not believe his stories.[1]

In most American eyes, the rebels were fighting for an independent republic and for such American-patent blessings as free enterprise, free schools, and free churches. Even the most isolationist American newspapers, such as the New York *Evening Post,* the Springfield *Republican,* and the Boston *Transcript,* expressed hope that the Cubans would succeed. The Boston *Herald* said on July 4, 1895, that if the rebels proved themselves in battle, it might become the duty of the United States to step in with good offices and secure for Cuba either independence or home rule.

The Cubans were not slow to capitalize on American sympathy. Some twenty thousand of them already lived in the United States. Many belonged to clubs and secret societies affiliated with the international Cuban Revolutionary Party. From these groups came the men, arms, and money to start the revolution. Though their leaders had mostly been working as common laborers, many were intellectuals—journalists, writers, or teachers. Some were active professional men, and there were special clubs of Cuban lawyers and doctors. All were dedicated to obtaining freedom for their homeland, and they worked as zealously and tirelessly as any of the American revolutionaries had or as any of the Russian Bolsheviks were to. Organizing rallies and going from community to community, they asked Americans of all nationalities to help with contributions and expressions of sympathy.

Their work was co-ordinated by a Junta or central committee sitting in New York. It undertook to arouse enthusiasm among the American public, obtain donations, and induce the American government to recognize the government which the rebels had organized and if possible to give it diplomatic and financial support.[2] Never well organized, the Junta rarely had enough funds to meet the ceaseless demands from generals in Cuba. Its members bickered with one another, but nevertheless it set out to win over two powerful allies within the United States: organized labor and the press.

Though many Cubans worked in cigar factories, most had resisted approaches from the national Cigar Makers' Union, preferring to remain within their own organizations. Then, when the revolution broke out, representatives of the Junta evidently suggested that Cuban cigarworkers might join the union if union leaders would help raise funds for the rebels. At any rate, cigarmakers' locals were soon passing resolutions of sympathy, and their leaders were obtaining similar declarations from municipal trade assemblies and state federations of labor. Samuel Gompers, the head of the American Federation of Labor, who had come from the Cigar Makers' Union, joined in arranging a mass meeting in New York, and the Federation's 1895 national assembly passed a pro-Cuban resolution.[3] Union labor seemed to take intense interest in the Cuban cause.

The other ally which the Junta sought was the press. It already had an agent on the editorial staff of the New Orleans *Times-Picayune*, and soon hired secretly a writer for the Washington *Star*.[4] There was a limit, however, to the number of journalists whom the Junta could plant or bribe. In most cases its agents could only approach editors and offer copy.

Few papers could then afford regular correspondents even through-out the United States. The wire services were relatively new, had slender resources, and could produce little more than laconic bulletins from Spanish official sources. Therefore when representatives of the Junta came to city rooms, offering as much copy as any newspaper could use, editors were quick to accept. Short on staff and funds, editors of papers outside of the great urban centers were especially eager for material to fill in space between advertisements. As a result many newspapers became voluntary propaganda organs for the Cubans.

Sensation-mongering sheets like William Randolph Hearst's and Joseph Pulitzer's later dispatched special correspondents to vie with shocking accounts of Spanish atrocities. They had been preceded by the Junta's own releases, which had appeared month in and month out in hundreds of papers across the country. Staid dailies like the Boston *Herald,* the Buffalo *Courier,* the Newark *Advertiser,* the Cleveland *Plain-Dealer,* the Omaha *World-Herald,* and the Portland *Oregonian* whetted sympathy for the rebels just as much as did the fiery New York *Journal* or *World.* The press as a whole, not just the "yellow press," aided the Cuban cause.

In Chicago a *Club Patriótico Cubano* had been at work for some time. The local cigarmakers' union had passed pro-Cuban resolves, and the municipal Trades Assembly and the state Federation of Labor followed suit. The city's dailies, all in financial straits, accepted and published regular handouts supplied by the Junta or the local club; all but one had come out editorially for Cuban independence.

Support was won for the revolutionaries in unexpected places. Edward F. Cragin, an active member of the Union League Club, had been approached earlier by a traveling representative of the Junta. As a leading promoter for the Nicaragua Canal Company, he had reason for wanting to arouse public interest in the Caribbean. He and perhaps others talked up the Cuban cause in the lobbies, dining rooms, and assembly hall of the club. They found sympathetic listeners, for the club's *raison d'être* was to preserve memories of the war for the union among its members, all veterans either of the war or of postwar political campaigns for harsh reconstruction measures in the South. They were of the group and generation which believed America had degenerated morally to become soft and materialistic since the great trial of 1861–1865. Since a large number of Cubans were Negroes, the rebel cause could appeal to Union Leaguers as a new crusade in behalf of oppressed blacks. Ardent Republicans, the club members could also see in it an issue embarrassing to a Democratic administration, safer for Republican campaigners than silver or the trusts, fresher than the tired tariff question, and possibly attractive to workingmen voters. Seventy to eighty members of the Union League Club joined Cragin in becoming sponsors for a mass meeting, organized by the Federation of Labor.

The Grand Army of the Republic and the officer veterans' Loyal Legion, the Sons of the Colonial Wars, and the Civil Service Reform Association joined in backing the rally. All four had campaigned for years for "Americanism" and for such specific measures as a law requiring schools to display the national flag, bemoaning the decline of patriotism and calling for a rebirth of crusading idealism. As in the Union League Club, so in these organizations, the majority of members were devout Republicans. Special pro-Cuban committees were created for Bohemian-Americans and German-Americans, groups generally identified in Chicago with the Republican party. On the German-American Committee, the two most prominent men were George Schneider of the Union League Club and E. S. Dreyer, who had served with Cragin on the 1893 World's Fair Committee; both were in serious though unsuspected financial trouble at the time. In addition to viewing the Cuban issue in patriotic and partisan terms, they may also have seen a chance to handle Cuban bonds or in some way win profits that would rescue them from their personal troubles. In any case, they helped to turn out crowds for the rally.[5]

When the demonstration took place, a number of Protestant clergymen appeared on the platform, among them Bishop Samuel Fallows of the Reformed Episcopal Church, an ex-Union colonel and chaplain for the G.A.R. and the Loyal Legion, Hiram W. Thomas of the then nondenominational but Methodist-oriented People's Church, chaplain for the Illinois National Guard, and Presbyterian John Henry Barrows, member of the Sons of the American Revolution

and a self-described "staunch Republican."[6] These clergymen may
have seen agitation in the rebel cause as a means of reuniting two
groups—the upper class and workers—for labor's alienation from
the churches and the peril of class conflict were constant themes in
Protestant preaching and writing. They were concerned also about
the apparent drift of workingmen into the Roman Catholic church.
Doctrinal anti-Catholicism had increased among Reformed, Methodist, Baptist, Presbyterian, and Congregational ministers, and this in
turn strengthened feeling against what one of Chicago's Baptists
called "Pope-ridden" Spain.

On the last day of September the Chicago mass meeting took place.
Four thousand people pressed into the Central Music Hall while an
overflow of nearly two thousand went to Association Hall. The City
Council formally adjourned in order to be present. Barrows said the
United States should break relations with "cutthroat Spain," and
Fallows called for raising an army to help the Cubans. They were
topped only by an ex-judge who advocated taking Cuba and everything else from the North Pole to South America. Most speakers,
however, took care to state that they wanted only freedom for Cuba,
not annexation. After the meetings a permanent Committee of One
Hundred was formed to keep the excitement alive.

With minor variations, subsequent demonstrations in New York,
Philadelphia, Kansas City, Cleveland, Akron, Cincinnati, and Providence followed the Chicago pattern. Cuban-Americans would begin
the agitation; labor organizations would join in, followed by the
G.A.R., the Loyal Legion, and other patriotic societies. The anti-
Catholic Junior Order of United American Workmen took a conspicuous role in Philadelphia and other places where it was strong. Protestant evangelists served as star speakers for the occasions. In New York,
it was Baptist Thomas Dixon, whose *Failure of Protestantism* was
one of the more widely read tracts on the churches' need to re-
capture workingmen and overcome the Catholic peril. In Philadelphia, it was the Reverend Russell H. Conwell, famous for his lecture,
"Acres of Diamonds." The Young Men's Congress of his Baptist
Temple formed itself into a city-wide Cuban sympathy committee.

In all of these cities, the Cuban cause was taken up in the name of Republicanism, patriotism, and Protestantism.[7]

By December, when Congress came into session, the movement had spread out from the cities and the groups involved in the urban demonstrations. Congressmen received resolutions for Cuban independence adopted at rallies in a dozen small towns near Cleveland and Cincinnati. They heard from labor unions in Houston, Denver, and Pawnee, Oklahoma; from units of the G.A.R. in Maryland, Wisconsin, and Minnesota; from numerous branches of the Junior Order of United American Workmen; and from Protestant churches scattered over the Northeast and Midwest. Petitions came in larger number and from more widespread sources than those on the Armenian and Venezuelan issues.[8]

Since the two senators from Florida had many Cuban-American constituents, they were quick to take up the cause. Wilkinson Call of Jacksonville arranged to have his son named by the Junta as agent for the sale of Cuban bonds in England, and put the Junta's Washington representatives in touch with Benjamin Le Fevre, an ex-congressman who had become a somewhat shady but nevertheless influential lobbyist. Le Fevre advised the Junta to make "arrangements for mutual benefit" with the Nicaragua Canal Company and the Standard Oil Company.[9] Though Cuban records are silent as to what happened afterward, it is possible that more than one politician took up the cause for personal profit or at the behest of business interests that had something to gain—not necessarily in Cuba. But the movement had so much inherent appeal and evident popular support that most public men probably came in on the leadstrings either of emotion or of simple political calculation.

Some Republicans saw Cuba as a major issue in the approaching Presidential campaign. In Philadelphia the leading Republican papers, the *Press* and the *Times,* had been fearful that silverism might capture their party, and they both quickly put forward Cuban independence as a better Republican battle cry. Former Governor Russell Alger of Michigan insisted that Republicans should stress foreign policy questions, and he sent an enthusiastic telegram to the Chicago demonstrators. So did Senator Shelby M. Cullom of Illinois, whose faint hope of nomination for the Presidency rested on his identification with jingoism, imperialism, and a strong stand on the Monroe doctrine. After Cleveland's Venezuela message, others seized upon the Cuban issue, if only to neutralize the advantage won by Democrats.

Despite the character of the 1895 demonstrations, a number of Democrats also took it up. Many of the party's silverites feared that the free coinage cry alone might not capture either the national convention or the autumn elections. Many conservatives worried lest the silverites succeed. To some in both groups the Cuban cause seemed made to order. By calling for Cuban independence, either faction might hope to win over labor, and in the campaign the party might make inroads on churches and patriotic groups that normally voted Republican.

Governor John Peter Altgeld of Illinois, the front-runner for the Democratic nomination, leaped into the movement. Congratulating the Chicago demonstrators, he called for intervention and annexation. Tillman of South Carolina, who was then regarded as Altgeld's chief competitor, did not lag far behind. He spoke in favor of the Cubans, and, dominating his state's constitutional convention, had it resolve in favor of immediate recognition. The silverite governors of Georgia, Arkansas, and Indiana joined in. When Congress convened, Morgan of Alabama, Mills of Texas, Vest of Missouri, and Allen of Nebraska spoke loudly in favor of the Cubans. So many southern and western silverites took up the issue that some subsequent students have thought the Cuban movement agrarian in origin. In fact, it probably attracted these leaders precisely because it had appeal for groups other than their own.[10]

Conservative, pro-administration Democrats saw the Cuban issue as one, like Venezuela, that might be exploited to restore party unity. The Ohioan who wrote Olney asking for "a little 'Jingo' " to help in the gubernatorial campaign suggested that Cuba would do as well as Venezuela. Dickinson of Michigan, who had been the first Cleveland man to speak out on Venezuela, urged some action to aid Cuba and established close relations himself with Junta agents in Washington. After the Democratic convention had turned to silverism and nominated Bryan, the former governor of Virginia who was Cleveland's consul general in Havana urged the President to form a party of gold Democrats, have it call for Cuban independence, and then intervene in the island. This party, he reasoned, "would get . . . the credit of stopping the wholesale atrocities . . . [and] the acquisition of Cuba. . . . [A] successful war . . . might do much towards directing the minds of the people away from imaginary ills, the relief of which, is erroneously supposed to be reached by 'Free Silver.' "[11] In the turbulent and confused times preceding the election of 1896, many politicians could see uses for the enthusiasm that had developed among some of the voters.

Some, it is true, could see disadvantages in the issue. Business-minded Republicans believed that agitation might bring war with Spain and feared that war might injure trade and upset the stock market. Though Cullom's candidacy was not taken seriously, his rivals could reasonably fear that if foreign policy issues became important, he might win enough delegates to be a force in the convention. William McKinley and Thomas B. Reed, the leading contenders, were undoubtedly restrained by recollection of how strongly businessmen had recently reacted against jingoism. They and their principal supporters were probably loath to see Cuba too much talked about. Democratic rivals of Altgeld and Tillman may have had the same feeling. Nevertheless, the interested groups were so strong and public enthusiasm so apparent that some action by Congress was almost inevitable.

Barely eight weeks after Congress convened, and only four weeks after Cleveland had delivered his thunderous Venezuela message, the Senate Foreign Relations Committee reported out resolutions on the subject of Cuba. Old John Sherman, the chairman, disapproved; he had said cautiously when interviewed in September that the rebels should be recognized when they controlled Cuba, but not before. Though seventy-two and practically senile, he had four times narrowly missed nomination for the Presidency, and he may have conceived himself a rival of McKinley and Reed. If so, he did not want to help the candidacy of Cullom. But his Republican colleagues on the committee were Cullom himself, Frye, Lodge, and Cameron of Pennsylvania, all of whom, for one reason or another, favored bringing the issue to debate. Among the Democrats were Morgan, Mills, and Daniel, who had all promised to help the Junta. Sherman and whoever stood with him could hope at best for a mild resolution, and the committee ended by reporting out two resolutions—one by Cameron threatening intervention, another signed by the majority, proposing merely recognition of Cuban belligerency.[12]

When presented to the Senate, the issue produced two full weeks of debate, more than that given any other topic of the session. Some orators called for action on economic grounds. Lodge declared, "Free Cuba would mean a great market to the United States; it would mean an opportunity for American capital." Mills asserted that the Monroe doctrine required the United States to restore order and throw Spain out. Not a few speakers argued from domestic grounds. Allen, Morgan, and other silverites asked for a strong resolution as a rebuke to selfish, timid men of wealth in the United States. In the House, Representative Henry F. Thomas of Michigan dwelt lovingly on the possibility of war, saying, "The blue and the gray shall be blended into one vast army, flying the banner of freedom, keeping step to the heartbeat of humanity, and moving upon the last contingency of despotism." Senator Vest of Missouri warned that failure to act would be defiance of destiny, and "the time will come when there will be retribution upon us as a people, because we have not been true to the task assigned us by Providence." In both the Senate and the House, the issue let loose cascades of imperialistic and moralistic oratory.

The minority in opposition produced little rhetoric. Representative Samuel W. McCall of Massachusetts said, "Our businessmen have been overwhelmed with burdens, almost crucified, during the last few years, and can ill bear any additional threats." Senator Hawley of Connecticut warned of America's possibly having to fight other powers besides Spain, and Hale of Maine, though a veteran navalist, cautioned the Senate against encouraging the spirit of militarism at home. Senator Caffery of Louisiana argued that the United States should not impose her will on others but should rest content with setting the world a virtuous example. To other southerners the capacity of Cuban Negroes to govern themselves was in doubt.

Only a handful voted against the final resolutions. A test vote in the Senate ran 57–12; the record vote was 63–6. The House measure passed 262–17. The minority in each case was made up of southerners and New Englanders, the one group affected by the color of the Cubans, the other in large part by a tradition left over from opposition to the slaveholders' annexationism of the 1850's.

Quite a few in both houses abstained. Many were either southerners or New Englanders; three of the Pennsylvanians were declared foes of organized labor; a few of the others were Catholics, sensitive to the militant Protestant drift of the Cuban crusade. Some may have felt that, if pressed, they could justify themselves by denouncing the resolutions as too weak. Nevertheless, seventeen abstentions in the Senate and seventy-six in the House suggested that not all professional judges of public opinion took the movement seriously as yet.

After the Congressional furor, it came to seem as if the skeptics had been right. Public interest in Cuba appeared to trail off. General Valeriano ("Butcher") Weyler took command in Cuba and began to herd the civil population into reconcentration camps, but his policy was ruthless without being spectacular. Tropical rains beat down on the island from April to September, and there were few battles to report. In a Presidential election year, moreover, editors had no shortage of copy—for little more than the price of the postage, McKinley's backers would supply two- or four-page mats complete with news, pictures, and advertisements. Even in papers committed to the Cuban cause, the rebellion ceased to dominate the front pages.

During the 1896 election, neither party talked much about Cuba. Both mentioned the subject in their platforms, but Bryan would not speak on any issue except free coinage, and McKinley had little to gain from worrying the financial community with doubts about his conservatism. Neither they nor lesser candidates could forget, furthermore, that Cleveland remained President and that he might act as dramatically in the Cuban affair as he had in the Venezuelan.

Only after the election did the issue rise again. Rain ended in the island late in September. As the ground slowly dried, Weyler mobilized two hundred thousand troops for an offensive in the mountainous eastern province of Pinar del Rio. The Negro general, Antonio Maceo, meanwhile led a rebel column westward to raid the central provinces and harass Havana. Exciting battles and skirmishes began to be reported once again. With the Presidential race over and little happening elsewhere, the Junta's releases appeared on front pages again, even in newspapers whose editorials opposed recognition of Cuban belligerency or independence.

In early December, 1896, Maceo was slain. Spaniards crowed with triumph. The Junta charged that he had asked for parleys, crossed the Spanish line under flag of truce, and been killed by the Spanish commander. As proof of Spain's brutality and faithlessness, the tale was told and retold.

Coincidentally, Congress convened and began again to debate recognition. When Cleveland made it plain in his annual message that he intended no action, Senators Cameron, Mills, Call, Cullom, and Morgan hastened to introduce resolutions. Cameron's, calling for good offices to secure Cuban independence, was the one most agreeable to the Junta and seemingly the one with most chance of passage. Maceo's death supplied emotional stimulus, while Cameron's resolution offered a practical outlet for passion.

In Allegheny, Pennsylvania, a G.A.R. meeting was adjourning when someone brought in the Junta account of Maceo's killing. The post commander hastily called the members back to read them the story. Some excitedly proposed the adoption of resolutions condemning Spain. Others suggested that the whole post volunteer for service in Cuba. Similar scenes were enacted at G.A.R. meetings elsewhere in Pennsylvania and in New York, Ohio, Illinois, Michigan, and South Dakota, and in gatherings of Sons of Veterans, Junior Order United American Mechanics, Sons of the American Revolution, Daughters of Liberty, and similar groups.[13]

Weyler was burned in effigy in small towns in New Jersey, Pennsylvania, Illinois, and Iowa. Public rallies were held in larger communities like Buffalo, Jersey City, Wheeling, Chattanooga, and Los Angeles. In Little Rock and Newark Negroes held large rallies of their own.

Atlanta reported the biggest public demonstration in many years.

A Dallas rally was claimed to be the greatest ever held in Texas. In New York a giant meeting at the Cooper Union was preceded by a parade of two thousand.

Unlike the carefully prepared demonstrations of 1895, those of 1896 occurred almost spontaneously, within a week of the story of Maceo's death.

In 1895 certain clergymen and individual officers of civic and patriotic organizations had become aroused. They organized rallies and drew crowds. Subsequently they went to churches, G.A.R. posts, lodges, and clubs, asked for resolutions, and obtained them. They had no proof that many shared their excitement. They merely had evidence that their acquaintances were not of contrary minds and were willing to oblige them.

The sudden manifestations of 1896 proved something else. This time G.A.R. posts, lodges, and assemblies in small towns acted on their own, before newspaper editors and clergymen and others had spoken publicly. According to newspaper fragments, opinion leaders in country towns and urban neighborhoods now knew their minds as they had not a year earlier. In tiny North Tonawanda, according to the Buffalo *Courier,* hotel lobby and police court orators demanded aid to Cuba the day after they read of Maceo's killing. So, it was said, did drugstore and barbershop experts in East St. Louis and Pittsburgh. Although the 1895 demonstrations had started in cities and then spread out, those in 1896 had no definable points of origin. They occurred everywhere. Nor did they burst from any particular class. The manifestants of 1895 had been Cuban-Americans, union workers, and middle- and upper-middle-class members of Union League Clubs, G.A.R. posts, and the like. While in 1896 a number of businessmen's organizations expressed disapproval of events, among them the Boston Merchants Association, the Milwaukee Chamber of Commerce, the Memphis Cotton Growers Exchange, the Fort Smith Commercial League, the Chicago Commercial Club, and the Indianapolis and Baltimore Boards of Trade, Presidents Alonzo B. Hepburn of the National City Bank of New York, Chauncey Depew of the New York Central Railroad, and Collis P. Huntington of the Southern Pacific joined in the rallies. These were far more prominent business figures than any who had taken part in the demonstrations of 1895.[14]

On the other hand, there had also been a distinct spread of interest in groups hostile to big business. In the labor movement the Cuban cause had originally been taken up by the Cigar Makers' Union, but at the A.F. of L. convention in Cincinnati in December, 1896, when conservative unionists opposed a prorecognition resolution, militants, among whom the cigarmakers formed only a small minority, carried the day for the resolution. Though agrarian leaders in Congress had begun talking about Cuba before there was any significant display of concern among their followers, resolutions in favor of aid to Cuba were now passed by such organizations as the Galveston Farmers Alliance, a Populist convention in Texas, a Democratic club in Manhattan, Kansas, and a Bryan Silver Club of Spokane, Washington. Similar motions were voted by agrarian-dominated state legislatures in North and South Carolina, Nebraska, and Wyoming.[15] The earlier excitement had arisen among people disquieted over the political, moral, or religious health of the country. That of 1896 occurred among people who were economically discontented. In places where depression had hit hardest, there were rushes of volunteers to the offices of Cuban recruiters. The Denver *Rocky Mountain News* interpreted the excitement in Leadville, Colorado, as a spillover of emotions roused by the battle between labor and management.

There were hosts of volunteers in many other places. More than twelve hundred offered their services in St. Louis. In Newark a boy of ten stole two pistols and set out along the railroad track to walk to Cuba. In Chicago a young stationer and a friend opened a recruiting office, explaining, "There may be a little business connected with it. We are agreed that Cuba presents a great field for enterprising young men, and believe this is as good a time as any to start a movement in that direction, and get in on the ground floor. If we don't succeed in helping Cuba, we may help ourselves."

A good deal of the apparent fervor may have been equally passionless. On balance, however, it seemed as if the mass of the people from coast to coast were in the clutch of feverish emotion.

In 1895 the Cuban question had seemed one that politicians might exploit; by the end of 1896 it had become one they could not escape.

Within two weeks after the rebellion's outbreak, a serious incident occurred in Cuban waters. The Colón-New York mail steamer, *Alliança,* passing near Cabo Maisi on the easternmost tip of Cuba, was chased by a zealous Spanish gunboat commander on the lookout for rebel provisioners. When the *Alliança*'s captain stubbornly though rightfully ignored his pursuer, the Spaniard fired several shots. The *Alliança* escaped harm, but its captain turned in an indignant report, and it became the duty of the Department of State to seek not only an apology but also assurances for the future.

The only real issue was whether the note to Madrid should be polite or not. There was no doubt about the public's preference. Even the conservative Philadelphia *Press* said Spain should be made to respect the American flag. The Democratic strategist, William C. Whitney, called for treating the incident as a "willful insult." Rumor had it that though Cleveland agreed with the mugwump New York *Evening Post* in believing the case should be considered a regrettable accident, he yielded to Secretary of State Gresham and a majority of the cabinet, Attorney General Olney included. In any event, a curt note was sent to Madrid. It demanded prompt disavowal and apology and declared that forcible interference with American ships could "under no circumstances be tolerated."

The Spanish government deferred replying till the gunboat commander could report. A change in the cabinet in Madrid served for still further delay. Almost a month passed before there was an interim answer, saying that Spain would regret it sincerely if investigation showed the gunboat commander to have "committed an error." Still another month went by before the Spanish government finally apologized and announced fleet orders to prevent future incidents. The affair had little lasting importance, for the same issue did not arise again. The *Alliança* case merely gave the administration its first choice between catering to domestic jingoism or placating Spanish pride and supplied a foretaste of the exasperating slowness with which Spain was to handle all American complaints.[1]

The only other case to produce anything approaching a crisis was that of the *Competitor* prisoners. Captured in April, 1896, while the schooner was landing arms for the rebels, crew and passengers were brought before a naval summary court martial and sentenced to death. The American consul general begged a new hearing for the American citizens in the group, citing a convention in which Spain promised civil trials for any Americans except those caught with arms in hand. The Spanish reply that the *Competitor* prisoners were not covered because not technically resident was hardly satisfying, nor were answers to the consul general's further protests that some of the prisoners had been unable to understand the trial because they knew no Spanish and had no interpreter and that none of the accused had been allowed to introduce evidence in defense. Secretary of State Olney wrote urgently, though privately, to the Spanish ambassador in Washington: "I must beg you to consider the serious consequences which I fear will result." He did not put such language into a formal communication, but it was evident that he might have done so if the Spanish government had not yielded and ordered a new trial. He did have to complain formally of "absolutely unreasonable delay" before the *Competitor* case was finally disposed of.[2]

Though the *Alliança* and *Competitor* affairs were the only two episodes deserving to be called incidents, the Cuban war caused constant irritation in Spanish-American relations. In the first two years of the war, more than eighty Americans were arrested in Cuba. Many were Cubans who had been naturalized in the United States. Most bore Spanish names. It was often hard for American authorities to discover whether claims of citizenship were legitimate. Sometimes it was harder still to learn the charges against them. Responses from the Spanish Governor General, especially during Weyler's tenure, tended to be haughty, uninformative, and sometimes insulting. In the meantime, relatives, friends, and Congressional representatives nagged the Department of State. When Congress was in session, pro-Cuban members asked embarrassing questions on the floor or in committee. The Secretary could hardly go to his office without finding on his desk some communication relating to Cuba or seeing in his waiting room a congressman or a relative of a prisoner. The President's situation was scarcely better. As each day passed, the administration came to feel more and more keenly that these annoyances had to stop.

Irritation and impatience were compounded by knowledge that the war was costing money. Investigations and representations on behalf of injured citizens were expensive. So were the coast patrols needed to intercept filibusterers. These costs seemed all the heavier because customs receipts on trade with Cuba fell to practically nothing. At a time when the federal budget still bore some resemblance to a household account, outlays and losses aggregating several million dollars were far from negligible.

The costs to the government were but a shadow of those to private citizens. Cleveland and Olney reckoned that Americans had some thirty to fifty million dollars invested in Cuban plantations, sugar refineries, and factories. As time went on, more and more of this property was destroyed or rendered useless. Though Olney remarked to Cleveland that the owners had taken conscious risks, neither he nor the President could feel free from all responsibility for their interests. In any case, they were inevitably concerned by the decline in trade. Both said publicly that continued fighting would soon make the island useless either as a source of supply, a market, or a place for profitable investment.

Potentially, too, the long-drawn-out war threatened even the safety of the United States. If Spain came to believe that she could not win with her own resources, she might appeal to some friendly power for aid. It was said that either of the major alliances, the Franco-Russian or the Austro-German, would pay a high price for Spanish partnership and that England would pay even more for the sake of protecting Gibraltar and winning Spanish support in the Mediterranean. If French or German or British troops should turn up in Cuba, the United States would face a clear infringement of the Monroe doctrine. After Cleveland's Venezuela message, there was no question but that such a case would require a threat of war. Cleveland may even have delivered the message partly as a warning to European powers that might ally with Spain. The continuance of the Cuban war, in any case, posed a real threat of eventual trouble.

That the risk was more than imaginary seemed to be proved in 1896. American newspapers and journals like the *Literary Digest* and *Public Opinion* had already compiled extracts from the European press showing sympathy for Spain in every capital from London to St. Petersburg. On September 3 the American minister in Madrid reported that the Spanish government planned to capitalize on this sympathy. The Spanish Foreign Ministry meant to send out a memorandum stating Spain's position and inviting the powers to express their approval and state that no other nation had a right to meddle or even criticize. Learning suddenly of this scheme, the minister hurried to the Puerta del Sol and declared that the dispatch of such a memorandum might be considered an unfriendly act. An embarrassed Spanish Foreign Minister, suspecting that the American had his information from the British ambassador and that this meant England would not co-operate, promised that the memorandum would not be sent. The American could report to Washington that the immediate danger was past. But the episode left officials in the United States to brood upon the possibility that Spain would sooner or later seek aid in Europe.[3]

Apart from this danger, there was also risk that some power might take advantage of American preoccupation with Cuba to launch an imperial venture of its own in the Western Hemisphere. Spanish-American relations were perpetually troubled by friction over filibusters or imprisoned Americans, anti-Spanish demonstrations in the United States, and anti-American demonstrations in Spain. As early as October, 1895, the Spanish Governor General in Cuba declared that war with the United States would have its advantages: "We would have real battles instead of ambushes . . . ; and as in these great moments of history, honor is more important than success, if luck were to go against us, if we were to be defeated, if we were to lose the island of Cuba, we would have lost it with honor."[4] The United States seemingly had to be ready at all times for a war that Spain might start. In these circumstances it was conceivable that some

European power might think it opportune to contest the Monroe doctrine.

The bloody, indecisive war in Cuba created irritations and harmed American business. As long as it went on, there was danger of conflict with Spain, of trouble with other European states, or of some challenge to American dominance in the hemisphere. Like other Americans, Cleveland and Olney were horrified by the misery and suffering which the war caused. As politicians, they were affected by the stir in Congress and the country. But even if they had set aside moral and domestic considerations, their sense of the national interest would still have obliged them to seek means by which the United States could help end the war.

At first they attempted gingerly to aid Spain. Active assistance by American ships and troops was never in question. Congress was no more likely to vote money for fighting the rebels than to legalize polygamy. Cleveland and Olney could, however, try to pinch off rebel supplies and reinforcements.

There was some doubt as to whether the neutrality acts could be put in force unless the rebels were recognized as belligerents, and the issue was not cleared up until 1896 and 1897 when the Supreme Court judged the cases of *Viborg vs. the United States* and *The Three Friends*. Yet the President proclaimed neutrality on June 12, 1895, and thus forbade Americans to enlist, recruit, fit out warships, or otherwise set on foot military enterprises for the rebels. On July 27, 1896, Cleveland issued a fresh proclamation warning that "any combination of persons organized in the United States for the purpose of proceeding to and making war" in Cuba would be prosecuted. Olney discouraged banks from lending money to the rebels, and the Coast Guard endeavored to patrol the myriad quays and inlets of the Carolina and Florida coasts.

As Spanish authorities constantly complained, these measures did not in fact dam the stream of supplies and volunteers. Neutrality was as hard to enforce as Prohibition proved to be later, and Cleveland and Olney felt themselves unable to interfere with the activities of the Junta. Nevertheless, during the first year of the war, the administration can be said to have made a fair trial, insofar as it could, of helping Spain to smother the insurrection.[5]

Increasingly, however, Cleveland and Olney came to doubt that Spain could triumph and to wonder if the right policy for the United States might not be support of the rebels. After the first season of campaigns, Olney concluded that Spain would have to win soon or never. He wrote the President an unusually long letter, mentioning the mounting injury to American economic interests, the danger that Spain might attempt to sell the island, and the fact that "politicians of all stripes, including Congressmen, either are already setting their sails or preparing to set them so as to catch the popular breeze." He recommended that the administration put itself "in a position to intelligently consider and pass upon the questions of according to the insurgents belligerent rights, or of recognizing their independence— questions, one or both of which is or are sure to be raised and the decision of which sooner or later cannot be avoided."[6]

The President and Secretary of State knew that their decision could have important consequences. Once recognized, the rebels would become much better able to float bonds, borrow money, and contract for supplies. More important, their confidence would rise to such a point that they would probably abandon any thought of a compromise peace. If they were merely a handful of bandits, as the Spaniards claimed, their recognition by the United States would be tragic; it would enlarge and prolong the war. On the other hand, if they represented ninety per cent of the population, as a leading Cuban landowner told Olney, recognition would not only be justified but would presumably help bring the war to a speedier end.[7]

Cleveland and Olney felt that they lacked the information on which to base an intelligent decision. The Secretary suggested a special investigating mission, and he and the President periodically discussed possible names. But the Spanish minister objected and would not withdraw his objections. The administration had to content itself with seeking a specially qualified man to serve as consul general in Havana. After much casting about, the President and Secretary of State hit upon Fitzhugh Lee, a former governor of Virginia and onetime Confederate major general. As a conservative southerner, the chubby, genial Lee could be expected to be free of imperialist or jingo biases. Northern newspaper editors feared, indeed, that he was likely to be prejudiced against the rebels because so many were Negroes. Cleveland and Olney hoped that he could supply the information they lacked.

The Secretary explained in specific instructions to Lee:

From such sources as are available, it is quite material to ascertain what sort of civil government and administration, if any, prevail in that large part of the island which is under the control of the insurgents. Is there any such civil government *de facto?* Has it any fixed seat? Are there any elections of legislators or other civil officers? Is there any Legislature which convenes and enacts laws? Are the insurgent forces under the control of any such civil government? What does this civil government, if any, do in the way of protecting life, liberty and property? Has it established courts which are actually administrating justice and whose judgments are executed by the ordinary civil processes? Does this civil government, if there is any, lay and collect taxes in accordance with general and special laws? Or is each military commander a law unto himself levying such contributions upon persons and estates as can be extorted in each particular case? Does this civil government, if there is any, provide any mail service, have any currency, do anything in the way of furnishing roads or of providing for the poor or of supplying the youth of the country with educational facilities? In short, what of the ordinary functions of civil government, if any, does the so-called Cuban Republic exercise? Or is it a mere government on paper?

Unhappily, Lee proved unable to satisfy the administration's curiosity. Not only did he fail to send back the requested data but he soon fell, as Cleveland sourly remarked, "into the style of rolling intervention like a sweet morsel under his tongue."[8] It was he who suggested, after Bryan's nomination in 1896, that the President foment a war with Spain in order to turn the public's mind from "imaginary ills." Lee hardly proved the cautious, reliable informant the administration wanted.

Such data as Cleveland and Olney did cull from Lee and others disposed them against recognition. American property owners told of raids, ransoms, and general anarchy. C. E. Akers, the London *Times* correspondent in Havana, wrote Olney that the rebel leaders were no more fit to govern Cuba than the Spaniards. By the end of 1896, the Secretary of State felt reasonably sure that they had not yet created even "the nucleus of statehood," and the President told Congress that the rebels had no government worthy of the name.[9] Insofar as both men could judge the situation, they believed that the facts did not warrant so decisive a step as recognition.

In the meantime, moreover, they had become conscious that a policy of supporting the rebels would have drawbacks. As Assistant Secretary of State Adee pointed out, recognition would make it harder to collect claims against Spain. It occurred to Olney at some point that recognition would make Cuba an American republic and that under the Monroe doctrine, as elaborated in the Venezuela message, the United States might be obliged to help her against Spain, a European monarchy. Toward the end of 1896 it also became clear that so risky a policy might undermine the gradual business revival. A correspondent for the Chicago *Tribune* predicted recognition of Cuban independence by Cleveland, and stock prices in New York tumbled. Secretary of War Lamont hastened to declare that no change in policy was contemplated, and Olney came out publicly against recognition and even advised against debate of the subject by Congress. He explained to his friend, Clifton R. Breckinridge, the American ambassador in Russia: "It looked very much at the time as if something must be done or another financial panic would be percipitated [*sic*]."[10] Adee's worries about claims, Olney's about the Monroe doctrine, and the financial community's nervousness made telling arguments against recognition.

Nor were these possible disadvantages offset by prospective political gains. In 1895 the President may have toyed with the thought of Cuba as a campaign issue. Two Democrats close to him, Charles S. Hamlin and Don M. Dickinson, came out almost simultaneously for recognizing Cuban belligerency. The Junta's Washington agent wrote on December 16, 1895, "Dickinson says that the President wants to do and will do much for Cuba, that he counts on this for his platform and re-election." But if Cleveland ever had such thoughts, they disappeared after Republicans and radical Democrats seized the initiative. Up to and after the end of February, 1896, when Congress passed its recognition resolutions, the President could not announce a new policy without seeming merely to jump on an opposition bandwagon.

After early summer, when Bryan had been nominated and Cleveland repudiated, there was no longer any point in doing so. When Lee asked that a warship be sent to Havana, the President refused, writing Olney: "I do not want *now* anything of that kind made a convenient excuse for trouble with Spain." A friend who visited him in early August noted: ". . . in a general way he felt it incumbent upon him to be extremely careful; as the public mind seemed to be in an inflammable state, and a spark might kindle a conflagration. He said there seemed to be an epidemic of insanity in the country just at this time."[11] Whatever he may have thought at first, the President eventually concluded that support of the rebels would be unjustified, imprudent, unwise, and potentially dangerous.

If the end of the Cuban war were to be hastened, there remained only the vaguer middle course of independent American intervention. In public and Congressional debate, many ideas had been put forward. Some voices urged seizure or purchase of the island. Others suggested buying it from Spain and making it independent. But Cleveland was not attracted by either of these notions. He wrote Olney that he doubted whether Cuba should or could be incorporated into the United States. Perhaps he shared Carl Schurz's feeling that one South was enough. And with regard to the alternate scheme he remarked, "It would be absurd for us to buy the island and present it to the people now inhabiting it, and put its government and management in their hands."[12] He wanted the war and its costs stopped, not extended.

Both Cleveland and Olney hoped for some compromise between Spain and the rebels. When they came to the conclusion that neither side was likely to overcome the other, they urged the Spanish government to consider possible reforms and concessions that might satisfy rebel grievances. On March 20, 1896, the Spanish minister reported to Madrid:

I saw the Secretary of State and found him very preoccupied with the difficulties which the Cuban question is going to make for this government. . . . He said to me that the reports he had from Cuba were that Spain could not triumph for a long time nor could the rebels do more than they were doing, and the result would be the total destruction of the island, its annihilation, with immense injury to the American interests which would like to be able to help Spain pacify the island; that he would oppose any measure that could be considered an infringement on our sovereignty . . . ; but that he was certain that if reforms were made which could be accepted by the neutral mass of the country and which would justify a declaration by this government that they were adequate, the insurrection would lose the moral strength which it has here and it would be much easier to subdue the rebels.

Finding that suggestions of this kind had no effect, Olney drew up a formal, confidential note which was sent to the Spanish government on April 4, 1896. Though the surviving drafts in the Olney papers show no markings by the President, Cleveland undoubtedly studied and approved the communication. It reiterated all that Olney had already said. It asked point blank for "some authentic declaration" by Spain of the reforms which she would institute "to remove all just grounds for complaint." Finally, it offered mediation by the President to obtain rebel acceptance of terms satisfying "the reasonable demands and aspirations of Cuba."

But Spain would have nothing to do with American mediation. Two months passed before any reply to the offer came from Madrid. When it did, it simply repeated earlier promises that "such reforms as may be useful or necessary" would be effected "as soon as the submission of the insurgents be an accomplished fact." Citing rebel demands for independence, the Spanish reply declared that American mediation could have no success. It left the matter at that, adding that the insurrection would certainly die out if the American government simply stopped the "constant violations of international law in its territory" and announced publicly that it believed Spain to be in the right. Olney showed his disappointment to the Spanish minister and termed the Spanish reply "a courteous refusal . . . to accept the good offices of the United States."[13]

Cleveland and Olney continued to hope. Learning that there was some sentiment in Spain for Cuban autonomy, they asked their envoy to keep them fully informed. Cleveland inquired of Olney if there were not unofficial channels through which the Spanish government could be encouraged to offer reforms. In his annual message in December, 1896, he openly advised Spain to grant autonomy, not conditioned on rebel capitulation. When the Spanish minister announced that extensive reforms would soon be instituted, Olney telegraphed excitedly to Havana, trying to learn whether the rebels would accept some form of dominion status. Though Lee replied that they would not, Olney and Cleveland both congratulated the Spanish government and expressed hope that some compromise might result.[14]

It was no longer within their power to volunteer good offices; that lay with the incoming President. To the very last, however, their highest hope was that some arrangement might end the war with the rebels satisfied and Spain still sovereign over Cuba.

Both men recognized that if peace were not restored in some such fashion, it would become increasingly hard to avoid more forceful action. Olney had been candid in his note proposing mediation. "It is not proposed now," he observed, "to consider whether existing conditions would justify . . . intervention . . . or how much longer those conditions should be endured before such intervention would be justified. That the United States can not contemplate with complacency another ten years of Cuban insurrection, with all its injurious and distressing incidents, may certainly be taken for granted." The President was no less frank in his last annual message:

It cannot be reasonably assumed that the hitherto expectant attitude of the United States will be indefinitely maintained. While we are anxious to accord all due respect to the sovereignty of Spain, we can not view the pending conflict in all its features, and properly apprehend our inevitably close relations to it, and its possible results, without considering that by the course of events we may be drawn into such an unusual and unprecedented condition, as will fix a limit to our patient waiting for Spain to end the contest, either alone and in her own way, or with our friendly cooperation.

It remained to be seen whether Spain herself could induce the rebels to make peace before that day arrived.

An old Castilian proverb has it that God granted Spain warm skies, good grapes, and beautiful women. When entreated also to provide good government, He refused, saying that if Spain had that too, it would be heaven on earth.

Long before any American officials called attention to the fact, Spaniards were well aware that Cuba's government was even more imperfect than Spain's own. In theory the island was an extension of Spain. Its elected representatives sat in the national parliament, the Cortes. Its taxes and tariffs, like those for provinces in the peninsula, were fixed in Madrid. At least in form, Cuba's administrators were answerable to officials in the capital. The island's government was much like that of French Algeria.

But ideal and reality were farther apart in Cuba than in Algeria or even in Spain itself. Spaniards who were stationed in the island as civil or military officials had a political organization, the Unión Constitucional. Controlling all election machinery, this Unión chose most of Cuba's delegates to the Cortes. These representatives in turn pretended to speak for Cuba on taxes, tariffs, and like matters. On the whole, however, the Unión was less interested in benefiting Cuba than in ensuring that the central government did not reduce garrisons and civil establishments in the island, curb privileges, or restrict opportunities for graft. The Unión's representatives had a working alliance with shippers and industrialists of the Barcelona region. These Catalonian businessmen profited from mercantilist laws that hindered Cubans from buying or selling except through Spain. Together the Unión and its allies had been able to form a parliamentary bloc, throw support to either the Conservative or Liberal party, and thus prevent any cabinet from laying hands on the colony's decrepit and misshapen institutions.

By the early 1890's, however, Cuban landowners and merchants were complaining loudly of corruption and unfairness. Some had organized against the Unión Constitucional a Reformist party demanding administrative and economic concessions. Others had formed an Autonomist party calling for outright self-government like Canada's.[1]

Many islanders were in a frame of mind to support these or even more radical movements. Not a few had had experiences like José Martí's. When a child, Martí had seen his father fired from the Havana police force because a Spanish official wanted the job for someone else. A teacher whom he idolized had been plucked one day from the classroom and summarily sent into exile. He himself had been arrested at seventeen for laughing at a troop of Spanish soldiers. Held in jail for a year before trial, he was then sentenced by a Spanish judge to six years at hard labor.[2] Men with memories such as these were ready to fight for reform or more.

And Cuba's masses had every reason for following them. In 1861, when Spanish officials took a partial census, Cuba had just under eight hundred thousand whites. Only a small percentage owned property. Most did menial work in the cities or sweated in mills or on sugar plantations. At the time of the census, the island also had over six hundred thousand Negroes. Though they had been emancipated from slavery shortly after those in the United States, neither law nor time had lifted their condition. At least two-thirds of Cuba's people, white, brown, and black, lived in poverty, ignorance, and misery. In 1868 a fraction of these people had revolted, and Spain then had to make war for ten years to win even a compromise peace. Now, hearing Cuba's upper classes importune for reforms, politicians in Spain became uneasy.

Late in 1894 the government finally made up its mind that some repairs were imperative. The Liberal party was in power. The Minister for Colonies was Buenaventura de Abarzuza. He and other Liberal leaders wrestled with the Unión Constitucional and its allies and finally succeeded in putting before the Cortes a set of laws under which Cubans would gain a bit more voice in their own governance and slightly more freedom in trade. These so-called Abarzuza laws were in process of being approved by the Cortes in February, 1895, when Martí and his associates sent up the *grito de Baïre* and proclaimed the revolution for Cuban independence.

The Liberal government hoped that these promises of reform would prevent the insurrection from spreading. The Premier, Práxedes Mateo Sagasta, had no expectation of winning over the rebels themselves. Against them he pledged "an energetic campaign of repression, persecution, and chastisement." He did believe the majority of Cubans might be kept loyal so long as the upper classes had faith that the Abarzuza laws would improve their lot. If so, the revolt could be kept within manageable limits. The swamps and jungles would not nourish the rebels. Want of food and supplies would drive them into the open, and there Spanish troops could destroy them. The Colonial Minister told the Cortes that the Abarzuza laws would provide the most effective defense against the insurrection, and the Liberal majority dutifully passed them.[3]

Before the government could frame administrative decrees to set these laws in force, however, it found itself in a crisis. A Madrid daily, *El Resumen,* had printed an editorial criticizing junior officers of the army for their laggardness in volunteering to serve in Cuba. The newspaper's offices were broken into by a band of about thirty subalterns and lieutenants. When *El Resumen* and another daily protested this violence, both were stormed and sacked by an estimated three to four hundred young officers.

In the Cortes the government was attacked, not so much for failing to protect the newspapers as for not having already dragged their editors into military courts. Why, asked one speaker after another, had there not been swift punishment for journalists who defamed the army? Why had it been necessary for officers to take matters into their own hands?

When official spokesmen apologized that the law had not permitted action, army commanders in the Madrid area caucused and demanded that the government act anyway. Neither the army, the *Guardia Civil,* nor the police, it was reported, would even protect the government.

The Queen Regent summoned the most eminent soldier in the realm, General Arsenio Martínez de Campos, to pacify the generals. After conferring with them, he promised categorically that the press laws would be made stricter. Sagasta refused to stand sponsor for such amendments as Martínez Campos declared indispensable. Aware, however, that no civil government could long resist the army, he gladly accepted the alternative. He and his colleagues offered the Queen their resignations. She accepted, and a Conservative government took power even though the majority in the Cortes remained Liberal. The War Minister in the new cabinet took occasion to declare at once, "I shall continue to be an energetic defender of all the rights of the army."[4]

The new ministry had at its head Antonio Cánovas del Castillo. The dean of Spanish politicians, he had been in public life for nearly fifty years. At twenty-six he had been reputed *eminence grise* to the most successful of the mid-century's several military dictators. Alternately cabinet minister, conspirator, agitator, exile, he had done much to kill the short-lived republic of 1873, bring about the re-establishment of monarchy in 1874, and maintain a delicate semblance of stability since. The restoration constitution was largely his creation. So was the *turno a la inglesa,* an informal arrangement under which his party and the Liberal periodically exchanged office and rigged elections so that first one party and then the other controlled the Cortes, thus preserving the appearance of parliamentary democracy with none of its suspected dangers.

The studious son of a Málagan schoolteacher, Cánovas had also found time to write many books, among them a distinguished *History of the Decadence of Spain from Philip III to Charles II.* Antonio Ramos-Oliveira has written that among his many qualities Cánovas had one great defect: "He did not believe in Spain. 'They are Spaniards,' he once said, 'who cannot be anything else.' . . . In his inmost being, Cánovas was convinced that Spain was finished." He had nevertheless immense capacity and intelligence. Even his friends called him "El Monstruo"; his opponents could believe anything of him. It was rumored after his death, for example, that he had neglected matters of state because of preoccupation, at sixty-nine, with a new mistress.[5]

Taking over the premiership, Cánovas had to decide whether or not to continue the Liberal policy of buying off the Cuban rebellion with promises of reform. He barely held control over his own party. A certain number of young Conservatives were radical enough to believe that popular votes should be honestly counted and that civil servants and army officers should live on their salaries. Knowing that such notions would never be accepted by Cánovas, these visionaries wanted him replaced by handsome, magnetic, simple-minded Antonio Silvela. Another faction in the party consisted of devout Catholics who disliked Cánovas's policy of mediating between the church and anticlericals. They wanted the veteran leader replaced by pious Alejandro Pidal.

In order to combat both Silvelistas and Pidalistas, Cánovas had to have support from other factional leaders. The most powerful of these was Francisco Romero Robledo, a dark, disfigured fellow Málagan, who was notorious both as an election manipulator and as a spokesman for Catalonian businessmen and the Unión Constitucional. Cánovas could not afford to tie himself too closely to Romero, for Romero's followers alone could not sustain him in power. Neither, however, could he afford to fight him, for Romeristas, combined with Silvelistas and Pidalistas, could almost certainly carry the Conservative caucus against him.

Cánovas adopted a characteristically devious policy. He appointed Romero and two of his henchmen to the cabinet. Having done this, he then announced that the Conservative government would carry out the Abarzuza program. His Colonial Minister met with Cuban Reformists and on March 26 declared that the government would spare no effort to remedy the legitimate grievances of the islanders.

Cánovas indeed improved upon the Liberal policy. He arranged for Martínez Campos, the senior general of the army, to take command in Cuba. No doubt he wanted the venerable soldier out of the peninsula, for Martínez Campos did not like him and had immense influence with the Queen Regent. Nevertheless, the appointment involved some policy commitment because it was Martínez Campos who had made the peace that ended the war of 1868–1878 and who was, as a result, identified with pledges of reform made then and never fulfilled. Given plenary powers, Martínez Campos at once announced amnesty for any rebels who surrendered. Cánovas delayed drawing up decrees to carry out the Abarzuza laws. On the other hand, he offered concessions not only to loyal Cubans but even to insurrectionists.

At first this policy seemed to promise success. Groups of Cuban

Autonomists ostentatiously denounced the rebellion and pledged loyalty to Spain. After touring the island, however, Martínez Campos turned in a gloomy report. "The few Spaniards who are on the island," he wrote, "only dare proclaim themselves such in the cities; the rest of the inhabitants hate Spain." Neither kindness nor cruelty, reform or repression, he declared, could guarantee their loyalty.[6] Coming from a general who had so long shown faith in the Cubans, this summation compelled Cánovas to reconsider his tactics.

Hoping against hope to halt defection among Cubans, he worked to make the promise of reform more alluring. On October 8, he spoke to a reporter from *El Liberal:*

After the war is finished, it is evident that there are great reforms to undertake.

And on this score I am intransigent on only one point: intransigent against separatism.

With this, it is necessary to have done for once and for all.

As to the rest, I have an open mind. I do not emotionally reject any idea. I am receptive to anything, will consider anything, and thus will form my conviction. And the ideas which I profess are those which seem to me best.

Cuba needs full freedom from the central government [*descentralización*]. She has a right to administer her own funds and public works, doing first the things that she thinks most useful.

It is necessary to go straight ahead on the road of reform.

The Premier took care, however, that no reforms should actually be put in effect. He delayed application of the Abarzuza laws ostensibly because he felt it necessary to wait until an election could be held so that the Conservative party would have a popular mandate. In addition, he pointed out that there had been no census of Cuba for nearly thirty-five years. If any form of self-government was to be introduced, this obviously had to be remedied. Equally obviously, the continuance of war made it difficult to do so.

Since Cánovas had never shown partiality for change of any kind, he doubtless felt little sense of urgency. Furthermore, he knew that once the laws were put into effect they would lose most of their allure. In drawing them up, the Liberals had made many concessions to

Romero Robledo and his associates. There was to be an administrative council for Cuba, for example, but half its members were to be appointed from Madrid. Local government would remain securely in the hands of the Unión Constitucional. So long as his aim was to keep reformist Cubans loyal, Cánovas had good reason for offering promises rather than deeds.

In the meantime, he hoped to crush the rebellion by military force. The only question was how much effort it would take. Martínez Campos had observed in his report that stronger measures might become necessary. Specifically, he had mentioned reconcentrating the rural population in towns so that there would be no crops to sustain the rebels. Such a policy, the general admitted, would require much force and "the misery and hunger would be horrible." He could not himself carry it out; he was not ruthless enough. Someone like Valeriano Weyler, who had earned the sobriquet "butcher" during the earlier Cuban war, would have to undertake it. Cánovas had to decide whether or not to chance an all-out campaign such as Weyler would conduct, even though it might temporarily make conditions in Cuba worse.

There was no doubt that influential public opinion leaned toward a more energetic military effort. A rumor spread that Martínez Campos had punished the officer who killed José Martí. A distinguished Liberal politician asked publicly if Martínez Campos was not excessively tender toward the rebels. At the end of 1895 a campaign against the general suddenly broke out among Cubans in Spain, the Madrid popular press, and all three of the major military journals, *Ejército Español, Correspondencia Militar,* and *Correo Militar.* The Queen Regent meanwhile became persuaded that the general's health was failing and that he was subject to fits of fatigued forgetfulness.[7] Reluctantly, she and Cánovas agreed that Martínez Campos should be relieved and replaced by Lieutenant General Weyler.

The press had already quoted Weyler as calling Martínez Campos the wrong man for the Cuban command, adding, "I believe that with regard to the rebels a policy should be followed diametrically opposite to the one being followed." Shortly before being named to the Cuban command, he declared in another interview, "a salutary rigor . . .

would deprive the rebels of the most effective means of war." No one could doubt what attitude Weyler would take.

Two weeks after arrival in Havana he justified all expectations. Concentrating forces to fight the rebels, he deprived civilians of protection. He decreed life imprisonment or death for anyone who aided the rebels, and he ordered the people of rural areas to move into reconcentration camps on pain of arrest and imprisonment. Eventually he directed troops in the depopulated areas to shoot anything that moved.[8]

At the time when the United States began to offer advice, Spanish policy thus had two distinct and almost contradictory sides. One, administered by Weyler, involved relentless prosecution of the war with little regard for the feelings, interests, or even lives of the neutral or uncommitted Cubans. The other, principally evident in Cánovas's speeches, entailed promises of immense improvements and reforms if Cubans would only remain loyal to Spain.

When addressed by Cleveland and Olney, Cánovas did no more than hold his ground. Officially, he returned a curt reply to America's tender of good offices, remarking simply that the rebels refused to negotiate. Unofficially, he explained his reason for refusing by delivering a speech to the Conservative caucus and then releasing it to the press on May 10, 1896. In it he said:

Dangerous and vain it would be to resolve only to seek an end to the war by war, without preparing for any case, for any eventuality, in which the national honor would consent to making certain concessions; but even more dangerous would it be in my judgment to think that with this or that concession it would be possible to win over a separatist party that wants nothing of the sort.

Cánovas took the position that the rebels themselves would accept nothing but independence and that it would be futile and humiliating to negotiate with them. In the same unofficial manner, however, he let the Americans know that he would continue to meditate possible reforms. There can be no doubt that he had some desire to meet American wishes. In 1895 he had apologized for the *Alliança* incident and paid one and a half million dollars to settle a long-standing American claim. In both cases he had had some evidence that contrary decisions would be popular, yet he deliberately passed up the opportunity to play demagogue. He obviously saw wisdom in avoiding friction with Washington.

Still, it seems perfectly clear the Cánovas's attitude toward Cuban reform was shaped almost entirely by domestic considerations. He wanted to hold elections in Spain so that he could turn out the Liberal majority and give seats in the Cortes to Conservatives. Since an election meant a pretense of voting in Cuba as well as the peninsula, he had to ask Weyler if polling in the island would interfere with military plans and operations. The question was a necessary formality. Putting it, however, made Cánovas seem almost under Weyler's orders, and, since Weyler was already linked with Romero Robledo and the Unión Constitucional, the result was to make the Premier appear more tied than ever to this one faction. He had to dispel this impression if Pidalistas, Silvelistas, and others were not to coalesce and oust him from the party leadership.

Especially was this so because the Queen Regent so evidently wanted him replaced. A powerful group of clergymen, led by the Cardinal Archbishop of Valladolid, had the ear of the court. This group wished a purged Conservative party loyal to the church and hostile to the patchwork compromises with liberalism and anticlericalism that were keystones in Cánovas's system. It was Cánovas's rooted belief that if this group prevailed, the whole precarious structure upholding the dynasty would collapse. Even though he sighed to friends that he wanted retirement and leisure, he regarded himself as indispensable. He had to keep a firm grip on his party, he felt, and to do so he had to escape complete identification with Weyler and Romero. For this purpose his simplest expedient was to part company with them on the issue of Cuban reform.[9]

In addition, it was this issue that Cánovas's opponents seemed most likely to exploit. Silvela, who in principle was no reformer, had come out publicly for applying the Abarzuza laws with as little delay as possible. Sagasta, the former Premier and chief of the Liberal party, went secretly to visit the American minister and urge that the United States press for Cuban self-government. It is at least possible that he did so hoping for overt American pressure which would embarrass Cánovas, make it a matter of pride for him to refuse reforms, and thus allow Liberals to attack him for doing nothing.

There is evidence indicating that Cánovas was in fact slowed by the American suggestions. After Olney broached the topic of reform, the Spanish Foreign Minister remarked that the government might have trouble doing what it intended because of the danger of seeming to submit to American dictation. After receiving the Olney note, he reiterated, "We must avoid any appearance of doing what we propose to do on account of foreign pressure."[10]

Nevertheless, after the elections had been held and the government's agents had ensured the return of a predictably large Conservative majority, the Queen Regent greeted the new Cortes on May 11, 1896, with an address from the throne promising Cuba "an administrative and economic personality of exclusively local character and one which facilitates the complete participation of the country in its particular affairs while maintaining intact the rights of [Spanish] sovereignty and the indispensable conditions for its subsistence." These phrases, no more precise in Spanish than in translation, contained one important word—"economic." The Abarzuza laws related almost altogether to administration. The speech from the throne hinted that Cuba might be released from her dependence on Catalonian merchants, shippers, and industrialists. And this one veiled hint was enough to draw angry invective from Romero Robledo.

The government's second step came in a speech by Cánovas on July 14. Romero had just spoken to prolonged applause from the Conservative majority, repeating what the Premier himself had earlier said: that war had to be answered with war and that reforms could only be effected after the war was over. He also said, "if any government, whatever it may be, establishes autonomy, it will be returned to private life, for it is understood that autonomy is synonymous with independence."

Cánovas did not directly contradict Romero, but he did declare: "The government recognizes the necessity for giving the island of Cuba great administrative and economic reforms which will mean complete freedom from the central government. . . . In a word, the economic reforms which the government will establish are equivalent to what the English call 'self-government' (administrative autonomy)." He went on to say that the reforms would be applied "when the triumph of our arms is a fact, a little before or a little after."

Not only did Cánovas commit himself to extensive reforms, but he also suggested that the government might not wait until the war had ended. He went even farther a few days later, saying: "It will be enough if the insurrection is broken. Once the principal centers of population are free from the menace of the enemy, we will not delay for a minute." Cánovas had still done nothing. He was only making promises. But he had begun making promises that could almost be felt and tasted.

In January, 1897, six weeks after Cleveland's annual message advised autonomy, Cánovas finally defined the reforms he was willing to offer to Cuba. At the time, he needed more than ever to detach himself from Weyler. The general's failure to achieve victory had produced disillusionment even among his erstwhile partisans. On October 6, 1896, the *Correspondencia Militar* suggested that he probably ought to be replaced. On October 9, the *Correo Militar* joined in. It was known that Martínez Campos had criticized the general and urged the Queen to replace him. Cánovas could not himself order Weyler home, for, as he candidly admitted, there was no other general with Conservative ties who could take his place. He did need to take precautions lest the general's critics assume that the only way of removing him was to remove the government, and, since Weyler's views were well known, he had only to take another step toward reform to prove that he and the general differed.

This course was also advisable because the Premier needed urgently to placate the Queen. He had had a serious falling out with her. In the Philippine Islands, where another revolutionary war was in progress, the post of commanding general had fallen vacant. Cánovas had promised it to Captain General Fernando Primo de Rivera, who needed a command in order to repair his finances. The Queen wanted to name Lieutenant General Camilo Polavieja, an adherent of the neoclerical faction captained by the Cardinal Archbishop of Valladolid. Each was determined to have his way.

Coincidentally, on December 8, 1896, the *Imparcial*'s correspondent in Cuba reported Weyler's allegedly impenetrable line, the *trocha,* to have been crossed by Antonio Maceo and a rebel troop. Havana seemed in danger. On the morning of December 9, Madrid papers were full of the rumor that the Queen would dismiss Cánovas and summon a different Conservative cabinet or perhaps a coalition ministry under Martínez Campos.

Cánovas was saved only by the killing of Maceo. Almost the only success reported for months, this event transformed the public mood. Newspapers described jubilation in the streets, coffee houses, and garrisons of Madrid. The Premier was safe.

Recognizing that his rescue was due to accident, Cánovas judged it prudent to make concessions to the Queen. First, he allowed Polavieja to be named to the Philippine command. Second, at a cabinet meeting on December 17, he approved draft decrees defining reforms to be applied immediately in Puerto Rico and later in Cuba. The Queen felt, as she told the French ambassador, that she had "wrenched" this concession from the Premier.[11]

Cánovas still balked at actually putting reforms into effect in Cuba. Friendly governments had begun to give the same advice as the United States. The French urged that reforms be granted the Cubans. The Vatican evidently seconded this counsel. More important, factions and parties within Spain became increasingly bold in criticizing the government's procrastination. Emilio Castelar, onetime leader of Spanish republicans, appeared at a banquet and broke a silence of nine years to call for extensive Cuban reforms. The republican splinter parties, long so divided that they could not assemble without fistfights, managed to form a partial union. The one plank on which they all agreed was autonomy for Cuba. Representatives of the Liberal left had already joined in the demand for more, ampler, and immediate reforms. Then on March 22, 1897, a leader of the Liberal right spoke. Antonio Maura, the real sponsor of the original Liberal reform project, told the Press Association: "It is necessary to do in Cuba whatever may be required to keep its heart and to win its will in favor of Spain." It was evident that the Liberals would soon call for autonomy and insist that only such a policy could keep the loyalty of the left. One Liberal leader, Segismundo Moret, warned at Zaragoza on

October 19, 1896, that if Cánovas refused this demand there would be danger of revolution. "If the government declines the responsibility," he said, "the monarchy will be responsible."[12]

On the other hand, Cánovas could see that there might also be peril in yielding too much or too quickly. It was rumored that Romero's supporters were talking of a republic with him and Weyler as its strong men. Zealots in the cause of the exiled pretender, Don Carlos, were reported gathering funds and arms. And, as always, there was evidence that a revolutionary *pronunciamiento* could light a wild fire. In October, 1895, a thousand manifestants had attacked a religious procession in Cádiz and stoned a bishop and a police chief. In Barcelona and Valencia riots had required the imposition of martial law. News in 1896 that the American government was threatening intervention brought fifteen thousand young men into the Ramblas in Barcelona, shouting against the United States and against any compromises with the Cuban rebels. Valencia had a similar demonstration, and lesser disturbances occurred in the north at Bilbao, Logroño, Oviedo, and Valladolid, in the east at Zaragoza, and in the south at Murcia, Granada, and Málaga. The Queen wrote her sister-in-law in March, 1897, that she feared "a revolt in the streets."[13] Though Cánovas endeavored to soothe her, he realized that it might be as dangerous to do something as to do nothing.

Nevertheless, when he published the decrees that were someday to go into effect, he weakened his earlier statements about how distant that day might be. "When the majority of provinces are cleared of rebels," he told the press on January 29, "that will be the moment . . . to apply the reforms." On April 24, a month before the Cortes were to reconvene, he said that he could not predict whether reforms would be put in effect before or after the sessions commenced. Then he received from Weyler an obviously exaggerated summary of the army's successes in the campaigning season of 1896–1897. He published it. Madrid newspapers remarked cynically that while there were only twenty-eight battalions in provinces described as still in rebellion, there were eighty-three in those allegedly tranquil. Yet this dispatch gave the Premier the pretext he needed. On April 29, more than two years after the Cortes's enactment of the Abarzuza laws,

Cánovas at last announced that reforms would be instituted in the pacified provinces of Cuba.

Though the outgoing Cleveland administration expressed pleasure over this announcement, assuming that it had resulted from American importunities, the fact was that the Spanish government had been moved almost entirely by domestic considerations. Cánovas had moved step by step toward reform because he needed to separate himself from Romero and Weyler. In the end he had seen the shadow of revolution lying across both the roads before him. Perhaps he chose as he did, reasoning that otherwise the Liberals would probably come to power and that if real danger lay ahead he was more fit to deal with it than they. Perhaps, in other words, the key to his whole policy was that trait of character on which so many of his contemporaries remarked—his haughty egotism or *soberbia*.

Though the Premier's decisions on Cuba were little influenced by American goading, his government did not entirely disregard the possibility that relations with the United States might become troublesome. While Cánovas concentrated over the chessboard of Spanish politics, his diplomats occupied themselves in a more fanciful game. They endeavored to find allies in Europe.

The Foreign Minister, Carlos O'Donnell y Abreu, Duke of Tetuán, was a polished, impetuous nephew of the ex-sergeant become military dictator whom Cánovas had served in his own youth. A mercurial optimist, Tetuán evidently assumed that the powers would be only too glad to lend Spain a hand. At about the time when the American Congress started discussing recognition, he began work on a formal memorandum stating Spain's case against American interference in Cuba. His expectation was that the powers would endorse the memorandum and thus implicitly commit themselves to oppose the United States. These endorsements could be exhibited in Washington, and the Americans would then presumably have better sense than to test their sincerity. Tetuán worked on this document intermittently. As a close friend of Martínez Campos's, he felt obliged to resign when the general was relieved. The Queen urged him to return so that he could continue with the memorandum. After a suitable interval, he did so. But it was summer in 1896 before he had it completed.

In the meanwhile he had made overtures to individual powers. Spain's one connection with the great alliance systems of Europe had been a pact with Italy of 1887, renewed in 1891, and allowed to lapse in 1895. Though formally tying Spain only to Italy, in fact it had connected her with the Triple Alliance and also with the more limited Mediterranean partnership of Italy, Austria, and England. Its effect had been to guarantee these powers that Spain would not support France in any North African adventures. The failure to renew it had been due to indiscreet revelation of its existence and resulting questions in the Cortes. At the time, Cánovas had not wanted to defend himself against doctrinaire isolationists, pro-French factions, and earnest Catholics who resented Italy's having taken Rome from the Pope.

By spring of 1896, the Premier and his Foreign Minister were willing to offer Italy renewal of the pact on condition that Italy, Austria, and England guarantee Spanish possession of Cuba. Tetuán did not make it clear whether he wished mere moral support or a promise of naval backing, but the Italians were not in either case prepared to sign. Nor were the English ready to offer support, despite Tetuán's argument that Spain and Britain had a common interest in curbing American aggressiveness. Nor did the French seem tempted even by hints of a possible alliance.[14] The failure of these direct approaches left the memorandum, an appeal to the Concert of Europe, as the only resort.

The document was not kept particularly secret. Tetuán spoke of it to various ambassadors. Press reports of cabinet meetings occasionally mentioned discussion of a circular intended for the powers. The *Imparcial* of May 14, 1896, carried a fairly full story on the project. Most of the ambassadors showed sympathy with its terms and aims. Though editorials in semiofficial Russian and French papers said Spain could not expect aid from Europe, the Spanish ambassadors in Paris and St. Petersburg reported more optimistically. Tetuán judged that his project was opposed only by the Russian ambassador in Madrid, not even by his government. He made a direct appeal to the Russian Foreign Minister and received the embarrassed reply that Russia had no objection. By the beginning of August, 1896, printed copies of the memorandum had reached Spanish embassies in all the major capitals. They were being translated and prepared for delivery on signal from Madrid.

At this point Tetuán met an obstacle. Hannis Taylor, the American minister, suddenly demanded a special interview. He announced dramatically that he had learned of the proposed memorandum. He asserted that if the memorandum were what he understood it to be, the United States would regard its dispatch as an unfriendly act. Unwilling to show the document to Taylor, Tetuán felt obliged to promise that it would not be sent.

He quickly recovered himself. The powers already knew the gist of the memorandum; they had been alerted to expect its delivery. Tetuán directed Spanish envoys to call on foreign ministers, explain that the memorandum could not be delivered on account of objections from the United States, but proceed to read aloud the principal parts of the document in the course of apologizing for its withdrawal. In most cases the foreign ministers listened attentively and said something kind but noncommittal. After all the responses were in, Tetuán concluded that all the powers were sympathetic and that "all are convinced of the European character of the problem." When he wrote his memoirs six years later, he still believed that the memorandum had laid a basis for successful appeal to Europe.[15]

The circulation of this memorandum and the proposal to Italy were the only steps that the Cánovas government took in direct response to American pressure. On rare occasions when Cánovas spoke of the United States, it was to say that he trusted Cleveland to keep the peace. He himself was simply too preoccupied in holding Spain together to give much thought to the distant future. Governing a nation that might fly to pieces any day, he could rarely afford to think beyond the next fortnight. During his premiership, the danger of war was never near enough to affect him deeply. Aside from sending out the Tetuán memorandum, the Cánovas government cannot be said to have made any effort to avert a Spanish-American conflict.

Perhaps Cánovas did begin to think more seriously of this danger during the summer of 1897. His own position had become almost unbearable. He had succeeded finally in winning out over the Queen, having Polavieja brought back from the Philippines, and fulfilling his promise to give the place to Primo de Rivera. But when Polavieja arrived in Madrid, greeted by throngs of Cánovas's enemies, the Queen made a gesture of defiance, appearing on a balcony of the Palace to wave a handkerchief at the general. Cánovas felt obliged on the following day, May 17, to publish an ugly editorial in *La Época,* his official organ, asserting that the Queen understood her constitutional duty to support her ministers, that she had stepped onto her balcony and fluttered the kerchief by sheer accident, and that she had apologized to the Premier for misinterpretations by the press. Although this humiliation of the Queen demonstrated Cánovas's strength, it gave him no added popularity.

Only a few days later he was compelled to raise formally the question of the Queen's confidence. Tetuán and a Liberal exchanged words in the lobby of the Senate. Tetuán gave emphasis to his statements by hitting his adversary on the mouth. Bystanders restrained both men, though the latter's son fell upon Tetuán and destroyed his hat. There was talk of a duel. The Liberals and the Silvelistas walked out of the Cortes, refusing to return till Cánovas had fired Tetuán. Cánovas refused to do so, knowing that the Duke's faction was indispensable to him. He had to ask the Queen to confirm him in power with his cabinet unaltered. Possibly he learned that she did so only after the Liberal leader had said, in effect, that he did not yet want the premiership. In any case, he must have suspected that the Queen would probably replace him as soon as the summer recess was over.

Cánovas had reason to believe that if he were to safeguard Spain from upheaval, he would have to mature some drastic solution for the Cuban problem. Despite optimistic reports from Washington on the conciliatory attitude of the incoming American President, Cánovas was aware that the United States might soon cause trouble. More than one of his friends recalled his saying that summer, "If, over and above what exists, we were to add thirty or forty thousand Americans landed on the island, the great fleet, and all the power of that republic, what would be our fate?" The editor of *La Época* recorded his declaring that war would be "the perdition and ruin of our country." But whether any means of meeting this danger had occurred to him, no one knows.[16]

On August 8, 1897, in San Sebastián, where the Queen kept summer court, Cánovas was shot and killed by a young anarchist. The War Minister became Premier. Romero Robledo, who had long since left the ministry on account of some contract scandals, went into open opposition, taking with him a third of the Conservative deputies. Pidal, Silvela, Tetuán, and others quarreled publicly over Cánovas's inheritance. The Queen meanwhile took the step which she had long been meditating. She sent word to the chief of the Liberal party, inviting him to form a ministry. She allowed the Conservatives to retain office only until her return to Madrid. As soon as opportunity offered, she dismissed them and summoned a Liberal government.

The American with whom the Spanish Liberals would have to contend was Cleveland's successor, William McKinley, one of the most enigmatic figures ever to occupy the White House. A man's character usually emerges for the historian out of private letters. McKinley wrote none. The hundred-odd volumes of his personal papers in the Library of Congress have practically nothing in his own hand. Collections of his friends' papers hold little more. At most there is an occasional note inviting someone to come talk something over. He simply would not commit himself on paper.

Nor, it seems, would he do so in public speeches. When young he had won a reputation as a convincing trial lawyer. During his twelve years in the House of Representatives he was looked upon as a formidable advocate of the protective tariff. Some of his extemporaneous sallies against free traders were long remembered and quoted. As a campaigner, he invented slogans that, if ponderous, were still telling: "not more coinage, but a more active use of the money coined. Not open mints . . . but open mills. . . ." But his statements after he began to dream of the Presidency held so many reservations and ambiguities as often to seem parodies. When questioned about the Cuban issue in 1895, for example, he declared, "I most politely decline to go on record. At this time I do not care to speak about it. In my position it were better that I say nothing now. Perhaps later I may have something to say."

Surprisingly, however, neither the public nor his acquaintances thought of McKinley as secretive or slippery. Two young men who spent much time with him, his private secretary, George B. Cortelyou, and Comptroller of the Currency Charles G. Dawes, revered him. When crisis came, Dawes wrote in his diary, "The President as always, remains the firm, cool, able leader of men. . . . In the greatness of McKinley the safety of the situation lies." It would appear that this worshipful attitude was shared by his wife. Julia Foraker recounts that, hearing an English visitor say she liked America but loved England best, Mrs. McKinley drew herself up and exclaimed frostily, "Do you mean to say that you would prefer England to a country ruled over by *my husband?*"[1]

Bits and scraps of others' reminiscences make McKinley seem a father character from a Victorian novel. He bore himself stiffly. In his heavy, handsome face, dark eyes flashed from shadows under thick, tufted eyebrows. Several times commended for gallantry during the Civil War, he had come out as a major at the age of twenty-two. He never swore. He sometimes reproved acquaintances who used bad language or told off-color stories. He always went to church and made a point of never working on Sundays. To his invalid wife he showed exemplary devotion. He would leave the cabinet table to perform minor services for her. The character that he exhibited to the world could have been invented by Louisa May Alcott.

His public career was consistent with the discreet silences of his private papers and the ambiguities of his speeches. Once out of the army, he set his mind on becoming a member of Congress. He married a banker's daughter in his home town, became prosecuting attorney, and went to Congress almost as soon as he was of age. There he deliberately became an expert on the tariff, later counseling younger members to make their mark in the House by becoming masters of some question, no matter what. On the floor he worked for the ironmongers, potters, and sheepgrowers of his district and for the Republican caucus. Climbing to the chairmanship of the Ways and Means Committee, he authored the McKinley tariff bill of 1890, which was a major issue in the elections of 1890 and 1892. He came to be talked of for the Presidency and from that time forward said and did practically nothing that could lose votes.

When as Governor of Ohio he found that a friend's bankruptcy had put him over one hundred thousand dollars in debt, he allowed some rich industrialists to pay off his notes. An adoring biographer records ingenuously that when McKinley first learned the news, "he paced the floor in agony. 'I have kept clear of all entanglements all my life,' he groaned. 'Oh, that this should come to me now.' "[2] One of those industrialists, Mark Hanna, managed his campaign for the Presidency. When Hanna then wanted a seat in the Senate, Mc-

Kinley created a vacancy by appointing the frail and doddering Senator Sherman Secretary of State. In McKinley's political career before 1897 one finds no sign of any ambition except to climb the greasy pole. There are traces of virtue but few of character.

Yet there can be little doubt that it was McKinley who made White House decisions. Hanna, whom some thought a power behind the throne, gave little advice to the President. Old friends from Capitol Hill were rarely seen at the White House. In the cabinet, the Secretary of State was senile, the Secretary of the Treasury often off at spiritualist seances, the Secretary of the Navy only faintly aware of what was going on in the White House, and the Secretary of War busy with his own department and his home state. Assistant Secretary William R. Day, who really ran the State Department, saw more of McKinley than anyone else, and Day was a model of self-effacement. No one around the President sought to wrestle away his responsibilities, and he himself trusted no one enough to make him a confidant.[3]

The enigma of McKinley's personality makes it exceedingly hard to plumb the motives beneath his policies. Though such reconstruction is always guesswork, one usually knows enough to feel that such and such an impulse was consistent with a man's character. In McKinley's case, there is nothing to make one interpretation inherently more convincing than another. His young friends thought he showed high principle and great courage. Theodore Roosevelt said he had no more backbone than a chocolate éclair. It may be that he was, in fact, a cunning and resourceful manipulator of events. The scanty evidence left behind can be fitted into any number of patterns.

It is clear that the Cuban question occupied McKinley's mind from the beginning and that he saw it much as Cleveland had. He inherited the duty of protecting citizens and preventing breaches of neutrality. At the very outset of his administration, he had to receive Congressional appeals for the rescue of putative Americans, Gustave Richelieu, August Bolten, George Washington Aguirre, and Ruis Rivera. Several unpopular trials were meanwhile in progress at home, especially that against members of the *Dauntless* expedition. In addition, the new administration's very first financial estimates had to include appropriations for patroling coasts, investigating violations of neutrality, and maintaining quarantines against Cuban fevers. It cannot have taken McKinley long to view the Cuban war as a nuisance and an expense.

There were some economic results of the endless rebellion that Cleveland may have foreseen but that only materialized as the new administration took over. The Democratic President had been worried mainly by destruction of American property. The Republican faced the consequences not only of these ravages but also of those on the other ninety per cent of Cuban plantations. By 1897 sugar imports from Cuba had fallen to almost one-fifth of the 1894 figure: from 956,524 tons to 209,433. Refinery inventories were exhausted, and the eastern "sugar trust," the American Sugar Refining Company, found itself having to import large quantities from other sources and to pay as much as three to four dollars more per ton. Much the same thing happened in the tobacco industry as imports of Cuban leaf fell off.

These consequences of the Cuban war were troubling for McKinley as a politician concerned with consumer prices. They had a bearing upon his hope for new tariff legislation and, indeed, on his leadership in the Republican party. Sugar was the one major commodity that had been made duty-free in the McKinley tariff act. The resultant loss of revenue, coupled with the expense of paying a bounty to domestic sugar producers, had been one justification for high schedules on other items. To McKinley and the Republican caucus this had seemed the best if not the sole means of ending surpluses and thus destroying the free traders' best argument for lower tariffs. The Democrats, in the Wilson act of 1894, had restored some duties on sugar and lowered those on wool, iron ore, and other articles in which Republicans, especially Ohio Republicans, were interested. McKinley wanted something like the McKinley bill re-enacted; his first act as President was to summon a special session of Congress and ask it for "the restoration of . . . protective legislation." But he could not hope for remission or reduction of raw sugar duties so long as a large percentage of the import was of beet sugar from Germany and other European countries. The beet sugar producers of Michigan,

Nebraska, Nevada, and California would not hear of it. The bill drawn up by the special session had to include levies on raw sugar and correspondingly lower rates on wool, iron ore, and the like. Only if peace came and Cuba resumed cane production could McKinley hope for more satisfactory legislation.

The sugar shortage also affected the President's party leadership because of the political power of the sugar trust. The profits of the trust, if not indeed its existence, depended directly on differential duties curbing imports of refined sugar. The President of the American Sugar Refining Company had a reputation as one of the most politically active of business magnates. It was known that he made large contributions to candidates in both parties. It was said that he distributed stock shares among congressmen who then took profits when their own legislation insured the industry continued protection. One senator was reported to have made two million dollars in one speculative coup. Three powerful Republican leaders in the Senate, Allison, Nelson W. Aldrich of Rhode Island, and Matthew S. Quay of Pennsylvania, were supposed to be linked with the trust. And the trust, desiring cheap raw sugar, had a keen interest in the restoration of peace in Cuba.[4] If the President failed to take steps toward that end, it was conceivable that the sugar senators might put forward a Cuban policy of their own.

Even without the tariff problem and the sugar trust to worry about, McKinley would have been able to see that the Cuban issue threatened political trouble. The manifestations produced by Maceo's death and the Cameron resolution were not events a politician could ignore. McKinley was visited by more than one congressman who advised prompt and energetic action. Senator John M. Thurston of Nebraska, a loyal Republican, long counsel for the Union Pacific Railroad and chairman of the convention that had nominated McKinley, emerged from a conference at Canton declaring that the new administration would have to intervene in Cuba: "the people out West are demanding that something be done." The Democrats seemed prepared to close ranks on Cuba; conservatives like Hill of New York and Gorman of Maryland joined agrarian agitators. There was obvious danger that Republicans like Thurston, Cullom, and Mason might combine with Democrats to form a majority against a too pacific administration. The President's House leader, General Charles H. Grosvenor of Ohio, wrote that the temper of the Senate chilled his blood: "I think I see everywhere all along the line a disposition to provoke hostilities and to bring about a condition that will ruin us all."[5] It was perfectly clear that if the President failed to offer leadership, there was danger of rebellion in the Senate, perhaps in the House, possibly even in the country.

Even if this had not been the case, of course, McKinley might have concerned himself with Cuba for moral reasons. He did give the appearance of being a devout Methodist. His mother had been a prop of that church in his home town. He himself had walked the sawdust to be converted at the age of ten and briefly considered the ministry as a career. It may be that he was inwardly antagonistic toward Popish Spain. Even if his piety was mostly outward, he could still have been moved by the suffering and brutality reported in Cuba. The consul general in Havana wrote, for example, of men hacked by machetes and dragged through village streets, of Spanish troops appropriating hospitals and churches as barracks, and of disease and starvation everywhere.[6] And similar tales came almost daily from other consular agents, newspaper reporters, and tourists. It is possible that even without economic and political considerations McKinley would have felt in his heart a need to do something for Cuba.

But what was he to do?

In the interval between election and inauguration, McKinley evidently hoped that Cleveland would solve the dilemma for him. Lodge wrote Theodore Roosevelt that he had seen McKinley in Canton: "Cuba . . . is very much on his mind and I found that he had given it a great deal of thought. He very naturally does not want to be obliged to go to war as soon as he comes in, for of course his great ambition is to restore business and bring back good times and he dislikes the idea of such interruption. He would like the crisis to come this winter and be settled one way or the other before he takes up the reins." The Cameron resolution aimed at bringing on the crisis, but Cleveland and Olney refused to be prodded. If the resolution passed and Cleveland stood his ground, McKinley would no sooner be in office then he would have to choose between yielding to Congress or fighting it. Once sure that Cleveland would not act, McKinley let it be known that he wished the Senate to table the Cameron resolution and leave him a free hand. He told a later visitor to Canton that he was glad Cleveland had been "conservative in his treatment and recommenda-tions, and not disposed to do or say anything likely to create an immediate ugly situation for the new administration."[7]

Despite arguments and pressures for some bold move such as recognition or a demand that Spain pacify the island within a given time, McKinley could no more have opened his administration in such a fashion than he could have come out suddenly for free coinage of silver. In the first place, he was too much dependent on the good opinion of businessmen. A Presidential intimate once made a list of the men whom McKinley looked up to; it included John D. Rocke-feller and other Standard Oil magnates, and George H. Pullman, Myron T. Herrick, Charles H. Cramp, J. P. Morgan, and Frank Thomson: "the President respects the opinion of a capable busi-ness man like Mr. Thomson who has shown himself worthy of re-spect on account of his talents and his having been placed in charge of such a large property as the Pennsylvania Railroad Company."[8]

Men who fitted this list were generally against any policy that risked war. McKinley would not have wanted to antagonize them. Believing that recovery from the lingering economic depression de-pended on business confidence, he hoped instead to calm and hearten them. And he must have known, at least intuitively, that he could not do without their backing. Other Republican leaders had more of a hold than he on the veterans, the religious denominations, the ethnic minorities, and other groups that composed the party. His own strong-hold was the industrial and financial community. Without its whole-hearted support, the status and power of the Presidency would have availed him little; he could have hoped for no more leadership or legislative success than Cleveland. It was simply out of the question for him to embark on a policy unless virtually certain that Republi-can businessmen would back him.

Even without this overriding consideration, McKinley might pos-sibly have been deterred from initial boldness by uncertainty about the diplomatic situation. Ever since the introduction of the Cameron resolution, there had been constant rumors of possible European combinations behind Spain. In January, 1897, the Berlin *Tageblatt* printed a sensational report that France and Russia had promised to intervene in Washington if necessary to prevent a Spanish-American war. Blowitz, the erratic but extraordinarily well-connected Paris correspondent of the London *Times,* confirmed the story. The most cautious and knowledgeable American correspondent in Europe, Isaac N. Ford of the New York *Tribune,* denied it but admitted that Paris financiers holding Spanish bonds and securities were restless. The St. Petersburg *Novoe Vremya* then launched a strong anti-American campaign, suggesting to at least some American observers that the *Tageblatt* and Blowitz stories were true. *Novoe Vremya* declared, "Europe has every reason to oppose the strengthening of the United States in the New World and must be ready to support Spain if she is threatened with the loss of Cuba"[9]

Nor was the rumor of possible Franco-Russian backing for Spain the only one about. Blowitz also reported the German Kaiser to have called for European unity not only in support of Spain but also against the Monroe doctrine. Though the tale was officially denied, American editors and commentators seemed unconvinced. Much was made of a speech in the Reichstag by a Prussian Conservative leader, calling for united resistance to the American economic menace. Editors pointed critically at Germany's official policy of directing emigration toward South America. Some commented on the extent to which Europe's action in the Cretan question, seemingly under German leadership, appeared to portend a revived Holy Alliance. The New York *Tribune* warned, "Its activities are not to be confined to Europe. All the world must come beneath its sway." Added to more improbable tales, such as one that Spain and Japan had signed an alliance to keep the United States out of both Cuba and Hawaii, these rumors could at least have made the new President a little uneasy. If nothing else, they helped to justify a cautious policy.

McKinley, even more than Cleveland, felt the drag of both the upper and the nether millstones. The constant irritation and expense resulting from the Cuban war, its economic consequences, and above

all its explosive potential as a domestic issue made it simply impossible for him to be an indifferent spectator. On the other hand, he
could not launch out on some bold course of interference. His own
national constituency, the community of rich businessmen, was not
ready to support such a policy, and he could not judge what international complications it might bring.

In the early months of his administration, he temporized. In his
inaugural address he scattered a little balm in both directions. After
declaring sternly, "It will be our aim to pursue a firm and dignified
foreign policy, which shall be just, impartial, ever watchful of our
national honor, and always insisting upon the enforcement of the lawful rights of American citizens everywhere," he went on to say sooth-
ingly, "We want no wars of conquest; we must avoid the temptation
of territorial aggression. War should never be entered upon until
every agency of peace has failed; peace is preferable to war in almost
every contingency." Newspapers that were supposed to have an inside track, like the New York *Tribune* and Hanna's Cleveland *Leader,*
repeatedly offered reassurance that McKinley intended to continue
the cautious, pacific policy of his predecessor. Businessmen and business journals sighed happily that McKinley would be as safe and
sound on foreign policy as on the gold standard and the tariff.

At the same time, the new President managed to keep up hopes
among jingoes. Sherman visited his former colleagues on the Foreign
Relations Committee and assured them that McKinley would co-
operate fully with Congress. Chairman Hitt of the House Foreign
Affairs Committee, after several calls at the White House, told Junta
agents that McKinley knew exactly what he was doing and would
help Cuba without any pressure from Congress. Lodge, who was
supposed to be in the President's confidence, had already assured a
Cuban representative, "This Congress will not end without McKinley's having done something far-reaching in the affair."[10]

By retaining Fitzhugh Lee as consul general in Havana, the President lent color to these statements, for it was already notorious that
Lee hoped for intervention and annexation. Sherman was reported as
saying that the State Department would no longer disregard the grievances of Americans, as Olney had, and it was ostentatiously an-

nounced from the White House that only three citizens remained in
Spanish prisons. When rumor got out that hundreds of Americans
were starving and dying of disease in Cuba, McKinley swiftly sent
a special message to Congress. He asked an immediate appropriation
of fifty thousand dollars for food and medicine. The new chairman
of the Senate Foreign Relations Committee, Cushman K. Davis of
Minnesota, went to the White House, and it was afterward reported
authoritatively, "the President will use his powers to stop the
bloodshed insofar as he can without involving the United States in
war."[11]

No sooner had the relief proposal ceased to be a sensation than
McKinley was speaking out against Weyler's reconcentration policy.
On June 8, three weeks after the special message, the Assistant Secretary of State put the Spanish ambassador on warning that the
President might have to protest formally if Spain did not immediately
remedy conditions in the camps. After the shortest polite interval,
the threat was carried out. The Spanish government was told officially:
"Against this deliberate infliction of suffering on innocent noncom-
batants . . . the President is constrained to protest, in the name of the
American people and in the name of common humanity." Though
the note was confidential, its text was probably shown to appropriate
members of the Senate. Republican jingoes were quoted in the press,
at any rate, as saying they now felt sure the administration would
"adopt a positive policy."[12]

McKinley bought time from the jingoes with every coin that came
to hand. He made judicious use of his patronage. He gave posts in
the cabinet to conservative men of such proven ineffectualness as to
calm the most skittish believer in *laissez-faire*. But he made other
appointments to please other people. Lodge, for example, had set
his heart on having Theodore Roosevelt as Assistant Secretary of
the Navy. The President pretended that there were great obstacles,
among them that Roosevelt was *persona non grata* to Platt, the party
leader in New York. Actually, Platt was thrilled at the thought of
having Roosevelt out of his state. At length McKinley pretended to
succumb. Lodge was overjoyed, more so than if the President had

yielded at once, and the appointment gave some additional pleasure to others whom Lodge had enlisted in the cause.

McKinley capitalized in much the same fashion on naming John Hay as ambassador to Great Britain, Henry White as Hay's assistant, and William W. Rockhill as minister to Greece. At the same time, he was offering posts which they could not or would not accept to General McCook, the Junta's banker, John W. Foster, and others. His use of the patronage extended to the very lowest offices. Chandler, for example, asked that one of his friends be named to a postmastership in New Hampshire. Gallinger, the state's other Republican senator, protested that the man was wholly unfit; he could not trust his own private mail to his hands. But the President appointed Chandler's nominee none the less. Gallinger was already tied to him while Chandler was not.[13]

In addition, the President did what he could to keep jingoes' minds off Cuba. Summoning Congress into special session, he explained that he acted reluctantly and only because the government had to have more money. Speaker Reed was reported to be following the President's wishes as well as his own inclinations in curbing House debate on any subject other than the tariff. Senators could not be harnessed in such fashion, but the President did refrain from putting temptation before them. Though he had commended the Anglo-American arbitration treaty in his inaugural address, he let the British ambassador know that he could not press for its prompt ratification; it was undesirable that chauvinists see any red rags. Such extraneous matters as he did put before the Senate were rather those that jingoes could be expected to welcome. He encouraged debate on the navy and the Nicaragua canal.[14] Despite earlier implied promises to leave the Hawaiian question alone, he also put a new annexation treaty before the upper house.

The timing of this treaty may have been fortuitous. Japan had protested the Hawaiian republic's treatment of Japanese nationals. Some Tokyo newspapers talked wildly of punitive expeditions, and Japanese warships were reported in the Central Pacific. Hawaiian agents in Washington gave wide and sensational publicity to the alleged danger of Japan's seizing the islands, and veteran advocates of annexation made the most of it. McKinley may have been worried about the risk. His minister in Honolulu was directed to proclaim a protectorate if Japan seemed likely to use force, and the fleet commander in the area was ordered to back him up. By the time the treaty was drawn up, however, even Roosevelt had been forced to admit that Japan posed no immediate menace. The President knew that the treaty could not win two-thirds of the Senate. He assured Carl Schurz that ratification was impossible. Smiling benignly, he explained that his aim had been simply to test public opinion. He may have meant the treaty as a warning to Japan. More probably, he intended it as a sop for the Cuban jingoes.

Since the navy, the isthmian canal, and Hawaiian annexation were all old Republican causes, the President's reserved support of them excited nothing but mild suspicion among his more conservative followers. At the same time, it quieted the jingoes. Theodore Roosevelt wrote to Lodge, "it would be everything for us to take firm action on behalf of the wretched Cubans, [but the] President has done so much that I don't feel like being discontented."[15] Partly by chance, partly by art, McKinley won time in which to seek some way out of the Cuban dilemma.

Groping for some possible escape, he toyed with the thought of buying Spain out. In the summer of 1897 someone approached the Junta on the subject. It was induced to offer one hundred and fifty million dollars in bonds to compensate Spain for granting independence, with the interest to be guaranteed by United States supervision of the Cuban customs. Through a Paris house with large Spanish holdings, the Junta's banker sought to put the offer before Spain. On the advice of their government, the Frenchmen refused to co-operate. The American banker nevertheless continued to visit the White House, and there were rumors from time to time of unofficial agents seeking contact with the Spanish cabinet. McKinley continued to dream of Spain's deciding to sell out. He could not, however, depend upon such a contingency to rescue him from his predicament.[16]

Like Cleveland, he had to pin most of his hopes on the possibility of a negotiated truce between Spain and the rebels. Not long before McKinley came into office, Cánovas published his long-deferred reform decrees. Cleveland and Olney had told the Spanish ambassador that these reforms were "as extensive as could be asked and more than they had expected," and McKinley and his friends were reported equally pleased. But the proclamation appeared to have little effect. Consul General Lee declared that rebel leaders would not even meet with Spanish emissaries and that he could find no one, Spaniard, rebel, or neutral, even showing interest in the reform scheme. It was his own grim view "that the war will drag its weary length so long as the insurgents can dig sustainance [*sic*] from the ground upon the one side or money be obtained by the other, with the continued result of untold human suffering, loss of human life, the murder of innocent men, women, and children by both sides, and the frightful havoc which disease makes."[17] Other consuls in Cuba rendered the same verdict (including, it should be said, the relatively unbiased representatives of Britain, France, and Russia). Any chance of a truce seemed therefore to lie in still further concessions by Spain.

It is not clear when McKinley reached the obvious conclusion that, like Cleveland, he would have to press for such concessions. It took him months to find someone for the thankless job of representing him in Madrid. He tendered the mission to Elihu Root, President Seth Low of Columbia, John W. Foster, and Dean Jacob D. Cox of the Cincinnati Law School. Eventually he found a man: Stewart Lyndon Woodford, a Brooklyn lawyer, brevet brigadier general of volunteers during the Civil War, office holder under Lincoln, Hayes, and Garfield, and defeated candidate for governor of New York in 1870.[18]

The formal instruction given to Woodford on July 16 was minatory without being explicit. Declaring that Spain could never hope to regain complete sovereignty over Cuba, the document asked if she would not "make proposals of settlement honorable to herself and just to her Cuban colony and to mankind." If peace were not shortly restored, it warned, the United States would certainly have to recognize the Cubans. "There is no longer question that the sentiment of the American people strongly demands . . . it." It went on to say that if peace did not come soon, the American government would have to think of intervention. The President volunteered his good offices but refrained from specifying what Spain might ask of him or what kind of arrangement he desired. He only insisted that the settlement "be a lasting one, honorable and advantageous to Spain and to Cuba and equitable to the United States."

What McKinley said privately to Woodford may have been more precise. The minister was to be his personal agent, sending back not only regular dispatches to the State Department, but also communications marked, "To be handed unopened to the President by his direction." In some of these private reports, the envoy mentioned words that had been spoken to him by McKinley. He recalled instructions to be "patient, courteous, kind, and firm." Though he also remembered that the President had advised against pressing for too much too quickly, remarking that time worked to the advantage of the United States, he told other diplomats in Madrid "that before Congress should meet in December some means must be found whereby this struggle shall be put in the sure way of being peacefully and finally ended." It seems likely that the President had himself mentioned such a time limit.

It is probable that McKinley talked with Woodford of what he might eventually have to do. The minister had been directed to go to Madrid via London and Paris and there to talk with the American ambassadors to Britain, France, and Germany. In these conversations Woodford was to ask how the powers would react in any number of eventualities, ranging from recognition of belligerency to forcible annexation. From the minister's later assurances to representatives of the powers in Madrid "that the United States does not seek to annex Cuba or establish a protectorate over Cuba," one suspects that the President had said he did not want annexation but might be driven to it. From other remarks, one gathers that McKinley also said, in effect: "If Spain grants autonomy on the Canadian model and asks American good offices, I will urge the rebels to accept. If they refuse, the only solution will be independence."[19]

The Spaniards did not respond to McKinley as they had to Cleveland. Cánovas was assassinated just before Woodford arrived in Spain. Woodford presented McKinley's demands and, as if in consequence, the Conservative government fell. A Liberal cabinet took office and promptly proclaimed a comprehensive scheme for Cuban

autonomy, much like the 1867 statute for Canada. The new government also removed Weyler and promised an early end to reconcentration. As Congress reassembled in Washington, administration spokesmen were able to declare that Spain was trying to obtain peace, that
there was promise of reduced suffering in Cuba, that there were no
Americans in Spanish jails, and that McKinley, whose bold and manly
diplomacy was responsible for all these changes, should be allowed to
keep up his good work.

Instead of announcing a new policy, McKinley felt it possible
merely to say to Congress what he had said to Spain. Rehearsing the
grim past of the Cuban problem, the obstacles in the way of recognition, and the favorable omens of change in Spanish policy, he declared: "The near future will demonstrate whether the indispensable
condition of a righteous peace . . . is likely to be attained. If not,
the exigency of further and other action by the United States will
remain to be taken." Elsewhere in his message, he indicated that this
"further and other action" would be "intervention to end the war by
imposing a rational compromise between the contestants" or intervention in behalf of one or the other party. "I speak not of forcible
annexation," he added, "for that cannot be thought of. That, by our
code of morality, would be criminal aggression." His kind words for
Spain, intimating that things might work out by themselves, soothed
his business supporters. The promise of action in "the near future"
heartened the jingoes.

But McKinley's message was probably more than a sop to both
sides. The language was not like most he used. Underneath the pulp
and water ran a sinew of meaning. "The near future" was not so
vague as other phrases he might have chosen. Everyone who had
followed the Cuban war knew that it progressed by winters. Each
April began a rainy season which made campaigning by either side
impossible until the following October. If the rains came in 1898 and
Spain's armies had not achieved victory, it would be perfectly evident
that they never could do so, for McKinley knew that Spain no longer
had enough young men even for replacements, let alone for reinforcements, and that she was having trouble paying and provisioning the
troops she had. The end of the 1897–1898 campaigning season

seemed the limit of any hope that Spain might have of overcoming the rebels.

McKinley must have felt that if by that time Spain still refused to face reality, he would have to demand that she do so. All the considerations that had affected both him and Cleveland were still in play. McKinley commented to Congress that the enforcement of neutrality was costing millions. In his instructions to Woodford he had spoken of the "ruin" of American property in Cuba and observed that it was doubtful if Cuba could be self-supporting even if peace were restored immediately. Conditions among the Cuban population had already come to seem almost intolerable even to people opposed in principle to American intervention. Men, women, and children were reported to be starving and dying of disease all over the island. A consul in Santiago declared, "As I write a man is dying on the street in front of my door, the third in a comparatively short time." Many stories reaching American newspapers were fictitious, of course, and even the best intentioned observers were so affected by what they saw that they exaggerated. Postwar calculations suggest that the number of Cuban deaths was probably around one hundred thousand. At the time, everyone, including Spaniards, reckoned the toll as nearer four hundred thousand, or more than a quarter of the island's population.[20] The thought that tens of thousands more would die and that the United States might save them weighed on many an American's conscience and perhaps also on the President's.

During 1897, furthermore, new practical considerations had come into view. No matter how the President conducted himself, he had to bear in mind the danger of war. Congressional debates on recognition had touched off anti-American riots in Spain. The Spanish government insisted publicly that the Cuban war went on only because it was nourished by American money and supplies. More than one Spaniard had said, as Martínez Campos had, that war with the United States would be a means of ending the Cuban war with honor. Against the danger that passion or calculation would lead Spain to force a fight, McKinley was obliged to hold most of his naval force together ready for combat. At the same time, he was under some compulsion to keep it out of the Caribbean, where its presence might alarm the Spaniards or encourage them to rashness. The possibility of war with Spain pre-occupied the resources of the United States more than war itself would have.

One resultant danger was illustrated by an incident in the winter of 1897. At Port-au-Prince, Haiti, Emil Lüders, a ne'er-do-well of alleged German nationality, was jailed. The German minister demanded his release. When the Haitian president refused, the Germans broke relations. Two of their warships promptly appeared and gave the Haitians five hours in which to release Lüders, pledge a thirty-thousand-dollar indemnity, and apologize, threatening in the event of refusal to bombard the presidential palace. The Haitians gave in. The United States Department of State declared that the Germans had been completely within their rights. Nevertheless, the incident followed repeated attacks on the Monroe doctrine by German newspapers and public figures, including Prince Bismarck, and it coincided with a giant German naval budget that provided, among other things, four new cruisers for the Caribbean and south Atlantic.[21] The preoccupation of the United States with Spain and Cuba gave obvious encouragement to German ambitions. So long as the Cuban war had not ended one way or another, there was even danger of a Spanish-German alliance. The President could reasonably have felt that the "exigency of further and other action" ought to arise before the new German warships were on the seas.

Still another consideration was introduced late in 1897 by the German seizure of Kiaowchow on the China coast. Diplomatic pouches and the columns of informed journals were filled with rumors of impending counterstrokes by Russia, France, and even Italy. Among American newspapers editorializing on the danger to trade and investment, not least were conservative Republican journals tied to the administration. After the British Chancellor of the Exchequer made a strong speech for the Open Door, many of them called upon the President to support the British stand. McKinley may have shared their optimism about the Chinese market. He may simply have felt that duty to the business community would eventually require him to do something. In any case, he had to recognize that he was practically impotent because of the situation in Cuba. News from Asia gave Mc-

Kinley another strong reason for not allowing the Cuban war to go on indefinitely.

Overshadowing all other factors, however, was the domestic political aspect of the Cuban problem. McKinley could conceivably have closed his heart to the suffering in the island. He could have continued negotiating about specific incidents, paying out more and more money for coast patrols and neutrality prosecutions. He could have abandoned hope of rescuing Cuban trade and the Cuban sugar supply. To meet the risk of a German challenge to the Monroe doctrine, he could, among other things, have launched a larger naval building program of his own. He could also have waited to see what the future held in Asia. What he could not do was allow the Cuban issue to be used against him as it had been used against Cleveland.

McKinley's duty to the Republican party was much clearer than his duty to the nation. Though later generations were to find the arguments against intervention overpowering, the same moral certitude was not so easy for people of the time. Many goodhearted Americans saw it as the only righteous course. They felt about the horrors in Cuba much as moral Englishmen had about the Bulgarian massacres. The counterarguments in 1897–1898 were mainly practical: conflict with Spain would hurt business and block recovery; it might unite Europe against the United States; it might entail annexation and hence the addition of undesirable racial elements to an already too-mixed population. By enlarging the army and navy and possibly creating a colonial service, it could increase the cost of government and the number of jobs not under civil service. Insofar as anti-interventionists were moralists, they based their case on the assumption that if America once yielded to the temptation of a foreign war, her soul would be lost to militarism and imperialism. McKinley was neither a Levite nor a prophet, nor was he any more experienced in applied ethics than in diplomacy. If he asked himself what Washington or Lincoln would have done, he probably could not have answered. Gladstone, whose spirit he might equally well have invoked, would almost certainly have favored intervention. The chances are that McKinley's conscience did not tell him very clearly what he ought to do.

His rational faculties, on the other hand, informed him that he had a duty to keep the Republican party together. Though his own stronghold may have been the business community, he presided over a coalition. To maintain a businesslike "hands-off" policy toward Cuba could easily infuriate veteran, Negro, church, or other groups in the party. Though they might not be driven to voting for Democrats, they could stay home or seek new leaders like those who had just captured the Democratic party. For McKinley it must have been disquieting that in the summer of 1897 the National League of Republican Clubs should have featured a speech by the more or less radical governor of Michigan, Hazen Pingree. According to press reports, representatives of the party rank and file cheered loudly when Pingree spoke of monopolistic excesses, strikers' rights, and maldistribution of wealth.[22] Control of Congress could easily be lost, if not to the Republican party, at least to conservative leadership, and the Presidency might pass in 1900 to Bryan or some other radical. In no circumstances could McKinley, either as a Republican or as a conservative, ignore his responsibility to maintain a united party.

Reasons of state and conscience and above all considerations of domestic politics made it almost necessary that McKinley fix a limit for patience. He did not set a date in so many words. Such precision would have been out of character. In any case, it would have been imprudent. He could not foresee the events that might supervene. He could not even be sure from day to day what jingoes would accept or what antijingoes would bear. From newspaper accounts and the reports of his minister in Madrid, he knew the danger of pressing Spain too openly, pricking her pride, and making it a point of honor for her not to yield to the inevitable. In a formal note to the Spanish government he went no farther than to use phrases identical with those in the annual message. Leaving Spain unembarrassed and his own retreats open, he merely let it be understood that a deadline was approaching.

PART FOUR

CRISIS

"Cuba—it is the flesh of the flesh of Spain; it is part of the history, the glory, and the grandeur of Spain. If you pick up any [Spanish] newspaper . . . Cuban affairs take up the first, the second, the third page. . . .

"Some soldiers pass by . . . along streets swept, in November, by the wind of the Guadarrama. You see them and point—'soldados para Cuba.' There are 20,000 about to go. That squadron that is going on maneuvers, this battery of artillery that returns to its barracks, they have but three young lieutenants and three old captains: lieutenants of eighteen, captains of fifty. Where are the rest? In Cuba. Thus, what you see and what you don't see—appearances, absences, departures—everywhere and every minute calls to mind Cuba."

> Charles Benoist, L'Espagne, Cuba et les États-Unis (*Paris, 1898*)

"As concerns Spain, Count Muraviev says . . . the dynasty can only be saved if the Queen puts herself in the forefront of chauvinistic agitation and, cost what it will, go to war, even if there is no chance whatever of a happy outcome. . . . Count Muraviev employed these words: 'If the Queen is wise, moderate, and truly patriotic, she will fall and be thrown out; if, on the other hand, she puts herself at the head of the column and is neither wise nor patriotic, she can save her crown. This is cynical but so.' "

> Prince Radolin to Count von Bülow, April 16, 1898, Grosse Politik, XV, No. 4141

Early in 1897, when Spain's first reforms began taking effect in Cuba, public indignation in the United States seemed to cool. Democrats in Congress, it is true, continued to talk about Cuba even after McKinley succeeded in appeasing Republican jingoes. When Morgan demanded a vote on a joint resolution acknowledging Cuban belligerency, insisting that "the mind of the people of the United States is agitated and all their hearts are full of this subject," only nineteen senators held out for rereferral to committee, even though passage was plainly not desired by the administration, and only fourteen refused to approve the resolution itself. The forty-five senators who voted "aye" foresaw that Speaker Reed would prevent action by the House; still they testified by their votes that they believed the public eager for some kind of action.[1]

Rank and file politicians certainly took this view. The National Association of Democratic Clubs, meeting in Washington in July, 1897, resolved: "The day should be hastened by all proper means which shall see the lone star of Cuba fixed forever in the constellation of American States, and we demand the immediate recognition of the belligerent rights of the Cuban people." The National League of Republican Clubs merely replied that the President could "be relied upon to interpose his good offices to end . . . [the] struggle with the greatest promptitude consistent with wise administration." Kentucky Republicans wrote a demand for intervention into their platform. Iowa Republicans almost did so. When Congress came into session in December, Democrats were reported as planning to press the Cuban issue. Many in the President's own party refused to say whether or not they would vote for a recognition resolution against opposition from the White House.[2]

On the whole, however, these senators and representatives seemed to be still under the influence of the Maceo incident and the excitement of the preceding winter. Though circulation-hungry New York dailies played up lurid events and other papers copied their stories, there had been only one eruption of public feeling on the Cuban issue since the inauguration of McKinley. The case of Evangelina Cisneros, a Cuban girl allegedly jailed for defending her honor against a Spanish officer, produced a petition signed by over a million women. But this petition had been circulated by and in Hearst newspapers, and the agitation died down as soon as a Hearst reporter aided the girl to escape.

When the session of 1897–1898 opened and McKinley asked the Congress to give him more time, his strong but vague message promised action if Cuba were not pacified in the near future. Administration spokesmen claimed that Spain's autonomy decree and the removal of Weyler were fruits of McKinley's diplomacy. A poll by the New York *Herald* showed majorities in both the Senate and the House privately opposed to any Congressional action, though Senator John H. Mitchell of Oregon, like other administration supporters, predicted that a recognition resolution would be forced through both Houses. Nothing of the sort happened.

Congressmen found to their astonishment that they were not pressed as they had been in the previous session. Only a few memorials and petitions came in. Morgan told a Junta representative that he and Lodge thought it desirable to fight for Hawaiian annexation before renewing a campaign for intervention in Cuba. Others tried to reassure the Junta that McKinley meant to do something more in the near future. This procrastination may have been in some cases reaction to a suit filed in Illinois by a printer who claimed that the Junta had never paid him $3,500 due for manufacturing bonds. At least two senators, Mason of Illinois and Hernando DeSoto Money of Mississippi, had been given some of these bonds.[3] But this would only explain why they failed to raise the issue on their own initiative. The more important fact was that the public did not appear to be clamoring for action as it had a year earlier.

Congress's inaction did not cause McKinley to become unwary. From time to time the White House issued announcements calculated to keep jingoes at bay. At the opening of the session, for example, it was made known that the North Atlantic squadron, the main force of the navy, would winter off Key West, as near as possible to Cuba. Both the Spanish government and American conservatives were told that the move was merely routine preparation for spring maneuvers. Jingo newspapers, however, interpreted it as preparation for the "further and other action" of which McKinley had spoken in his annual message.

The President took precautions lest congressmen return from the Christmas recess fired up to gratify bellicose constituents. The New York *Herald* reported the White House increasingly concerned about suffering among Cubans in reconcentration camps. If deaths from sickness and starvation did not lessen, said the *Herald,* the President might well feel that conditions had reached the breaking point he had forecast. On Christmas Eve the State Department issued an appeal in the name of the President for private contributions to help relieve the suffering, and it was noised about that the President himself contributed the first five thousand dollars. Moreover, by arrangements pressed on the Spanish legation, the money, food, and medicine were to be sent in naval vessels.[4] The announcement of this departure from precedent, more than the relief appeal itself, was sure to warm and quieten the jingoes.

Almost immediately, events required the President to do more. On January 12, 1898, riots broke out in Havana. Led by soldiers still loyal to Weyler, the demonstrations were really directed against three newspapers that had criticized the departed general, and violence subsided as soon as their presses had been smashed. To Consul General Lee and American reporters, however, the commotion had seemed at first the beginning of anarchy in the city. The President evidently paled at a nightmare vision of Americans being shot, hanged, and butchered while Congress was in session, for the State Department signaled Lee that if communications were interrupted the fleet would move. Subsequent dispatches showed the riots to be over and Americans in no danger, but the Spanish minister was informed that a fresh outbreak might oblige the President not only to send ships but also to land troops.[5]

The riots, brief and harmless though they had been, revived the danger of Congress's taking up the Cuban issue. As it happened, diplomatic and consular appropriations were being considered by the House at the time. Not even the best efforts of Speaker Reed prevented

Democrats from dragging Cuba into the debate. At least one Republican, William Alden Smith of Michigan, went to the Speaker and eventually to the White House to say that he could not afford to remain silent much longer; the pressure from his constituents was too great.[6] Despite the relative quiet in the Senate, conservative leaders confessed that they were only half-sure of their ability to keep the Senate in line behind the President.

Chairman Hitt of the House Foreign Affairs Committee, who was widely regarded as an administration spokesman, finally rose in the House to declare that since the Democrats insisted on talking about Cuba, it was well that the subject be discussed openly and candidly. He went on,

We have seen in the time that the President has been in charge what he has tried to do and how much he has accomplished. Can we not trust him? We know that spirit that animates the captain of the ship. Events that have recently transpired at Havana and are impending warn us how grave is his responsibility . . . and . . . indicate how near we may be to a critical hour. What will be done? The President, while he does not favor the recognition of belligerency as a specific cure or as advisable, has intimated where the line of duty will take him, acting not by halves, but facing the whole question.

He quoted McKinley's comments on possible armed intervention, and concluded, "We should all of us be ready to do our duty like patriotic Americans, standing firmly behind the President when he takes a step necessary for the vindication of the honor and protection of the interests of our country."

An unnamed high official denied that Hitt had spoken for the President, and even such a practiced observer as the American correspondent of the London *Times* remained unsure whether the speech had been inspired. But the possibility that Hitt's words were McKinley's was enough to force the Democrats temporarily to lay aside the Cuban issue.

Before they could rally, the President had taken the further step of posting the *Maine* to Havana. The question of stationing a warship there had been discussed ever since the outbreak of the rebellion. Cleveland and his Secretary of the Navy had refused appeals from

Lee on the ground that there was too much risk of an inflammatory incident. The McKinley administration, bent on keeping Congress cool, could not be so indifferent to Lee's warnings of possible danger to American residents.

Lee was advised in June, 1897, that a naval vessel would be sent if he ever thought its presence imperative. As soon as he began telling of possible Weyler-ite uprisings, the Department of State arranged with the navy for the *Maine* to go to Key West. Following the Havana riots the State Department directed Lee to send out some message every day. If a day passed without one, the *Màine* was to sail.

This arrangement had obvious disadvantages, since Spaniards were apt to feel affronted if the ship suddenly turned up after a new riot. Even the cautious, pacific Secretary of the Navy concluded that it would be safer on all counts simply to station the ship at Havana, and on January 24 Day asked the Spanish minister blandly if, in view of the improvement in Spanish-Amercan relations, the *Maine* could not pay a courtesy call at Havana. The President knew that dispatch of the ship would arouse little criticism, for even the New York *Evening Post* and the New York *Staatszeitung* had said editorially that the Havana riots might signal the failure of autonomy and hence make necessary some new gestures by the administration. He could take comfort principally from the fact that the *Maine*'s dispatch would help to calm the zealots.[7]

Hardly had the ship reached Havana, however, before a sensational news story broke at home. A New York newspaper published a private letter written by the Spanish minister, Dupuy de Lôme. In it the minister described the President, according to the official translation, as "weak and a bidder for the admiration of the crowd, besides being a would-be politician (*politicastro*) who tries to leave a door open behind himself while keeping on good terms with the jingoes of his party." The minister admitted to the letter, and the administration had no choice but to demand his recall. The Spanish government meanwhile hurriedly accepted de Lôme's resignation and the State Department was left to plead with Madrid for some apology that it could exhibit to Congress and the press. A few grudging words of regret sufficed, and the administration declared the episode closed.[8]

The de Lôme incident marked the point at which time began to run out. In the week following publication of the letter there was every indication that Congress and the country verged on new demonstrations like those that had followed Maceo's death. Three recognition resolutions appeared in the Senate. One came from Allen, a Kansas Populist, one from Frank J. Cannon, a Utah Silver Republican, the third from Mason of Illinois, who, as an orthodox Republican, had usually been found on the administration's side. In support of his resolution, Mason made as fiery a speech as any other, damning unpatriotic Wall Street speculators who would not let the nation do its duty to humanity.

In Mason's home state, Governor John R. Tanner issued an official proclamation, asking contributions for Cuban relief but declaring that the real remedy was not charity but recognition. The New York state assembly passed a recognition resolution despite opposition from all Republican leaders in the body. Lodge wrote Henry White even before the de Lôme letter, "feeling in this country is steadily rising in favor of active intervention." Three days after de Lôme's letter had been published, a worried Bostonian wrote the Secretary of the Navy: "The jingo members of Congress and vile unscrupulous, jingo, yellow journals have so wrought up and stirred popular feeling that we seem to be slanting on the verge of a war with Spain with all its terrible consequences." One newspaper with supposed inside sources of information reported on February 13 that a delegation of Republican congressmen had visited McKinley to demand that he force a crisis with Spain.[9]

Nowhere was there clearer evidence of the threatened public outbreak than in McKinley's own state of Ohio. During December and early January, the President had fought to have the state legislature elect Hanna to a full six-year term as senator. Though Day, other Ohioans in Washington, and even outsiders like Theodore Roosevelt had been pressed into service, Hanna triumphed by only one vote. In mid-February the state Republican League met. Representatives of Senator Foraker's faction were prepared to do battle with the followers of McKinley and Hanna. The issue they chose was a proposed resolution for recognition of Cuba. Though the President's friends fought it stubbornly, contending that it was insulting to the administration, their fight was useless and the resolution passed 437–283.[10] Coupled with indications from other states, this vote showed beyond any doubt that Republican jingoes would not long remain patient.

On February 14, notice to this effect was formally served. The Foreign Relations and Foreign Affairs Committees introduced almost identical resolutions which the two Houses passed without delay. They called upon the administration to publish the reports of American consuls in Cuba. Some members of the two committees presumably knew that these reports drew an unrelieved picture of Spanish military failure and of suffering among the Cuban civil population. It had already been noised in the press that all the consular corps regarded autonomy as a failure. McKinley did not have to deliver the correspondence at once, but he knew that the moment when he did would be the moment when Congress began to discuss a declaration of war.

Then, early on the morning of February 16, the President was awakened to receive a telegram from Lee. Dated 12:30 A.M., it read: "*Maine* blown up and destroyed to-night at 9:40 P.M." Subsequent telegrams reported the dead at about 260, the cause of the explosion unknown.[11]

The initial reaction seemed, it is true, to be merely dismay. Hearst and a few other publishers denounced Spain and called for war. In search of support, their reporters interviewed hundreds of erstwhile jingoes. They found many who would say that war would be inevitable if Spain had deliberately blown up the *Maine,* but surprisingly few who held Spain to blame or advocated immediate war. Ordinarily bellicose journals such as the St. Louis *Republic* and the New York *Press* said the *Maine*'s explosion was a misfortune that need not affect Spanish-American relations. Publisher Whitelaw Reid of the New York *Tribune* wrote optimistically to his Washington correspondent, "In one way the horrible disaster . . . may prove a sort of blessing in disguise. It really looks as if it might sober our . . . jingoes a little."

Momentarily, indeed, there seemed a reaction much like that which had followed Cleveland's Venezuela message. Many businessmen had already come out against intervention in Cuba, and business journals promptly called for patience and self-restraint in the *Maine* case. In

New York "all the reputable community" was reported against war and incensed at yellow journals that called for it. In Chicago financiers were said to be resolutely in favor of continued peace. One Chicago broker criticized the Cubans as "nothing but mongrels, not fit for self-government." Two eminent business figures, Cleveland industrialist Myron T. Herrick and Omaha railroad lawyer Charles F. Manderson, wrote the President assuring him that no one they knew was even excited about the *Maine*.[12]

Many of the clergy suddenly joined businessmen in calling for peace. On the first Sunday after the explosion, three Methodist ministers in Brooklyn gave pacific sermons. So did a leading Methodist in Cleveland. A week later an Episcopalian in Washington denounced "wild clamors for blood, blood, blood." In Chicago a Baptist, a Methodist, and a Universalist all called for peace. Boston Congregationalist and Unitarian groups issued similar appeals; so did religious newspapers, including some that had long been bemoaning Cuba's condition. The Baptist Chicago *Standard* declared, "The religious weeklies . . . have been almost without exception opposed to war. . . . A great conservative force thus exerted has done much to guide public opinion in safe channels." The French ambassador reported to his government, "In nearly all the churches pastors have given pacific sermons; this is especially noteworthy because there is in the passions aroused against Spain something of old Huguenot and Puritan hatreds."[13]

Jewish spokesmen took the same side. In Chicago, Reform leader Emil Hirsch pleaded for cautious diplomacy, and orthodox Rabbi Joseph Stolz denounced "savages" who cried for war. Though the Roman Catholic clergy feared the charge of sympathizing with Spain, Irish and Italian clerics both deplored the possibility of violence. Some went so far as to say that it would be sinful for American Catholics to fight Spanish Catholics.

Joined with businessmen and clergymen were German-American leaders. A *Literary Digest* survey of the German language press found only one sheet, Hearst's New York *Morgen Journal,* that was not firmly for peaceful arrangements with Spain.

There was some reason for believing in the spring of 1898 that a movement for peace, even more powerful than the one of 1895–1896, was getting under way. There was even some evidence of backtracking on the part of important jingo groups. On March 2 representatives of the national G.A.R. met jointly in Atlanta, Georgia, with representatives of the United Confederate Veterans. Though the Commander-in-Chief of the G.A.R., General John P. S. Govin, had been active in the Cuban agitation in Pennsylvania, he now made a speech calling for cool heads and support of the President, whatever direction he took. The Chicago Union League Club, where the Committee of One Hundred had had its start, listened to advocates of peace, gave them standing ovations, and booed members who sought to speak for war. The Union League Club of San Francisco passed a resolution condemning war agitation and backing the President. Many of these sermons, editorials, and resolutions were ambiguous; nevertheless they served to create an appearance of stiffening opposition to jingoism.

The passing days brought little evidence, however, that utterances by peaceful-minded clergymen and businessmen were having any effect on the general public. A minority of Protestant ministers joined the public clamor. In Chicago Baptist Poindexter S. Henson blamed the *Maine* sinking on "the procrastinating policy of those at the head of our nation, who have failed to deal honestly and courageously in behalf of an oppressed people." Newspapers reported sermons for intervention by a number of Baptists, Methodists, and Presbyterians. In Boston, where peace sentiment was supposed to be strongest, a Congregationalist equated "jingoism" with "strong and pure patriotism." In Chicago a leading Campbellite minister pleaded for war, and in San Francisco a Unitarian declared that it would be a service to Spain as well as to Cuba. In Terre Haute, Indiana, an Episcopal clergyman promised to do all in his power "to make Spanish the prevailing language of hell." In an address before a ministerial association in St. Louis, Methodist Bishop Charles C. McCabe declared, "There are many things worse than war. It may be that the United States is to become the Knight Errant of the world. War with Spain may put her in a position to demand civil and religious liberty for the oppressed of every nation and of every clime." Another Methodist bishop, John F.

Hurst of Washington, D.C., wrote the President, exhorting him to free Cuba, adding, "Who knoweth whether thou art not come to the Kingdom for such a time as this?"[14] Since, as in 1896, manifestations of public feeling preceded utterances by clergymen, this bellicose minority of preachers did not supply the only leadership, though their dissent may have fortified in favor of war laymen who would otherwise have had sober second thoughts. The public movement, however, was independent of them or any well-defined leadership group.

Across the country, thousands gave themselves up to emotional excesses like those of tent-meeting revivals. Theater audiences cheered, stamped, and wept at the playing of the Star-Spangled Banner. The antiwar New York *Herald* reported "war fever" in Jersey City and Hoboken. The conservative Portland, Oregon, *Morning Tribune* admitted that enthusiastic war talk could be heard on every street corner. Similar reports came from smaller towns. There were mob scenes in which effigies of Spanish statesmen were burned in Troy, New York, Metropolis, Illinois, Pittsburg, Kansas, and Somerset, Kentucky. The St. Louis *Republic* reported fervor for Cuban independence and war with Spain in suburban communities like Kirkwood, Webster Groves, and Ferguson, Missouri, and in Clay City and Mount Vernon, Illinois. Colonel Henry A. Newman, coming in from Randolph County in central Missouri, said he himself opposed war, but "everything is war talk up in our part of the country, and patriotism is oozing out of every boy who is old enough to pack feed to the pigs." The editor of the Carson City *Appeal* declared that in Nevada, "the clamor for war is heard everywhere. Many people . . . are for war . . . on general principles, without a well-defined idea of the why or wherefor." A New York Democratic leader, just returned from a southern tour, reported resentment against Spain to be intense throughout the South.

Some of the fervor was anti-Catholic. In St. Louis the utterances of those few Catholic priests who spoke up for Spain were reproduced on "Cuba Libre" handouts. In Boston the Reverend Justin D. Fulton, Baptist author of such tracts as "Washington in the Lap of Rome," charged the administration with failing to act through fear of seven hundred thousand armed Catholics. In New York the editor of *The*

Converted Catholic accused all Catholics of treasonable sympathy for Spain.

A number of Catholics retaliated by testifying their enthusiastic willingness to fight. An Indiana unit of the Catholic Knights of America offered to volunteer. A priest in Los Angeles declared, "The butcheries in Cuba must cease at any cost," and another in New York told his congregation, "We must show our true spirit as American citizens." Irish Catholic groups in Boston, New York, Chicago, Denver, and San Francisco proclaimed their enthusiasm for the Cuban cause and willingness to fight. Italians in Missouri and Alabama offered to raise companies for war. One said, "every Italian who has made America his home is only waiting a call to arms in order to prove his loyalty to this country."

Congressmen and cabinet officers received increasingly offensive letters, many scrawled in pencil on crude paper. Two typical examples came to Navy Secretary John D. Long (from Haverhill, Massachusetts): "If we wer in Spaines place and they in ours they would wipe us of the map as regards the Maine it was a planed plot and De Lome is at the bottom of it . . . the people are indignent wake up the president people in general will not stand it much Longer"; (from Chicago): "Who else is to blame but you McKinley & Hanna & Reed. Who are working for the interest of the monied people of the U.S. between the actions of you three demagoges you have caused the Glorious Maine to be blown up . . . Why on earth don't you resign you *old fosil*."[15]

By the seventh week after the *Maine* disaster, these passions were beginning to take the form of anger against the President. In a Colorado community McKinley was hanged in effigy. In New York theaters, as the Hearst papers gleefully reported, the President's picture was sometimes hissed. A Massachusetts man wrote to Senator Chandler, "There is a growing discontent every where in the East in the dilley dally of the Administration on the Cuban question." The French ambassador, writing to Paris of spreading anti-McKinley feeling, observed, "A sort of bellicose fury has seized the American nation."[16]

In the face of this undiminished mass passion, some pacific business and church leaders showed signs of weakening. The ordinarily staid

New York *Journal of Commerce* published an almost hysterical edi-torial: "if popular passion is permitted to force the Administration into war, what is the conclusion suggested to our own masses? Simply that they may have whatever mad follies they hanker after, provided they raise their clamor to the requisite pitch." Wall Street was reported increasingly gloomy and convinced of the inevitability of war. Busi-ness journals swung toward the position that war might be necessary, and the same shift occurred among religious weeklies like the *Chris-tian Index,* which warned, "the president will have to act, or an outraged nation will, through its congress, act for themselves."

Though the President's own views and acts were closely guarded secrets, businessmen, lawyers, and clergymen could see with increas-ing clarity the danger that McKinley might change front and make himself leader of the war forces. The further peril, if business and religious leaders appeared isolated and antipatriotic, was all too ob-vious. By conscious or unconscious processes of rationalization, ci-devant leadership groups eased from resolute pacifism toward a more ambivalent position. Whitelaw Reid wrote to McKinley: "The impres-sion I got on crossing the continent was that the more intelligent classes are not greatly affected by the sensational press; but . . . I have never seen a more profound or touching readiness to trust the President, and await his word."[17]

Many in "the more intelligent classes" needed no more than an excuse to abandon their obviously unpopular pacifism and, like other minority groups, to affirm their patriotism. In the middle of March Senator Redfield Proctor of Vermont returned from a brief trip to Cuba and delivered a speech in the Senate. He described the suffering that he had seen, and declared that Spain would never give up and the rebels would never give in; the only solution was American inter-vention. A relatively undistinguished Vermont politician, once Sec-retary of War under Harrison, Proctor said little that was new. His conversion to interventionism would not have caused great remark nor would his speech have been published across the nation had it not been for the widespread rumors that he had gone to Cuba as McKin-ley's observer and that his speech had been cleared with the President.

Businessmen, clergymen, and previously conservative newspaper editors seized upon this straw in the wind. The *Wall Street Journal* reported that Proctor's speech "converted a great many people in Wall Street who have heretofore taken the ground that the United States had no business to interfere in a revolution on Spanish soil." Clergymen and religious newspapers began dissociating themselves from businessmen. A San Francisco Congregationalist preached, "If there is to be a war with Spain it will be on the ground that humanity is our republic, our country the world. The passion for business is the least Christian." A Congregationalist in St. Louis declared his mind changed by Proctor's speech: "It were better far to paralyze the business of Wall Street than paralyze our national life." Consciously or unconsciously, many public leaders decided that it was no longer safe to resist the passion for war.

Politicians had naturally been even more alive to these currents in public emotion. Some Populists and agrarian Democrats had begun calling for war as soon as the *Maine* sank, among them Senator Marion Butler of South Carolina, the Populist Governor of Kansas, and William J. Stone, a Bryan Democrat from Missouri. So had local Populist and Democratic groups in Indiana, Illinois, Colorado, and California. Later, some historians were to suppose that the clamor for war originated among southern and western farmers. On the evidence, however, they were no more in a frenzy than northern and eastern urbanites. Their political leaders had simply broken already with most conservative community leaders on account of the free silver issue and thus had nothing to lose by speaking out.

Before long, Democrats who were not silverites showed willingness to gamble that war fever could not be cured. Hannis Taylor, who had been Cleveland's minister to Spain, called for immediate intervention, not on account of the *Maine* but simply to free Cuba. Olney said, in a rare public appearance: "No foreign question arises nowadays, but as soon as it is hinted that the United States should interfere and play its part in a manly fashion, the cry of 'jingo' goes up." Bryan, as the national party leader, was careful not to commit himself too soon. At first he refused comment other than to say that in a crisis the country would be united. At the end of March he called in newspaper reporters and announced, "the time for intervention has arrived. Humanity demands that we shall act. Cuba lies almost within sight of our shores, and the sufferings of her people cannot be ignored unless we, as a nation, have become so engrossed in money-making as to be indifferent to distress." If the administration failed to act, it was evident that Democrats would exploit the Cuban issue to the full.

Many Republicans made it clear that they could not support the administration if it resisted the public demand. Republican governors in Illinois, Indiana, and Vermont joined the war movement. Speaking to the State Board of Agriculture, Vermont's governor said: "The spirit of Bunker Hill still lives, and 'Uncle Sam' will soon stretch out his long, bony hands and give those who are seeking freedom their liberty." Republican senators and representatives in Congress began hinting broadly that if the President failed to move, Congress would do so.

Administration supporters began to tremble. The conservative Chicago *Times-Herald,* published by H. H. Kohlsaat, suddenly abandoned its pacific stand, declaring: "Intervention in Cuba . . . is immediately inevitable. Our own internal political conditions will not permit its postponement. Who that has marked the signs of the times does not see that 'war for Cuban liberty' looms before us as the only rallying standard of the legions of our national discontent." Senator Lodge, who, though a jingo, was also a firm supporter of the administration, wrote an earnest letter to the President, reporting virtual unanimity among the voters in Massachusetts. He cited a staunch Republican, the chairman of the Board of Selectmen in Nahant, who said that if the Cuban question were not settled at once, "it will become very hard to vote for the Republican party." Lodge went on to report:

I put the same questions over and over again & always got answers like these & was told that "Everybody felt that way." . . . [I]f the war in Cuba drags on through the summer with nothing done we shall go down in the greatest defeat ever known. . . . I know that it is easily & properly said that to bring on or even to threaten war for political reasons is a crime & I quite agree. But to sacrifice a great party & bring free silver upon the country for a wrong policy is hardly less odious. On a great, broad ques-

tion like this, when right & wrong are involved I believe profoundly in
the popular instinct & what that instinct is no one who goes out among
the people . . . can doubt for one moment.

Some conservative Republicans and Democrats continued to believe that public feeling would come under control if the administration only waited the clamor out. The majority in Congress evidently
did not agree. Senator Spooner wrote gloomily at the beginning of
April: "Apparently Congress cannot keep its head. It looks . . . as
if a majority had their watches out, waiting for the arrival of a particular hour . . . to force the hand of the President, and let loose the
dogs of war."[18]

At the outset of the Cuban rebellion, few in the United States except a handful of Cuban-Americans had been intensely interested.
Now, three years later, neighborhoods, suburbs, small towns, and
rural counties simply caught fire. No section, no type of community,
no occupational group was immune. Vocal opposition by much of
the Protestant clergy and the religious press, silence on the part of the
G.A.R. and other organization leaders, and resolute disapproval from
the most successful businessmen—many of whom had sympathized
with the rebels from the beginning, but who now dreaded an open
conflict—barely checked the fever for war. In numberless and nameless leaders and followers, emotion had become unshakable conviction. A frightened elite retreated from resistance to acquiescence. Politicians in one party, the Democratic, prepared to make capital of
the issue, while those in the other, the Republican, more terrified of
the opposition than of Spain, begged the administration to capitulate
and make war for the sake of party survival and domestic peace.

Ever since the beginning of his administration, McKinley had been maneuvering to prevent just such an eruption of emotion as that which swept Congress and the country. Hoping to end the war in Cuba, he had demanded that Spain grant the island autonomy. To placate jingoes, he had promised in his annual message for 1897 that he would move to "other and further action" if fighting in Cuba continued. As earnests of his intentions, he asked Congress for relief funds and, after the Havana riots, ordered the *Maine* to the city. When the de Lôme letter was published, he had done his best to obtain a formal apology from Spain. After the *Maine* exploded, he had immediately ordered an investigation and allowed it to be reported authoritatively that, if evidence appeared of Spanish guilt, he would not allow the deed to go unpunished.

In the hectic weeks that followed the explosion, McKinley obviously could not tell whether or not he would be compelled to go farther. The reaction among business groups and the clergy did resemble that after Cleveland's Venezuela message, and it seemed possible that public excitement might die down. The New York *Herald* reported that McKinley would use the *Maine* incident as a pretext for withholding the consular correspondence from Congress. The same journal also gave a detailed account of a cabinet meeting on February 25, ten days after the explosion, in which the President allegedly said that, even if the *Maine* proved to have been sunk by a Spanish mine or torpedo, he might be able to settle for a large cash indemnity. At the same time he was speaking to callers, such as Senator Fairbanks of Indiana, about preparing for war, and his Secretary of the Navy was writing in his diary, "Public sentiment is very intense. . . . The slightest spark is liable to result in war with Spain." The President simply could not judge how the winds would blow.[1]

By the beginning of March, he had evidently begun to sense that neither Congress nor the public would be tamed. According to the San Francisco *Examiner* for February 26, the Iowa Congressional delegation had notified him that they would disapprove unanimously if he tried to settle the *Maine* case for dollars and cents. Preliminary indications were that a naval investigating board would report the explosion to have been externally caused, probably by a Spanish mine or torpedo. On March 3 Assistant Secretary of State Day summoned the Spanish minister for an informal conference. There he warned solemnly that the public temper was rising and that a crisis might be inevitable if Spain did not soon terminate reconcentration, proclaim an armistice, and announce that she would accept American mediation. This was no ultimatum. The terms were not written out, and no report of the conversation was made to the American minister in Madrid. But the Assistant Secretary's words foreshadowed an ultimatum that might have to be sent at any time.[2]

McKinley still hoped somehow to escape the necessity for making formal demands upon Spain. In talks with congressmen, he found some who feared that America was not prepared for war, and he played on this concern. On March 6, he conferred with members of the House Appropriations Committee and said, according to the later recollection of Representative Joseph G. Cannon of Illinois, "I must have money to get ready for war. I am doing everything possible to prevent war but it must come, and we are not prepared for war. Who knows where this war will lead us; it may be more than war with Spain." Hanna subsequently voiced the same warning in the New York *World*. Europe was "an armed camp, a tinderbox that a spark might ignite," he said, and cautioned that Spain might find powerful allies. The House reacted by appropriating fifty million dollars for military and naval expenditures, and the President was reported by the Boston *Evening Transcript* as saying that this money would help him keep the peace. The Secretary of the Navy explained in his diary that the administration hoped for some moral effect in Spain. No less important, probably, the request gave the jingoes something to occupy their minds.[3]

In the meantime, the President searched fretfully for new alternatives. One, which he had considered earlier, was the possibility of somehow buying Cuba. Not long after the sinking of the *Maine,* McKinley had received a message from the publisher of the New York

Herald, reporting that this possibility was being suggested by Americans in Madrid. Myron T. Herrick, one of the Ohio financiers who had rescued McKinley from his indebtedness in 1893, was visiting the White House at the time. The President questioned him about financing a Cuban settlement through a bond issue. Subsequently, he talked with one of the Junta's bankers, with Prince Albert of Belgium, and with Archbishop John Ireland, who could pass the President's views on to the French and Austrian ambassadors and to the Vatican. According to rumor, McKinley went so far as to have legislation drafted that would give him three hundred million dollars to use as he saw fit. His Secretary of Treasury remembered later that McKinley's most ardent efforts had gone into promotion of this scheme. But the New York *Herald* polled the House of Representatives and found less than a quarter of the members ready to vote money for purchasing Cuba's independence. Since Minister Woodford also reported that the Spanish Queen had said she would abdicate before agreeing to sell the island, the project came to nought.[4]

Another possibility which the President explored was one suggested to him by Oscar Straus, a Macy's executive in New York and a former Republican minister to Turkey. The United States might urge Spain to deal with Cuba as Turkey had with Egypt, Straus wrote. Spain could retain nominal sovereignty, as the Porte did, and share in the customs revenues, while Cuba governed itself under American supervision. This notion interested McKinley. He sent the letter to Day and invited Straus to the White House. According to Straus's diary notes, "The President said he regarded the plan in all its aspects the most practical of any that have been brought to his attention, but intimated, not in so many words, but by the general drift of the conversation, such a plan would not stop the Jingoes." An outline of the scheme was submitted to the Junta, but the Cubans replied that they could not even consider such an arrangement.[5]

McKinley saw but one other chance of averting the necessity for an ultimatum. He learned that while a naval investigating board would report the *Maine*'s explosion to have been externally caused, it would also suggest the possibility of an accident, due to a free-floating, forgotten mine or torpedo. It occurred to the President that he might send this report to Congress, announce that he was demanding a large indemnity from Spain, and at the same time request a huge appropriation for relief of suffering in Cuba. Antiwar senators and representatives would undoubtedly support such financial intervention as a substitute for armed intervention. If enough others could be persuaded to accept the same view, Congress could at least be kept occupied until the beginning of the rainy season in Cuba. Then it could be contended that military operations were impossible and that the administration should have another few months in which to seek a negotiated settlement.

Such an evasive tactic would probably not have occurred to the President had he not possessed some leverage with Democrats in the Senate. Morgan, the party's most bellicose leader, was so devoted to the proposed Nicaragua canal that he could be expected to do almost anything in return for administration support of that project. McKinley talked with Morgan. Subsequently, when the senator sent him a memorandum on the canal, he forwarded it to Day with instructions that it receive the Assistant Secretary's personal attention. There is no clear evidence that a deal had been made, but it is an easy inference. The Junta's banker discovered that the administration planned to maneuver for delay and that "the chief Democrats" had agreed to co-operate. "Unless Spain commits some act of aggression . . . ," he wrote, "this policy of the President . . . will result in a postponement of the Cuban question until December."[6]

But neither the banker's fears nor McKinley's hopes were realized. Senator Chandler was writing almost daily to Paul Dana of the New York *Sun,* telling him of developments in Congress. On March 29 he wrote: "The democrats who for 2 or 3 days thought they ought to encourage a halt have given up that feeling and are for action. The Republicans in Congress feel that if the President will not formulate a policy it must be put forward by the Republican leaders in Senate and House."[7] Perhaps Democrats in Congress had learned that Bryan was about to call for intervention. Whatever the case, if Morgan had endeavored to use his influence, he had failed. Day cabled Woodford:

You should know and fully appreciate that there is profound feeling in Congress, and the gravest apprehension on the part of most conservative members that a resolution for intervention may pass both branches in spite of any effort which can be made. Only assurance from the President that if he fails in peaceful negotiations he will submit all the facts to Congress at a very early day will prevent immediate action on the part of Congress.[8]

From McKinley's standpoint there no longer seemed any alternative to an ultimatum. The antiwar front had practically disintegrated. After Proctor had declared himself for intervention, other previously conservative senators followed suit. The New York *Herald* changed its editorial policy just as the Chicago *Times-Herald* had. Its city editor wrote confidentially to McKinley, "Big corporations here now believe we will have war. Believe all would welcome it as relief to suspense." Whitelaw Reid advised the managing editor of his New York *Tribune* that war was inevitable and "it would be unwise for us to be the last persons to assent to it, or to seem to be dragged into the support of it." Elihu Root, then one of the leaders of the New York bar, wrote Theodore Roosevelt, "I sympathize with McKinley . . . ; but . . . if the administration does not turn its face towards the front and lead instead of being pushed, it seems to me it will be rolled over and crushed and the Republican party with it."[9]

Even accepting the necessity for an ultimatum did not, however, relieve the President of his embarrassments. Jingoes were allies of the Junta; some held Cuban bonds; all had clamored for recognition of the existing insurgent government. Though erstwhile conservatives might have reconciled themselves to war, they were not ready to fight it solely in the interest of the Cubans. Chandler wrote to Dana, quoting Senator Elkins as saying it would be "folly . . . to spend 500 millions in a war for Cuba and then not get the property fought for. That he says is a plain business proposition."[10] In drawing up his demands on Spain, the President felt he had to satisfy these divergent opinions, for he could still divorce himself neither from the jingoes nor their opponents.

He and Day solved this problem in characteristically subtle fashion —so subtle, indeed, that the surviving documents were later to mislead historians. At Senator Fairbanks' home, Day met with a group of conservatives from the upper house. Chandler, who heard about it later, listed Hanna, Allison, Aldrich, Hale, Spooner, and Platt of Connecticut as the others present. The last of these was Chandler's source, and Chandler quoted him as saying, "The understanding was that an armistice would be agreed to and negotiations opened with Spain for an autonomous government to the insurgents in Cuba, Spain not to relinquish her sovereignty. The final arbitration was to be left to the President of the United States if Spain and the Cubans couldn't agree." In accordance with this understanding, Day drew up a formal message for Woodford. Presumably he showed it to one or more of the senators. The concessions which it demanded from Spain were:

FIRST. Armistice until October 1. Negotiations meantime looking for peace between Spain and insurgents through friendly offices of President United States.

SECOND. Immediate revocation of reconcentrado order so as to permit people to return to their farms, and the needy to be relieved with provisions and supplies from United States cooperating with authorities so as to afford full relief.

Add, if possible:

THIRD. If terms of peace not satisfactorily settled by October 1, President of the United States to be final arbiter between Spain and insurgents.[11]

That was all. And since the Spanish government subsequently complied with the two essential conditions, granting an armistice and ending reconcentration, later readers of this document were to suspect that the American government wanted, not a negotiated settlement, but merely an excuse for war.

The fact was, however, that Day also sent Woodford other messages explaining that these itemized conditions did not limit and define all of America's demands. Indeed, on the very day before, Day had cabled the minister, suggesting in the name of the President that Spain offer the Cubans "full self-government, with reasonable indemnity."

After receiving the three-point message, Woodford asked what these earlier words meant, and Day replied: "Full self-government with indemnity would mean Cuban independence. . . . Very important to have definite agreement for determining peace after armistice."

When Woodford reported later that he thought he could achieve an armistice and peace, Day asked him worriedly, "Would the peace you are so confident of securing mean the independence of Cuba?"[12] Since the State Department's security procedures were lax enough so that reporters often read and quoted from the most confidential dispatches, Day and McKinley could not afford to be more explicit in advising Woodford that their minimum terms included one which the conservative senators had not and would not have approved. In reality, their demands were that Spain end reconcentration, proclaim an armistice, *and* acknowledge that she would make Cuba independent if the President deemed it necessary.

Believing that Woodford would make these requirements plain to the Spanish government, McKinley employed all his resource and guile to give Spain time to comply. Consul General Lee telegraphed that Americans still in Havana would be in danger if war came, and the President immediately called in members of Congress and sent copies of Lee's message to Capitol Hill. Even the most fevered of jingoes could see the force of Lee's advice. Chandler reported to Dana that no one resented an enforced wait, even though some radicals remained suspicious, "feeling that the delay will be utilized to get up some new scheme for holding on some terms the Spanish flag in Cuba." McKinley dealt with these suspicions by completing a message to Congress asking intervention to end the Cuban war. He exhibited it to a number of members of the Senate and House while declaring, "That message shall not go to Congress as long as there is a single American life in danger in Cuba."[13]

With Congress temporarily appeased, the President employed every moment to persuade Spain that she should meet his conditions. Knowing Archbishop Ireland to be in direct communication with the Vatican, McKinley not only told him America's conditions but declared that he would be glad of any help the Holy See could give. He dared not entreat assistance too openly, and he was embarrassed when the Spanish government claimed that he had invited papal mediation. He had to deny having done so or having made any suggestions to Spain except through formal diplomatic channels.[14]

Nevertheless, he continued these efforts furtively. He remained in

contact with Archbishop Ireland; he invited the good offices of the
House of Rothschild; he even went so far as to agree to combined diplomatic intervention by the great powers. Secretary of State Sherman,
whose failing talents had been little used by the administration, was
so thoroughly opposed to war that he spoke on his own initiative to
the Austro-Hungarian minister, Baron von Hengelmüller, urging that
the Austrian Emperor offer to mediate. Because he knew Sherman to
be only nominally head of his department, Hengelmüller prudently
consulted Day and was told that the President would reject any such
European intervention out of hand. Others close to McKinley voiced
the same opinion.[15] Yet in the final period of grace, when Congress was
only waiting for Americans to be evacuated from Cuba, both the
President and Day relented.

The French ambassador suddenly heard what he regarded as inspired rumors that McKinley would welcome some European overture. Not long afterward Archbishop Ireland came to the French embassy, directly from the President's study, to urge that the powers
appeal to Spain to meet America's conditions and to the President,
"*in the name of humanity*," to accept. When the British ambassador
called at the State Department to tell Day that the powers were discussing just such an appeal to the President and that his own instructions were to do whatever the United States requested, the Assistant
Secretary did not reiterate what he had said earlier to Hengelmüller.
On the contrary, he told the Englishman that while he doubted if any
result could be achieved, he did not see how such action could do
harm. When shown a collective note drawn up by the ambassadors,
Day gave his full approval. Presumably he acted with the knowledge
of the President.[16]

The results of this truly extraordinary action by the administration
were, in the first place, a little ceremony that took place in the White
House on April 6. The envoys from Britain, France, Germany, Austria-Hungary, Italy, and Russia presented themselves. The Englishman, having served longest in Washington, read the note which they
had all signed. It simply made "a pressing appeal to the feelings of
humanity and moderation of the President and of the American people" and expressed the earnest hope "that further negotiations will

lead to an agreement which, while securing the maintenance of peace, will afford all necessary guaranties for the reestablishment of order in Cuba." The President replied by reading a formal text expressing hope for peace but also speaking of America's "unselfish endeavors to fulfill a duty to humanity by ending a situation the indefinite prolongation of which has become insufferable."[17] Owing to the caution which McKinley and Day had shown, this exchange produced no unfavorable publicity. Indeed, it created almost no stir in the press.

In the second place, and of far more importance to the President, there also resulted a *démarche* by the powers in Madrid. Though the Pope had already begged the Spanish government to grant an armistice, Woodford reported the cabinet as still divided. Then, on the morning of April 9, the six European ambassadors called on the Spanish Foreign Minister, just as they had earlier called upon McKinley. In the name of Europe, they asked that Spain accede to the request from the Vatican. And before the day was out, the government had agreed. Woodford, who had already declared that he would regard an armistice as equivalent to peace, cabled jubilantly to McKinley that victory could be and was being won.[18]

The President felt no less elated. The first to bring him the news was Archbishop Ireland. Subsequently Ireland told the French ambassador that McKinley had been "delighted." Considering the assurances that Woodford had been sending him, the President must have believed that Spain had yielded to all his demands. After having wriggled and squirmed through so many tight places, McKinley could have a momentary feeling that it had all been worth while—that he had prevented a domestic rupture, brought peace and independence to Cuba, and spared his people a war.

But illusion was followed by disillusion. Even in his initial delight, McKinley may have been troubled by the fact that Ireland gave him no assurance of Spain's willingness to make Cuba free. He had made it quite clear to the Archbishop that this was an essential condition, and Ireland's silence hinted at a fact that McKinley did not know— that Spain had told the Vatican she "would accept no arbitration having as a condition the independence of Cuba." Unhappily for the President, the Spanish attitude soon stood revealed. When informing the State Department of the armistice decree, Dupuy de Lôme's successor took pains to state in writing, "The autonomic constitution . . . gives to the inhabitants of the island of Cuba a political system at least as liberal as that which exists in the Dominion of Canada . . . ; and the franchise and liberties granted to the Cubans are such that no motive or pretext is left for claiming any fuller measure thereof." The Spanish minister had actually drawn up this memorandum on his own initiative, but the Americans could not know this fact. When Day asked him whether Spain would leave to the United States the final decision with regard to Cuba's sovereignty, the minister drew himself up and stiffly said, "No."[19] The Assistant Secretary had to go sadly to the White House and inform the President that America's conditions had not been met.

McKinley may have made one last effort to bridle the Congress. There was a long cabinet meeting on the evening of April 10. According to a rumor picked up by the French ambassador, the President spoke at this meeting of asking for delay in order to observe the effects of an armistice. Subsequently, however, he discussed this possibility with the Vice-President and various Republican senators and was warned in the strongest terms against changing the message he had already drafted and locked in the safe. Despite counterefforts by Democratic Senator Elkins and other conservatives, the President heeded this advice. At another cabinet session on the following morning, he announced that he would merely add to the original message a postscript mentioning the armistice decree and saying that Congress might take it into account. Though even the usually uncritical Secretary of the Navy regarded this postscript as a *non sequitur,* McKinley kept it as it was. Later on the morning of April 11, he sent it to Capitol Hill.[20]

McKinley had drafted the message almost in the presence of jingo congressmen, yet had so written it as to ensure a little more delay. When perplexed by the necessity for navigating between radicals who wanted recognition of the insurgents and former conservatives who desired annexation, he had considered the possibility of just leaving the issue to Congress. In his papers there is a draft of a paragraph which would have done exactly that. But McKinley chose instead to take a stand characteristically somewhere vaguely between the two extremes. While advising Congress not to recognize the existing rebel regime, he proposed that an independent Cuban government eventually be given recognition. All he asked was power "to take measures to secure a full and final termination of hostilities between the Government of Spain and the people of Cuba," including authority to use the armed forces.

The vagueness of his words on the point of recognition guaranteed at least a delay of several days while Congress debated the more clear-cut alternatives. As a matter of fact, the Foreign Relations and Foreign Affairs Committees differed within themselves, and the two chambers differed with each other. The Senate committee reported out a resolution demanding Spanish withdrawal from the island and promising eventual independence. A minority of the committee urged an amendment recognizing the Republic of Cuba as then constituted, and this amendment carried. In the House, on the other hand, a resolution passed 324–19 which merely parroted the words of McKinley's message. As both Chandler and the French ambassador recognized, this uncertain language could conceivably allow the President to continue negotiations.[21]

In all probability, McKinley had no thought of evading the manifest will of Congress and the people. During the time that was left to him, he did continue efforts to persuade Spain that she should declare her willingness to grant Cuba freedom. Woodford was informed in detail of the differences between the two chambers. The French ambassador, who was believed to have a direct channel to Madrid, was told that the President did not necessarily desire independence, that he might be able to preserve some semblance of Spanish sovereignty, but that he could do nothing unless assured by Spain that she would concede independence if necessary.[22]

But Congress soon took away his initiative. Speaker Reed, who staunchly opposed war, had probably been responsible for the mild resolution enacted by the House. After the issue went to a conference committee, compromise was inevitable. The House conferees accepted the Senate's text. A vote in the lower chamber struck out the provision recognizing the insurgent government, and the upper body yielded to this verdict. Both agreed to demand that Spain relinquish sovereignty over the island, to authorize the use of armed forces by the President, and to pledge that the United States would not assume "sovereignty, jurisdiction, or control" over Cuba. On April 19, this resolution came to the President's desk.

He had no choice but to sign it, and once he had done so, he no longer possessed any power to prevent war. The only faint chance of peace that remained lay in a voluntary decision by Spain to abandon Cuba. McKinley had capitulated to the jingoes.

It is hard not to sympathize with him. Even after his message had gone to Congress, his secretary wrote that he looked unwell, that his face was haggard, and that he made "anxious inquiry for any news which has in it a token of peace."[23] He had used all his talent, tact, and charm to prevent war. Time and again he had succeeded in some maneuver, as in obtaining autonomy for Cuba, posting the *Maine* to Havana, or flourishing Lee's warnings about the safety of Americans in the island, but each time he found himself overtaken by events and compelled to devise new gambits and ruses.

He worked always in terrible consciousness of the division in public opinion. Not only respecting the wisdom of clergymen and rich businessmen but politically dependent on their support, he felt he could not attach himself to the jingoes or simply pose as a leader of the masses. At the same time, he did not dare to align himself with the elite and defy the popular clamor, as Cleveland had. He could only remember that Cleveland had also resisted the silverites and seen his party explode beneath him. McKinley was not a brave man. In his whole political career, there had been no act of boldness. And the one resource which he did not employ in 1898 was courage. Rightly or wrongly, he conceived that he had some justification for demanding a final end to the violence in Cuba, that his highest duty lay in keeping his own country united, and that the alternative to war might be a domestic crisis tantamount in his eyes to revolution. For these reasons he led his country unwillingly toward a war that he did not want for a cause in which he did not believe.

In Spain, the Liberals had come to office in October, 1897, committed to a new course. It was unusual for Liberal policy to be distinguishable from Conservative, for Sagasta, the party's seventy-two-year-old chief, had taken turns with Cánovas ever since the beginning of the regency. His following was fully as faction ridden as Cánovas's, and his hold over subordinate leaders was no more secure. Without the talent and brilliance of Cánovas, Sagasta served blandly, smilingly, and tactfully as a mediator, appeasing each faction as much as he could without alienating others. In peacetime, members of the Cuban oligarchy had constituted one of these factions. After two years of war, however, Cuba had become impoverished, her oligarchs were politically weaker, and Spanish merchants and industrialists had lost interest in the island. In the Liberal party, other factions had grown proportionally stronger. While Sagasta endeavored to keep to the middle of the road, he found that that road was veering leftward. By June, 1897, he felt compelled to declare, "In the reforms of Sr. Cánovas, whether considered together or in detail, one sees nothing more than the principles of autonomy. Let us go on then to autonomy."

In office, Sagasta found himself committed to an even more drastic policy, for the leaders of the Liberal right wing, Maura and Gamazo, declined to serve with him. The most powerful figure in his cabinet was therefore the intense, dynamic left-wing leader, Segismundo Moret, the Minister for Colonies. At Zaragoza on July 19, Moret had hinted that Cuba should have dominion status like Canada's. In words recalling those of 1878, which led to the "shameful" Pact of Zanjón, he also said, "Military force will tear the flesh of Cuba; but autonomy will staunch the blood that gushes from wounds opened by the steel." With Moret in the Colonial Ministry, it could be assumed that Weyler's successor would be free to do what Martínez Campos had done at Zanjón—to negotiate with the rebels and offer their chiefs posts and privileges under an autonomous regime. It was to be Liberal policy to seek a negotiated peace.

Needless to say, the Liberals did not devise this policy in order to placate the United States. Indeed, Sagasta tried to defer taking office so that granting autonomy and relieving Weyler would not seem responses to an alleged ultimatum brought by Woodford. He wanted to wait until late winter or even spring. But María Cristina would not let him do so. A Carlist bishop in Palma de Mallorca charged the Conservative Treasury Minister with having seized goods belonging to a sanctuary and excommunicated him. The Queen seized the opportunity to say that she could not side against the church. The Conservative cabinet, which could only defend its own member, had to resign. Sagasta was compelled, against his will, to form a government. The Liberals took office in spite of, not because of, the fact that their policies would satisfy American demands.[1]

Nevertheless, the new cabinet was more interested in the United States than its predecessor had been. Sagasta and his colleagues took the view that the Cuban rebels would refuse a negotiated settlement so long as they hoped for eventual aid from the United States and would only accept the half-loaf of autonomy if persuaded that they had no chance of American help.

The cabinet therefore kept a close eye on Washington. Spanish diplomats were asked to report in detail on American reactions to autonomy and the relief of Weyler, and ministers in Madrid scrutinized McKinley's annual message, not for indications of American intentions toward Spain, but for words that might hearten or discourage the rebels. A translation circulated to the cabinet is in the Spanish archives. It has innumerable marginal marks and underlinings, but none around McKinley's warning of "other and further action" in the "near future." The Spanish government was not yet concerned with anything McKinley said or did, except as it seemed likely to affect rebel morale. Since the message contained passages discouraging recognition and praising the offer of autonomy, the Foreign Minister advised the Spanish ambassador in Paris that the cabinet found it "very satisfactory." This surprising reaction to an ominous warning indicated the government's absorption in the one aim of achieving a settlement with the rebels.[2]

The same single-mindedness characterized negotiations with the

United States. In mid-November Moret visited Woodford to propose a Spanish-American commercial treaty giving the United States virtually free access to Cuban products and the Cuban market. Many detached observers, among them the French ambassador, believed America's real interest in Cuba to be economic and thought that if Spain removed barriers to trade, interest in Cuban independence would fall off. Though Moret himself had long advocated expanding Spanish commerce, he approached Woodford with political rather than economic considerations in mind. When Woodford agreed to negotiate, Moret speedily brought forward a project so liberal that it delighted the American. When the de Lôme letter was published, saying that a new commercial treaty might be discussed "even if only for effect," Moret hastened to assure Woodford that he at least was in deadly earnest. He even offered to go in person to Washington. Rumor had it that there was opposition in the cabinet. Certainly many members, including Sagasta, had little sympathy with Moret's free-trade inclinations. But the commercial treaty project had approval even from the most protectionist ministers.³

At one point, the Queen Regent and Moret combined in a desperate attempt to achieve understanding with Washington. The solemn, humorless, homely Hapsburg Archduchess had no concern but to save the throne for her twelve-year-old son. From Weyler's successor, General Ramón Blanco, who was a familiar of the court, she received early warnings that conditions in Cuba were nearly hopeless. On January 17, 1898, she asked Woodford to pay her a private visit. She said that in Spain only Moret would know of the interview; she requested Woodford to inform no one but McKinley. When he agreed, she proceeded to speak of the autonomy decree and the relief of Weyler as if, contrary to all that had been said, they were concessions to American demands. Cleveland, she asserted, had promised to denounce the rebels publicly if Spain would grant autonomy. Would not McKinley now do so, she asked, and also break up the Junta in New York?

When Woodford spoke of difficulties, she broke in: "The President can do this and if he does it . . . the insurgents will know that they cannot get help; and their chiefs will accept autonomy and surrender;

and this will stop the war and I shall have peace." Afterward the Queen sent Moret to him to reiterate her pleas. Both insisted on the utmost secrecy. As Woodford explained to McKinley, "neither the Liberal Ministry nor the Queen could hold their places if it were suspected that they had so far violated Spanish traditions and offended Spanish pride."[4]

When even this personal appeal to McKinley produced no results, the Queen and her ministers had to face the fact that the United States would not help to bring about a negotiated peace. At the same time, they learned how unlikely it was that Blanco would achieve any more military success than Weyler had. Shortly after the Liberals took office, editor José Canalejas of the Madrid *Heraldo* went to Cuba to make a personal investigation. Reporting to Sagasta, he described a sick and spiritless army facing an enemy it could never defeat. Soon the Premier received a private letter from Blanco confirming the worst:

The army, exhausted and anemic, filling the hospitals, without the force to fight or hardly even to hold up its weapons; more than three hundred thousand concentrados dying or starving, perishing from hunger and misery around the cities; the people of the countryside terrified, prey to genuine horror, forced to abandon their farms or lands, suffering under the most hideous tyranny, with no recourse to escape their terrible situation except to go strengthen the rebel ranks.[5]

After the Queen's interview with Woodford and this report from Blanco, though the cabinet might continue to hope for pacification through autonomy, it faced the probability of failure.

The Queen and her ministers had to search the grim alternatives that remained. Abandonment of the island was simply out of the question. Spain could not desert the loyal Spaniards still there. More important, to give up the struggle would be to insult the sensitive and dangerous vanity of the army. Weyler's supporters scarcely waited for his return to Spain before beginning to claim that in another few weeks or months he would certainly have crushed the insurrection. To Weyler had already rallied not only Romero Robledo's cohorts but all the inchoate forces that opposed the dynasty—Carlists, republicans, Catalonian separatists, and even, it was said, some anarchists.

Few other generals had as yet joined him, but it was easy to foresee their doing so if the Queen and her government surrendered to the rebels.

Short of this drastic course were several other alternatives that began to receive serious consideration. Most of them, as it happened, assumed a crisis with the United States. The movement of American warships into the Caribbean, the dispatch of the *Maine* to Havana, the de Lôme letter, and the *Maine* disaster had gradually awakened Spanish statesmen to the increasing likelihood of war. In their desperation they began to wonder if this contingency might not somehow be turned to account.

One possibility was to accept war as a means of abandoning Cuba gracefully. As far back as 1895, this thought had been mentioned by Martínez Campos. In November, 1897, the French ambassador reported the Queen as believing that Spain had only two choices: "to reach an understanding with the Washington cabinet . . . or to push things to the limit by forcing a war with America, in which the result will be the loss of Cuba, but taken by force and not ceded out of free will." As the ambassador also reported, "this thought today haunts the brains of many politicians."[6]

There was, however, another, more complex, and more tempting possibility. It involved recourse to the Tetuán scheme of 1896. By appealing to the powers, Spain might obtain their support against the United States. If it was given unreservedly, the Americans could be forced to back down. The Cuban rebels would then lose all hope of foreign aid. They would have to take what they could get by negotiation.

Even if the powers should refuse, as seemed more likely, it was still possible that they might insist upon Spain and America putting their differences to arbitration. After all, that was what America had demanded in the Venezuelan case. As early as December 2, 1897, Moret approached the Austrian ambassador, saying that if the United States recognized Cuba, "in order to protect Spain from great domestic dangers, it will be necessary to throw down the gauntlet, break diplomatic relations, and face up to the serious consequences. Of course, with the *ardent* hope that friendly powers will intervene to mediate and bring the conflict before a court of arbitration."[7] If that occurred, the United States would obviously be unable to help the rebels until after the court ruled. Proceedings before arbitral tribunals had a way of going on for years. The rebels might grow discouraged and decide to accept autonomy. If not, the court might render a judgment which would give Spain some face-saving means of abandoning the island. On all counts, appeal to the powers seemed the government's best hope.

Though individuals doubtless differed among themselves, the Queen and the entire cabinet settled on a double course of action. On the one hand, they determined to do what was necessary to postpone a crisis. The Foreign Minister gave de Lôme's successor, Polo de Bernabé, verbal instructions to gain as many days as possible. Directing the commander of the Atlantic squadron to have his force battle-ready by the end of April, the Navy Minister observed, "We shall have to be very careful and if possible avoid *till then* any conflict with the United States."[8] By that time, better preparations for war could have been made. Blanco would also have had the entire campaigning season for a last-ditch attempt at victory. And there would have been opportunity for approaches to and negotiations among the powers. One major object of the Spanish government was to win delay until at least the beginning of the Cuban rains.

The other was to obtain support from Europe. In 1897, Moret, the Queen, and the Foreign Minister had taken some preliminary soundings. Moret had spoken with the English and Austrian ambassadors, the Foreign Minister with the French and Russian. The Queen had communicated with her relative, the Austrian Emperor, and received from him a promise that Spain's plight would be discussed with the German Kaiser. As early as December 17, 1897, the Spanish ambassador in Paris was talking with the French Foreign Minister about intervention by the powers, " 'not with cannon or warship' but with remonstrance and counsel." Despite universal expressions of sympathy, the results of these soundings had not been encouraging. Until after the Queen's failure with Woodford, the idea of appealing to Europe seemed to be discarded. Then, as the French ambassador reported on January 23, it was suddenly taken up with new enthusiasm.

"It has become quite difficult," the Frenchman commented, "to demonstrate here today the vanity and danger of it."[9] By February it had become Spain's principal aim.

The Spanish government did not cease to consider other possibilities. At one time there was even serious discussion of selling the island to the United States. An American dentist in Madrid had planted the suggestion in various quarters. Though no one knew if he had authorization from Washington, the notion kindled a surprising amount of interest. The French ambassador remarked that many Spaniards were more pessimistic and realistic in private than they dared be in public.

Some saw special reasons for favoring a negotiated transfer to the United States. Recognizing that Cuban Catholicism might suffer if Protestant America conquered the island, some church officials favored sale as a means of making provision for the rights and properties of Catholic congregations. This consideration appealed especially to prelates who were not averse to a public storm against the dynastic parties.

The Cardinal Archbishop of Valladolid, whose aim was to build a new clericalist party, issued a pastoral letter on February 26, observing that Spain had not been able to preserve the loyalty of Cuba in time of peace, that autonomy faced "almost certain failure," and that the external situation of Spain was more perilous than at any time since the Napoleonic invasion. A bishop in Barcelona subsequently came out flatly for selling the island in order to protect the interests of the church.

Romero Robledo wanted support from this clericalist faction, and his newspaper, *El Nacional,* astonished Madrid on March 5 by printing an editorial in favor of selling Cuba. The Queen's almoner, who was one of the Cardinal Archbishop's correspondents, became an advocate of the project, and the Queen herself studied it.[10]

Woodford reported to McKinley that on March 11 a member of his staff received a mysterious visit from the Queen's private secretary. The minister inferred that she wished to meet him privately and arrange for sending to Washington by courier an offer to discuss possible American purchase of the island. On the following day, however, he was told that the Queen did not wish to see him after all, and he commented to the President, "The Queen evidently lost courage between Friday afternoon and Saturday noon." The Marqués de Lema, a young Conservative politician, relates in his memoirs that the Queen discussed the possibility candidly with various party leaders. None opposed the solution outright. The French ambassador reported that Silvela, who had become majority leader among the Conservatives, promised not to raise opposition. But Lema understood that no one in either party would consent to take responsibility, and the Queen discarded the idea. On March 18 Moret spoke to Woodford, saying, as the American reported:

. . . that justice to the Queen required him to assure me in the most positive manner that she had not been privy to or cognizant of any suggestion that she wished to talk with me about any possible cession of Cuba, either to the insurgents or to the United States; that she wished to hand over his patrimony unimpaired to her son when he should reach his majority; and that she would prefer to abdicate her regency and return to her Austrian home rather than be the instrument of ceding or parting with any of Spain's colonies.[11]

Other remedies were probably studied with equal care. At least as early as March 3, the Spanish government knew McKinley's three formal conditions: an end of reconcentration, an armistice, and acceptance of American final arbitration. The chargé d'affaires in Washington reported Day as having said that only speedy acceptance of these terms by Spain could prevent intervention. The possibility of accepting them was undoubtedly canvassed even more seriously than the drastic recourse of sale. It may be that some ministers early decided upon concessions that might be made at the last minute. Woodford believed Moret to have steeled himself for any alternative to war.[12] But the record of negotiations suggests that the cabinet as a whole, regarding McKinley's conditions as unacceptable, had no other object than to delay an inevitable crisis.

In all conferences with Woodford, Spanish ministers sought to tantalize him with hope that Spain would cave in if the United States only waited. Even before the chargé's report of McKinley's terms, Moret told Woodford that everything would depend on Cuba's new autonomous parliament. After the American warned that Spain would have to act at least before mid-April, Moret and the Foreign Minister conferred with him formally, reiterating that it was necessary to await formation of the Cuban parliament. The latter asked explicitly for "delay until beginning of the rainy season." A formal memorandum handed to Woodford on March 25 declared that nothing could be done without participation by the Cuban parliament which would not meet until May 4. Then, however, steps could be taken promptly to restore "lasting peace."[13]

After the American greeted this memorandum as vague and unencouraging, a conference was arranged with the Premier. Sagasta asked Woodford to understand that the Spanish government would find it hard even to offer an armistice. "He suggested," Woodford reported to McKinley, "that there are difficulties in the Spanish situation here in the Peninsula which I, as a stranger, could hardly understand." But the Cuban parliament, Sagasta ventured, would be freer, "and he hoped that the United States, which had waited so long, would now wait for these few weeks."

When Woodford responded that his government demanded immediate peace in the island, the Premier returned another formal memorandum, reversing the manner but not the sense of what he had said orally. The Spanish cabinet would have to leave preparations for "an honorable and stable peace" up to the new Cuban government. In the meantime, it would only accept an armistice if the rebels asked for it. In all these conferences and memoranda, the Spanish ministers implied that they had less objection to the substance of the American demands than to their form. Woodford was led to conclude, as he telegraphed the President, that "the ministry have gone as far as they dare do" and "are ready to go as far and as fast as they can."[14] Had he been more practiced or less trustful, he would have found it suspicious that they asked neither compromise nor concession. He would have realized that all they sought was time.

There were differences, to be sure, within the cabinet. Woodford was led to believe that Moret and a peace-at-any-price faction battled constantly against a bellicose wing led by the Foreign Minister, Pio Gullón. Though the extent of disagreement was exaggerated for his benefit, the division did lie between a compromising and an intransigent faction. After learning of McKinley's three demands, the cabinet agreed that reconcentration could easily be ended. The policy had few remaining partisans. Conditions in the camps had disturbed Spaniards as much as Americans, and Blanco was ready to do away with them. The cabinet also agreed, it would seem, that American mediation or arbitration could never be accepted. At no time was it even rumored that any minister favored this concession. Where the difference arose was over the granting of an armistice.

To this issue the cabinet devoted long and heated debate before arriving even at a compromise. Though ignorant of the cause, newspapers reported meetings from which ministers emerged with tight mouths and flushed faces. Moret told Woodford that he himself favored an armistice if the rebels could be induced to ask for it. Gullón declared that he opposed. Army spokesmen, it was said, flared up at any suggestion that Spain make the offer herself. Despite the practical advantages of a truce lasting through the rainy season, when no operations could be conducted in any case, the army believed it would be dishonorable to seek it. Only after much argument and a final conference with the Queen was a solution found. The cabinet decided that while armistice could not be proposed by Spain at the behest of the United States it could be conceded gracefully if either the rebels or the European powers made the request.[15]

In the end, after still another long debate, armistice was granted at the instance of the Pope. Behind both the papal initiative and the decision to accept it, however, lay developments from the other, the main line of Spanish diplomacy, the effort to secure backing in Europe.

Ever since February, when the double course of seeking delay and aid had been decided on, Spain had been doing her utmost to forge a combination among the powers. Experience with the 1896 memorandum and soundings taken in 1897 had encouraged belief that support would come automatically from most European capitals. The Triple Alliance—Austria-Hungary, Germany, and Italy—had tacitly endorsed the Tetuán memorandum. The British ambassador, despite his suspected rôle in sabotaging Tetuán's *démarche,* had virtually promised moral support in any new move. The French government was plainly sympathetic. The only hitch was that all powers consulted had insisted on united action, and the Russian government had indicated it would not join. In December, 1897, the Russian ambassador had revealed that he held "very precise instructions" to abstain from involvement in the Cuban question and not to commit his government to any act that might irritate the United States. The key to Spain's success or failure seemed to lie in St. Petersburg.[16]

The Spanish government resolved to appeal to the Tsar through the Emperor of Austria. Since France was Russia's ally, the first impulse had been to work through her. The Spanish ambassador to France, Fernando de León y Castillo, was called to Madrid for consultations. He advised that while the French government would do everything it could, reasons of international and domestic politics made it preferable that someone else take the initiative. The French Foreign Minister nominated the Queen's relative, Emperor Franz Josef of Austria, suggesting that as a monarch, he could perhaps appeal to the Tsar more effectively than could the President of the French Republic. The traditional antagonism between the Austrian and Russian courts had been eased by the recent signature of a secret but not unpublicized understanding on the Balkans. In addition, Austria, unlike France, had ties with Germany and Italy through the Triple Alliance and with England through the Mediterranean agreements. If France would not take the initiative, Austria certainly seemed second best.

On March 11, the Queen called in the Austrian ambassador and tearfully declared that Blanco would be master of Cuba in three months if it were not for American aid to the rebels. Just as Spain's prospects for triumph improved, she lamented, America supported the Cubans "all the more ruthlessly." An "unholy conflict" was fast approaching, and for that reason she begged "mediation and aid."[17]

Even after the Emperor had consented, the Spanish government kept up its own efforts to win over the Russians. The Queen called in the Russian ambassador, had a long talk with him, and evidently asked him to transmit her appeal directly to the Tsar. In the meantime, the Foreign Ministry repeatedly urged the French to bring pressure on their Russian ally. León y Castillo promised that Spain would do

anything France asked, "no matter how much or how little." He also
declared that the Queen and the new leader of the formerly isolationist
Conservative party were ready to put Spain on the side of the Franco-
Russian alliance. On March 24, Gullón telegraphed the ambassador,
". . . on the intelligence and zeal of Your Excellency depends in great
part whether we shall dominate or at least attenuate the grave circumstances in which we find ourselves." The French government ultimately agreed to urge Russian participation in a *démarche* by the
powers. On March 27 the Spaniards delightedly received word that
the Tsar's government would join in any action agreed upon by the
rest of the powers.[18]

Meanwhile, however, the Spanish government learned to its annoyance that the English were holding back. At the outset there had been
some, like León y Castillo, who doubted that the British government
would actually be as sympathetic as the British ambassador in Madrid
promised. But León y Castillo's view had been that if the continental
powers united, Britain would not be necessary. Only further conversations in Paris disabused him of this hope, for the French Foreign Minister insisted on England's participation. The French did agree to
exert such influence as they could in London. On their recommendation, María Cristina addressed a personal appeal to Queen Victoria,
much like those to Franz Josef and the Tsar. Though no direct answer
came from Victoria, León y Castillo telegraphed jubilantly on March
30 that the French Foreign Minister now reported all the powers ready
to join in giving moral support to Spain.[19]

For one brief moment, Spain seemed to have achieved her goals.
Moret, Gullón, and Sagasta could believe that their temporizing had
slowed up McKinley and that in the time gained they had won the
united support of Europe. The cabinet had already agreed to arbitrate
differences with the United States, so long as Spanish sovereignty over
Cuba was not questioned. Since this condition had been made known,
the powers presumably would heed it. Subsequently, in the debates
provoked by McKinley's demands, it had also been decided to grant
an armistice if the powers proposed it. The same condition was to
hold. It appeared, therefore, that the powers were ready to step in,
provide an honorable pretext for an armistice, insist on arbitration,

and in the arbitration ensure that Spain kept control over Cuba. No outcome could have been more satisfying to the Queen, Sagasta, and other members of the cabinet.

No sooner had the sun broken through, however, than clouds closed in again. In the first place, the British ambassador contradicted the assurance that had come from Paris. His government, he said, thought intervention at this stage premature. This attitude, Gullón exclaimed, was so "strange and surprising" that it might be due "to calculation or interest contrary to ours." In the second place, the Spanish ambassador in Berlin telegraphed that the German government probably would not join in. Since the Germans had been among the first to give an explicit promise of support, this news drew from Gullón an angry comment: "It will be incredible and of the gravest consequence if the deception by the Kaiser and his government is confirmed."[20] With both Britain and Germany hanging back, the momentary illusion of safety vanished.

It was at this stage that the Pope stepped in. The Spanish government knew that Cardinal Rampolla, the Papal Secretary of State, sympathized with Spain; Rafael Merry del Val, the Spanish ambassador at the Vatican, had reported him as terming McKinley's demands "insulting . . . and contrary to all the principles of international law." The Spaniards also knew that Rampolla had been using Archbishop Ireland to sound out McKinley's views on arbitration. Nevertheless, it came as a surprise when on April 2 the Pope offered to request an armistice, if such a request would enable Spain to escape her predicament with honor.[21]

This offer divided the cabinet. Gullón, the Foreign Minister, who had been thrown into despair by Germany's change of front, telegraphed the ambassador in Berlin, "This action falls all the more grievously on us because it will not be possible even to gain time so that the monarchical powers might in some fashion relieve the pressure which the North American republic endeavors to exert on the Spanish government. . . . I now doubt if after this they will want to do anything to relieve it." Since the papal proposal had been encouraged by Germany, it was barely possible that it might reunite the promised combination of the powers. At least, acceptance might win Spain some time. Both Gullón and Moret took the view that the Pope's offer had to be accepted.[22]

The opposite position was taken by both the War and Navy Ministers. Despite detailed memoranda on the weakness of the fleet, the Navy Minister still believed optimistically that the Spanish navy might be a match for the American. The War Minister was more gloomy, and on April 6 declared publicly, "I am not of those who boast of the certainty of victory . . . ; but I am of those who believe that, of two evils, this is the better; the worse would be the conflict which would rise in Spain if our honor and our rights were compromised. . . . I do not think the situation as extreme as my colleague, Sr. Moret." The minister's opinion was more guarded than those of the military press. The *Correspondencia Militar* had already begun calling for war; the *Correo Militar* had declared that victory was sure. Even the semi-official *Ejército Español* had said that a truce dictated by America would be shameful. The War Minister's hesitancy reflected the mood of the army, and the army was a force that the cabinet could never disregard.[23]

The Queen threw her influence behind Moret and Gullón. The German ambassador had earlier quoted her as terming Cuba a burden and a source of constant danger and declaring that she would gladly be rid of it. The Austrian ambassador, who knew her better, thought this report exaggerated, and the Queen herself later denied ever having made so strong a statement. On the other hand, it was true that she stood in much closer relationship than her government to the clerical faction which was ready, for reasons of church, to abandon Cuba. Owing to her friendship with Martínez Campos and other generals, she had less reason than her ministers to fear the army. Her interest was never to save the government or the traditional parties or even the constitution, but only to protect the dynasty. Possibly she believed that anger over an armistice or humiliation in Cuba would fall upon the government while anger at a disastrous war would fall upon her. In any case, she had quietly encouraged the Vatican to make its offer, and she let it be known, not so quietly, that she regarded acceptance of it as the best solution to Spain's dilemma.

Even with her influence in the balance, the outcome was by no means certain. Some minister, probably Gullón, put forward a compromise formula. Spain would accept papal mediation if the United States agreed to it first. Spain would further grant an armistice at the Pope's request provided the United States withdrew its naval vessels from the vicinity of Cuba. This formula was obviously intended to attract the Navy Minister and separate him from his military colleague, for the Atlantic squadron was just on its way to Cuba; plans for a naval war had not yet been completed by the staff; various vessels were still refitting; and negotiations were in progress for purchase of foreign warships. If the armistice resulted in withdrawal of the American fleet, it would be most advantageous for the navy, and the Navy Minister seems, albeit reluctantly, to have accepted the compromise.[24]

The actual vote in the cabinet may have been influenced by a misunderstanding. Merry del Val telegraphed from the Vatican that McKinley had "solicited" a papal armistice proposal. As soon as the Spanish Foreign Ministry published this message, Woodford and the State Department at once denied that McKinley had done any such thing. It turned out that Merry had been misled by a communication from Archbishop Ireland saying that the President would welcome the Pope's "help." Merry's message came just before the cabinet sat down to vote, and it may have affected some ministers. But the decision was not reversed, even after the misunderstanding had been explained. Some may have believed, with Gullón, that McKinley had really made the request but had felt compelled to deny it on account of Protestant feeling in his own country. In any case, the government voted to invite a papal request for an armistice.[25]

After the Pope made his plea, another accident almost caused the cabinet to refuse the armistice. On April 6, Woodford presented Gullón with a sudden note, saying that he had expected an armistice proclamation by noon of that day. McKinley's message, he understood, was already being delivered to Congress. Only if Spain made her announcement before midnight, he warned, would it be possible for the President to advise of the fact before Congress acted. This peremptory note offended Gullón and others. The Foreign Minister telegraphed vexedly to Polo, "The proceedings of the United States and the singular tactlessness of Woodford have made it difficult for the Spanish

Government to follow its own inclinations and concede to His Holiness a suspension of hostilities."[26]

Only renewed intervention by the Queen rescued the cabinet from return to indecision. She had been indirectly responsible for Woodford's *démarche,* having asked him confidentially what would be the effect if she proclaimed an armistice by April 6. When his surprise note threatened to prevent any armistice at all, she asked if the ambassadors of the powers could not add their urgings to those of the Pope. The ambassadors in Washington had already addressed their joint appeal to the President, Germany having consented to support the papal action and England belatedly and conditionally having agreed to participate. The Queen called in the Austrian ambassador and asked him to arrange a similar visit to her. It was quickly done, and on the morning of April 9 she was able to tell her ministers that all the powers joined with Cardinal Rampolla in strongly urging acceptance of the papal offer.[27]

When the cabinet met later in the day, it had before it the advice of the Queen, the Vatican, and the powers. Gullón could quote the Spanish minister in Washington as predicting that while the United States would never promise to withdraw its fleet, it would in fact do so if an armistice were proclaimed. Also on the envoy's authority, he could state that there was a good chance of McKinley's being able to hold off Congress if the armistice were granted. The Navy Minister, who was in receipt of anguished pleas for further delay from the commander of the Atlantic fleet, could see that an armistice offered Spain her only chance of winning time and preparing for combat. Aware of Blanco's low estimate of army materiel and morale, the War Minister could perceive the same truth.

More important, all members of the government could understand that failure to grant an armistice might end any prospect of European support. The ambassadors were now pressing Spain rather than the United States, yet the very fact that they were acting together was encouraging. Some of them suggested that if the armistice were proclaimed the powers might really back Spain up, and Rampolla warned that if their advice were ignored Spain would thenceforth be friendless. The government thus had reason to see an armistice as the only re-

maining act that might improve Spain's position and somehow eventually win for her the aid of Europe. After a brief, solemn debate, the
cabinet approved an armistice proclamation, and it was issued on
April 10.[28]

After that, nothing more could be done. All the powers, including
England and Germany, exhibited sympathy. The British government,
however, indicated that it saw reason for not offending the United
States. The German Foreign Minister said with curt candor that the
powers were preoccupied with more important affairs.[29] Further support from Europe would come only if the English and Germans
changed their minds, and no new gesture by Spain was likely to influence them.

Nor did there remain any feasible method of stalling the United
States. McKinley had delivered his message; Congress now held the
decision. The Spanish ministers did not regard the message itself as
unduly provocative. Sagasta and Gullón both commented that it contained more good than bad and that a rupture need not come unless
the Congress voted recognition of the rebels or demanded that Spain
abandon Cuba. The cabinet still had the option of asking McKinley to
mediate. Any such plea, however, would clearly imply that Spain was
willing to make Cuba independent. And this—the crucial concession
—no responsible official was ever disposed to approve. The Queen
denied the report of her views given (and probably invented) by the
German ambassador. Moret contradicted every rumor that he ever
considered Cuban independence preferable to war.[30]

Indeed, after McKinley's message to Congress, members of the
government found reason to worry that they might already have made
too many concessions. The armistice announcement brought angry
crowds into the streets of Madrid, Barcelona, and Valencia. Weyler's
friends, Carlists, and republicans were whipping them up. The military press shouted for war. So did journals like the *Imparcial* and the
Heraldo that posed as interpreters of independent public opinion.
Despite the private views of ministers on McKinley's speech, the
cabinet felt obliged to issue a resolute statement condemning it and
promising that there would be no retreat. By April 14, the situation
had become so serious that the aged and sick Martínez Campos came

forth, issued a soothing statement, and declared that, if necessary, he would form an all-party government. To admit the possibility of peaceful independence for Cuba or to accept American mediation had probably never seemed feasible to the Queen and her ministers. In the face of public feeling after the armistice decree, these steps could hardly even be discussed.[31]

As long as the two houses of Congress quarreled about their differing resolutions, hope flickered in Madrid. The minister in Washington reported that Congressional fury might die out in talk. The result might be a vague resolution empowering the President to continue negotiations. More important, he described the powers' ambassadors as vexed that McKinley paid so little attention to their joint note. He reported the English ambassador even angrier than the rest. Rumors followed that the ambassadors would call for acceptance of Spain's armistice offer and condemn intervention as immoral. There was even talk of simultaneous notes from the powers, as a more solemn and effective method of stating this opinion. But at the last moment the British government showed reluctance to proceed, the Germans reneged, and nothing was done. The Spanish government drew up a long memorandum, much like the one Tetuán had distributed in 1896, and sent it to all major capitals. Gullón urged the Spanish ambassadors to obtain prompt responses, but he could not have held high hopes.[32]

The Queen and the cabinet had in fact reconciled themselves to war. When the final Congressional resolution was cabled from Washington, the ministers met with the Queen. Gullón recommended that relations be broken as soon as it had been approved by the President. Moret did not dissent. He said it was still possible for Blanco and the rebels to come to terms or for McKinley to advise nothing more than extended autonomy. Unless these unlikely conditions developed, he favored rupture. The cabinet seemed unanimous, and the Queen unhesitatingly approved their decision. She agreed to summon the Cortes and put the country on a war footing. As soon as McKinley signed the joint resolution, the Foreign Ministry recalled the minister in Washington and handed Woodford his passports. Moret telegraphed Blanco, "Consider war as declared. Hostilities will begin immediately."[33]

PART FIVE

TURNING POINT

"The Cuban question has for Europe an interest that is not only local but also general. The excessive enlargement of the Monroe doctrine menaces all European states. . . . It is necessary to recognize that the governments of Europe have contributed to the growth in the pretensions of the American republic by having done absolutely nothing to prevent a possible conflict. . . . The Spanish government, for its part, has done all that it could to satisfy the Cuban populace. . . . The insurrection would have halted long ago if it had not been artificially sustained. . . . Have American politicians understood this situation as they should? Or do they suppose that the European powers will continue to stand by indifferently while events take their course?"

St. Petersburg *Novosti,*
February 10, 1898

XIV · THE VIEW FROM EUROPE

During all the months when this climax was building, the European powers had seemed to pay scant attention. Their ambassadors visited both McKinley and the Queen Regent to urge a peaceful settlement, but little came of these gestures, and otherwise they did nothing. Few historians of the period have even thought it worth while to mention the collective *démarche* in Washington.

Despite its seeming inconsequence, this joint *démarche* represented Europe's one united response to the emergence of America as a power. Europeans might well look back upon the episode as their great lost chance—the moment when, in Arnold Toynbee's terms, their civilization failed to produce the necessary creative response to a challenge. In this perspective, the hesitancy, torpor, and disunity of the powers in 1898 might be said to resemble that of the Greek city states when confronting Rome in the second century B.C. or that of the Italian principalities facing France in 1496. It may be that this was an instance of momentous inaction. In any event, it is worth while to inquire why the powers failed to exert themselves.

Certainly it cannot be said that Europeans were ignorant of America. Few literate travelers had failed to publish their impressions. Even before 1860, at least 330 such works had been printed in England, and more than a thousand came out in France before 1900. Innumerable emigrant guides were issued by steamship lines and similar agencies. Periodicals devoted exclusively or in part to American subjects were not rare. Though most of these writings were mere travelogues, many called attention to America's rising population and production. Early nineteenth-century commentators had been interested mainly in American democracy. Those after 1870 tended to remark more on America's richness.[1]

In the 1870's, Hungarian, Prussian, and French grain and live-stock growers became concerned over American competition. They persuaded their governments to put up tariffs against agricultural imports. By 1882 Hungarian ministers in the Austro-Hungarian Empire were speaking of America as Hungary's foremost competitor, and by the 1890's German officials were resorting to such devices as impossibly high sanitary requirements in order to keep out American foodstuffs. By that time, too, the fears of agriculturists had come to be shared by industrialists. Tariffs were laid on manufactures as well as farm products, and spokesmen for affected interests warned, as a German pamphleteer did in 1881, that Europe might "succumb to the United States in the battle for supremacy in world trade."[2]

Frenchmen were especially impressed by data on American economic growth. Scholars as well as propagandists made comparative studies. Detailed work was done on land distribution, railroad development, and labor organization in the United States. Several writers who examined American secondary schools and universities reported that their accessibility, coupled with their tendency to stress practical subjects, contributed to building relatively larger groups of entrepreneurs, managers, and skilled workmen. In effect, they warned their countrymen that the American boom was not, as had been first supposed, a mere result of immigration and a large cheap labor force.[3]

At the Collége de France, the acme of the French academic world, Émile Levasseur, one of the nation's leading economists, devoted himself almost exclusively to American studies. Investigating agriculture, labor, and capital formation, he produced a series of works so solid that they still have value. The abundance of natural resources in America, he contended, made possible mass production on scales almost inconceivable in Europe. The individual American farmhand or factory worker turned out more than his French counterpart. What he produced could be sold at a lower price while he himself received a higher wage. According to Levasseur's calculations, the real earnings of American unskilled laborers were higher, not lower, than those of Europeans. Standards of living were also higher and were certain, he thought, to rise relatively much more. And the tendency toward trust and monopoly formation would, he believed, bring larger scales of production, lower prices, and even higher real wages. To him, as to most French investigators, it seemed depressingly clear that the United States had competitive advantages which France simply could not match. Some concluded, as did Paul Leroy-Beaulieu, the editor of *L'économiste français,* that America could "aspire to . . . commercial and financial supremacy."[4]

Italian scholars tended to agree. Though not preoccupied with declining relative population as the French were, Italian economists and sociologists nevertheless saw indications that Italy was falling behind. As early as 1873 a Florentine agronomist published a work making unfavorable comparisons between Italian and American methods of using agricultural land. In the 1880's Bolognese and Milanese students brought out detailed studies on American agriculture and industry. These writers tended, on the whole, to praise American institutions and methods. But their findings caused more than one Italian, even in the 1880's, to foresee an "American peril." Egisto Rossi warned of it in a work published in 1884. "The rapid economic evolution of American society is destined to produce in European civilization the same effects that the Darwinian 'struggle for life' produces in the animal kingdom."[5]

For some Frenchmen and Italians, uneasiness over America's economic growth was compounded by antagonism toward American ideas. Simply as a republic, the United States was odious to conservative monarchists. This irritation increased in proportion as America endured and thrived, and conservative landowners and industrialists tended to see in American competition a moral as well as an economic threat. Agricultural prices in France were forced down by a flood of imports not only from America but equally from Tsarist Russia. The republican *Société nationale de l'encouragement à l'agriculture* protested against both. The royalist *Société des agriculteurs de France* talked only of the menace from America.

Sometimes this antirepublican anti-Americanism lost touch with reality. The Paris daily, *Figaro,* was a sophisticated, cosmopolitan, right-wing journal published for an upper-class audience. It often mocked American manners and customs. On July 12, 1896, however, it printed an article by Denis Guibert making involved comparisons between the United States and Rome and between Bryan and Julius Caesar. At the end, Guibert warned in all seriousness that if Bryan were elected, Europe should prepare for an armed American invasion.

Though it seems improbable that many Europeans shared this particular worry, a number of conservatives did feel uneasy about America for reasons that had little or nothing to do with economic competition. In both France and Italy the Catholic hierarchy discouraged members of the church from holding office or even voting: in the one state because it was an anticlerical republic; in the other because the government had dispossessed the Pope. Some Catholics had begun to feel, however, that the French republic and the Italian monarchy were there to stay and that churchmen would only hurt themselves if they continued to abstain from political activity. A few had even begun to advocate that Catholics steal a march on anticlericals by seizing leadership in mass movements for social reform, and these progressives made much use of America's example.

They took their texts from American priests. The Abbé Felix Klein brought out in 1894 a translation of speeches by Archbishop Ireland, and in 1897 he edited and prepared an introduction for a French edition of Walter Elliott's life of Father Hecker, the founder of the American Paulist brotherhood. In these and numerous other writings, the United States was pictured as a model for Europe. Church-state separation, it was argued, allowed concentration on spiritual aims and swept away the old antagonism between nationalism and Catholicism. The exponents of this almost modernist doctrine called it "Americanism."[6]

Conservative Catholics, on the other hand, saw in "Americanism" a heresy at least as dangerous as the liberalism condemned by Pius IX in the Syllabus of Errors. *La Verité* in France and the Jesuit *Civiltá Cattolica* in Italy assailed both the doctrine and its presumed source. The latter in its chronicle for May 2, 1897, asked if the United States could even be considered a Christian nation. The former published serially, March 3–19, 1898, an attack by Father Charles Maignen of the Brothers of St. Vincent de Paul on Klein, the life of Hecker, and the whole "Americanist" movement. Among other things, Maignen wrote that "Americanism" implied the superiority of republics to monarchies; true philosophy proved the contrary to be true.

Though written debate among priests turned on technical issues, the controversy stirred emotion among laymen. A Belgian aristocrat, Charles de Ricault d'Hericault, wrote in the *Revue générale* for June, 1899: "Americanism is not only a movement toward heresy; it is an *invasion of barbarism* . . . : it is attack by a new power against society, against Christian society . . . ; it is money against honor, coarse brutality against delicacy, . . . machinery against philosophy . . . , the insolent triumph of brute force. . . . This new barbarism is represented by Yankeeism, and religious Americanism is nothing but one of the assaults of pan-Americanism."

As Spanish-American relations worsened through 1896 and 1897, doctrinal antagonism toward the United States merged with emotional sympathy for Spain. *Figaro,* the monarchist *Gaulois,* and the clericalist *Echo de Paris* came virtually to advocate support of the Queen Regent by the French government. So did other Paris newspapers which were not ordinarily identified with protectionism, monarchism, or Catholicism. The *Petit Journal* and the *Correspondant* were both journals for the masses. Distinguished by their chauvinistic hostility to Britain, the sheets had applauded the United States during the Venezuela crisis but turned about when America composed its differences with Britain. When the United States Senate resolved to recognize Cuban belligerency, they charged that America meant to conquer the Caribbean, including the French islands there. They called upon Europe to defend Spain. The *Petit Journal* termed it a necessity for the survival of the Latin race.

More staid and sober dailies adopted a similar line. *Le Temps* declared in an editorial for November 12, 1896, that all colonial powers should take warning from America's treatment of Spain and consider banding to resist the trans-Atlantic republic's imperialism. The *Journal des Débats* expressed exactly the same view. According to the *Literary Digest* for November 27, 1897, the *Matina* and other Italian journals also urged or hinted at the wisdom of Europe's going to Spain's defense. In Latin Europe there were important and vocal groups exercised at the potential American menace and actively sympathetic toward Spain.

In Central Europe there was even more widespread anti-Americanism. Despite the fact that German Catholics were not by and large aristocrats, some priests and laymen expressed sympathy with French

and Italian opponents of "Americanism." Especially was this so because the hero of the movement, Archbishop Ireland, had a reputation as an enemy of the German-American clergy. Against his
battle to stop preaching and teaching in the German language, the
German-Americans had rallied support in their homeland. Groups
led by a Limburg businessman, Peter Paul Cahensly, had even appealed to the Pope to appoint a German cardinal for America.
"Cahenslyism" had then been attacked by Ireland's followers and
even more violently by the American secular and Protestant press.
When "Americanism" came under attack, therefore, few Germans
defended it. Even a virtual modernist like Hermann Schell refused
to identify himself with it, and far from conservative journals of the
Catholic *Zentrum* party, such as the Berlin *Germania,* sided with
Maignen and the anti-"Americanist" faction.[7]

The German aristocracy's Lutheran majority did not prevent it
from joining the Catholic aristocracy of Latin Europe in distaste for
the United States. Prussian Junkers were landowners hurt not only
by American competition but also by falling world prices for which
the huge American output was blamed. The bitterest German criticisms of the United States appeared in speeches in the Reichstag by
members of the Conservative party, predominantly Prussian, agrarian, and Protestant. Conservative newspapers such as the *Kreuzzeitung* and the *Deutsche Tageszeitung* used "American" and
"Yankee" as scornful epithets, and the Conservative monthly *Grenzboten* abandoned all restraint when it commented on American
affairs. Even when commending Cleveland's Venezuela message in
its editorial notes for January, 1896, it referred to the United States
as a "realm of ruthless slavery" ruled by "grasping money princes."

The Berlin *Post,* which spoke for the urban Free Conservative
party, joined the agrarian press in calling for a tariff war. So did the
Bismarckian *Hamburger Nachrichten,* published ironically in a city
that profited greatly from trade with the United States. And the
smart comic magazine, *Kladderadatsch,* which circulated through all
of Germany, pictured Uncle Sam with porcine eyes and a large hook
nose. Newspapers advocating imperialism tended to be anti-American. The Berlin *Vossische Zeitung,* the *Kölnische Zeitung,* and the

Frankfurter Zeitung, all of which were relatively liberal, assailed Cleveland for reasserting the Monroe doctrine and warning Europeans to stay out of the Western Hemisphere. When the Senate tried to recognize Cuban belligerency, the *Kölnische Zeitung* accused the United States of a "lust for conquest" and warned that Europe might have to combine to check it. After the settlement of the Venezuela dispute, the *Frankfurter Zeitung* predicted a British-American partnership in imperialism. Dr. Karl Peters, a leading Anglophobe as well as a leading colonialist, charged in *Zukunft* that Americans were slaves of British capital and that the eventual German struggle with England would be one with the united Anglo-Saxon race. In Vienna the Anglophobe *Politische Korrespondez* similarly identified the United States with Britain, and so did even the responsible middle class *Neue Freie Presse.*

In Germany as elsewhere, imperialism and navalism went hand in hand. As Eckart Kehr has shown, the German navalist movement was led by industrial and business groups, both Protestant and Catholic, which were normally antagonistic toward Prussian agrarians. In order to succeed, these groups had to enlist Conservative support. Seeking it, they played upon such emotions as antirepublicanism and anti-Americanism. Some navy propagandists asserted that Germany needed agricultural colonies in South America and a navy in order to get them. Others stressed American competition and the necessity for naval protection of Germany's expanding overseas commerce. In a speech in December, 1897, the Navy Ministry's economist ranked the American economic threat above that from England. Still others made much of an alleged need to protect German citizens abroad. Both in the Reichstag and in the press, navalists exploited this argument after the Lüders episode in Haiti in late 1897.[8] Though England served as the chief target of navy propagandists, the United States drew some fire, and navalism stimulated anti-Americanism.

Antagonism, mistrust, and even fear were more widespread in Germany probably than in any other European country except Spain. The groups that were identifiably anti-American overlapped. More than one German was a Catholic, a rightist, a member of the Colonial Society, and a member of the Navy League. But each group also contained distinctive elements, and Conservatives, agrarians, Catholics, colonialists, and navalists combined to form a large proportion of German public opinion.

Not even among these groups, however, was there much sense of affinity for Spain. In 1885 the German government had posted a claim to the Caroline Islands. Spain protested, and Bismarck withdrew the claim, but only after many bitter words spilled in the press of both countries. The sores left by this episode were reopened in 1894 when Spain suddenly and cavalierly abandoned a commercial agreement and began shutting out German products. When agitation on the Cuban issue developed in the United States, German periodicals sometimes criticized American methods and aims, but few took the part of Spain. *Grenzboten* remarked, for example, that Germany had no more historic reason for sympathizing with Spain than with the United States.[9] Anti-Americanism tended to focus on such projects as naval building, colonial conquest, and tariff wars rather than aid to Spain.

The situation in Russia was somewhat different. Though the interests of Russia's ruling class were also mainly agricultural and prices in the world market had fallen as an apparent result of increasing American exports, nevertheless Russian landowners were large-scale exporters. Their competition with America was abroad rather than at home. As a result, they blamed their ills on European tariffs as much as on American surpluses. And unlike their counterparts in Central Europe, they had no traditional dislike for the United States.

True Russian conservatives, like Konstantin Pobedonostsev, the Procurator of the Holy Synod, scorned all Western civilization. In their eyes, rationalism and belief in human goodness were evils beside which republicanism, universal suffrage, and capitalism seemed venial. Since few unhappy Russian emigrants returned and few American tourists crossed the Vistula, "the American" was not a type in Russian literature. Novelists and dramatists mocked their own *nouveaux riches*. Actually, as Louis Perlman has pointed out, they tended not to condemn the rags-to-riches businessman but to make a hero of him.[10] Few felt any special philosophical animosity toward the United States, and, on a practical level, even conservatives still reckoned England as Russia's principal enemy and America as England's foe and hence a natural ally for Russia. The right-wing journal, *Russkii Vestnik'*, commended Cleveland's Venezuela message as astute and well-timed. The moral it drew was that while the United States proclaimed "America for the Americans," Russia should proclaim "the East for Easterners."[11]

Some Russian conservatives naturally found it hard to stomach American principles. Revolutionaries had appealed to the American example, as the Decembrists had in 1825 and as Herzen, Chernyshevskii, and others had later. The radical Russian Populists were making much of Henry George. When the American republic threatened the Spanish monarchy, some Russian conservatives did find this too much. *Russkii Vestnik'* now suggested that in her own imperial sphere Russia might do well to be as wary of the United States as of England; America might eventually seek to control the Pacific. Even the moderate and sometimes semiofficial *Novoe Vremya* declared, "Europe has every reason to oppose the strengthening of the United States . . . and must be ready to support Spain if she is threatened with the loss of Cuba."[12] Such pronouncements, however, were much rarer in Russia than in western Europe. Important St. Petersburg journals commented much less frequently than those in Berlin and Paris on the developing Spanish-American crisis.

There was relatively little anti-Americanism in Russia. What there was, however, existed in circles close to the court and therefore formed an important segment of what passed in Russia for public opinion.

Among powerful groups in all continental lands, there was thus irritation over American economic competition, animosity toward American ideas, and some alarm at a prospective American menace. In no nation were these groups absolutely dominant. On the other hand, nowhere were they impotent, and their public and parliamentary backing was potentially available to any government that chose to resist the United States and support Spain.

This anti-Americanism had an offset, however, in surviving pro-American sentiment. In the late eighteenth and early nineteenth centuries, American democracy had aroused great enthusiasm among liberals and reformers. Gilbert Chinard, Carl Wittke, and Max

Laserson have described the impact of the American Revolution on Condorcet, Herder, Goethe, Radishchev, and other intellectual leaders. In *The American Spirit in Europe,* Halvdan Koht points out American influence on pacifist, feminist, and temperance movements. It was said that few really knew anything about Americans, even "that they are white as other people, that they live in houses, that they boil and roast their meat, and that they speak the English language." Yet Michael Pupin learned of Benjamin Franklin when growing up among peasants in a tiny village on the Sava. As a young nobleman in Russia, Baron Rosen read the novels of James Fenimore Cooper and dreamed of finding himself some day "in the wondrous land that had been the home of the 'Leatherstocking.' " Washington, Franklin, Jefferson, and Patrick Henry were his boyhood heroes, and he learned the Declaration of Independence by heart. Many, like Heinrich Heine, dreamed of traveling "To that place of freedom, where/All alike may live in clover." As emigration statistics show, millions were not deterred, as Heine was, by fear that it would be a land "Where tobacco's 'mongst their victuals,/Where they never use spittoons,/And so strangely play at skittles."[13]

There were obvious survivals of earlier romantic beliefs about America. Alongside warning reports on American economic growth ran a continuing flow of admiring commentary on American political institutions. Edmond Demolins in his widely read *À quoi tient la superiorité des Anglo Saxons?* of 1897 counseled Latin Europe to learn individualism, self-reliance, and a higher patriotism that could manifest itself in antimilitarism and arbitrationism. French political scientists like Auguste Carlier and Émile de Laveleye urged that their nation adopt at least some of America's political lessons. Federigo Garlanda and Francesco Racioppi gave the same general advice to Italians. More than one Russian liberal recommended following America's example.[14]

American millionaires, trusts, tariffs, and the all too frequent sight of tasteless tourists did test their faith, however. Some travelers to the United States, like Pierre de Coubertin, had to admit that its urban scenes were no more idyllic than those of Europe. To sustain his preconceptions, Coubertin had to postulate that the countryside was different. There, he felt, the wives of farmers must spend their evenings reading the best journals and reviews while their daughters played music of Chopin and Liszt. Others also, like the historian Ernest Lavisse and the humorist Paul Blouet, imputed amazing virtues to American women.[15]

Pro-American feeling was, nevertheless, on the wane. The newer reformers were not Jeffersonian liberals. A few drew on other American sources, as did the Russian Populists, but most were socialists of one school or another. Some, like those in England, looked upon the United States as a stronghold of capitalism and hence an ideological enemy. Socialists in France, Italy, and Germany took America's side against Spain on the ground that Americans would at least give Cuba better rule, but they viewed the choice as one between evils. The working-class left of the 1890's was not attached to the United States as the bourgeois left of the 1840's had been. Nor for that matter were all middle-class liberals. In *Ein neuer Pharao,* the German novelist, Friedrich Spielhagen, cast the United States minister as a spokesman for reactionary ideas.

The change in America's reputation was probably best mirrored in imaginative literature. In early nineteenth-century fiction, Americans were either strong, virtuous, simple types, like Cooper's heroes, or they were kindly rich uncles who rescued young lovers in the nick of time. Harold Jantz in a study of America in German literature and thought comments that until the 1890's American characters "remained ordinarily in the old tradition of simplicity, straightforwardness, and sincerity." Jantz found only two exceptions among earlier German novelists—the pioneer realists Theodor Fontane and Rudolf Lindau.[16]

The type, as Europeans then conceived it, appeared in two popular French plays of the 1870's. Edmond Gondinet's *Jonathan* depended for its plot on the audience's believing that a young American would go to any lengths to avoid breaking a promise and would be capable of superhuman chastity. Eugéne Labiche's farce, *Les trente millions de Gladiator,* also had an American hero. Evidently ignorant of the lengths to which democracy had gone in the United States, he called him Sir Richard Gladiator. He was recognizably American, however, in being honest, open, generous, continent, and somewhat simple. Just before the final curtain, Labiche had him resolve the play's last dilemma by giving 100,000 francs to an erstwhile rival who would otherwise have been too poor to marry. At the time, this was how the rich American was expected to act.

By the 1890's other types had appeared. A common figure was the enterprising bunko artist—Mark Smallbones in Henri de Pène's *Les demi-crimes* and the elder Mr. Curtis in Spielhagen's *Neuer Pharao*. Even the mold for women had changed, enough at least to admit adventuresses like those in Claude Vignon's *Une étrangère* and Jules Claretie's *L'Américaine*. There were survivals of the Cooper type and plenty of heroic, virtuous females, as in Sophie Junghans's novels and Pierre de Coulevain's *Noblesse américaine,* but the older stereotype was fading.

The more common new image appeared in a work by Abel Hermant, a writer who had become famous by publishing an antimilitarist romance, which he had not realized was antimilitarist until an officer challenged him to a duel. In a novel in dialogue entitled *Les transatlantiques,* he portrayed Jeremy Shaw, an American millionaire, as a man of relatively good heart but otherwise as a quite different character from Gondinet's Jonathan or Labiche's Gladiator. Shaw appears as efficient, calculating, and, in a good cause, ruthless. He has, moreover, a tendency to value everything in dollars, including suitors for his daughter's hand, and he carries doctrines of equality to disturbing lengths. He assumes not only that he is the born equal of monarchs but that because he has earned more money than they he has become their superior. He is by no means a villain, but neither is he so simple a figure as either Gladiator or Jonathan Carpett.

The contrast between the new type and the old is perhaps even clearer in the work of Paul Bourget. He was fascinated by national types and wrote essays as well as fiction about them. In *Une idylle tragique* he included an American, again a millionaire, Richard Carlyle Marsh. Early in the book, another type, a Provençal gifted with gypsy insight, points out Marsh at the gaming table:

That's the man. He isn't fifty, and he's worth ten million dollars. At eighteen he was a trolley conductor in Cleveland. . . . His fortune he has made literally with his hands. They show up clearly against the green cloth just now. Study those workman's hands. . . . Look how strong they are, but not rough. The knuckles speak of reflectiveness, judgment, coolness. The tips of his fingers are a little too broad; that comes from the tyranny of action, the urge for movement, and a tendency toward unhappy thoughts. . . . You see the thumb? The two joints are large and equal; this shows will and logic combined. It curves backward; that shows excessive generosity. . . . And watch his gestures—what decisiveness, what calmness in his play, what nervelessness! That's a man, that one, isn't he?

Later, the author intrudes to say of Marsh that he "basically detested the empty and vain society in which he lived. He lived there, however, because this world of the high aristocracy was another conquest to make." At another point, he has a French aristocrat generalize: "The Americans and I, we hardly understand one another. The pointless energy of these people exhausts me, even in thinking about it. And how many of them there are, how many!"

Bourget was a liberal and a believer in Catholic "Americanism." He had also visited the United States and published a book about his travels. Nonetheless, in his novel he was seeking to portray the national type, and the result was a figure no less admirable than Jonathan or Gladiator, but a good deal more fearsome.

Still and all, stereotype characters are not yet villains, and the very existence of laudatory writings by economists and political scientists indicated that there were some intellectuals who might speak out in opposition if their governments launched a crusade against the United States. No one could tell how many people might be influenced by them or by such childhood recollections as of Baron Rosen.

Some elements from business, banking, and shipping circles could be expected to oppose anti-American policies on entirely realistic grounds. The French investment in Spanish bonds and securities amounted to nearly eight hundred million dollars, but that in American securities was estimated to be considerably larger. Germany's annual trade with the United States was worth ninety-four million dollars. The prosperity of Le Havre and Hamburg depended partly on trans-Atlantic commerce. So did the marginal economic health of Fiume, where the Hungarian government had built up a subsidized grain and passenger traffic.[17] Continental businessmen, no less than those of England and America, favored cautious, unadventurous foreign policies. In view of the amount of investment and trade involved, they were apt to resist with special force any new departure in dealings with the United States.

In some countries, many people had personal or family ties with the United States. Relatively few Frenchmen had emigrated to America. Germans, on the other hand, had crossed the Atlantic by the millions. So had Italians and Hungarians, Poles, Slovenes, and others from the Austro-Hungarian Empire. Large numbers had come back, some no doubt embittered. The poet, Niklaus Lenau, returned to Germany damning Americans for their "stinking-to-heaven shop-keeper souls." Theodor Ladenburger, a German-American who revisited his homeland, found America considered "a refuge for the human refuse of the Old World" and returnees respected "only by virtue of the almighty dollar."[18] But some must have retained happy memories and had some influence on public opinion in their communities.

At least a few had influence at the court level. In Russia, Prince Mikhail Ivanovich Khilkov had worked in American railway shops before becoming director of railways and subsequently Minister of Communications. A Russian civil servant speaks of Khilkov in his memoirs as an American "self-made man." Relatives and friends of emigrants who remained overseas had an emotional tie to America. In some cases, whole villages took pride in a faraway son, as Idvor did in the inventor, Michael Pupin.[19] Returned emigrants and families and acquaintances of those remaining in America formed an indefinable but numerous augment for potential opposition to an anti-American policy.

While it is true that governments could have found backing for a policy of supporting Spain against the United States, it is also true that they would have had to expect resistance. In France, the veteran breaker of cabinets, Georges Clemenceau, stood ready to rally forces on any issue, and his *Justice* was one of the few French papers to side with America on the Cuban issue. In Germany, suggestions of discriminatory tariffs and of assistance to Spain drew hostile comment from business organs like the Berlin *Börsenzeitung,* the *Weser Zeitung,* and the *Hamburgische Korrespondent,* and in *Die Nation* from the liberal intellectual leader, Theodor Barth. In the Austro-Hungarian Empire, national minority groups opposed the imperial government at almost every opportunity, and their organizations and publications were assumed to be financed by contributions from emigrants in the United States. Since the issue never arose in concrete form, it is impossible to guess how public opinion might have divided. But it is a certainty that no statesman anywhere could contemplate an anti-American policy in full assurance of united popular backing.

When cabinet ministers considered Spain's appeals, they conversed mainly in terms of external conditions and interests. Behind their cautious words, however, lay realization that decisive commitment for or against the United States could arouse and divide public opinion, as had issues rising from the American Civil War. In many cases they were already near panic on account of existing unrest. In France, the Dreyfus case threatened the survival of the republic. In Vienna, street demonstrations brought down ministry after ministry. Italy suffered sporadic but widespread food riots which were to culminate in the bloody May outbreaks (the *fatti di maggio*) in 1898 in Milan. The statesmen of the powers were not averse to dramatic diplomatic gestures diverting public attention: the winter of 1897–1898 saw the Austro-Russian truce and seizures of ports in China; but few governmental leaders were willing to risk acts that might prove unpopular. Pure calculations of interest affected the handling of the Spanish-American crisis; so did the personalities and temperaments of ministers in the various European cabinets. But every continental government was at least partially paralyzed from the outset by awareness of the deep ambivalence with which their people viewed the United States.

The German government had been the first seriously to consider aiding Spain in the crisis over its relationship with the United States. In the early autumn of 1897, Kaiser Wilhelm II was at Rominten, one of his hunting lodges in the gloomy forests of East Prussia. Just back from a wearing but stimulating trip to Vienna, he found among correspondence forwarded from Berlin a dispatch from his ambassador in Madrid reporting the arrival of McKinley's new envoy, and predicting an American ultimatum with which the Spanish government would have to comply.

The fact that some such action by the United States had long been expected did not appear to modify the Kaiser's astonishment and outrage. He looked upon the regency in Madrid as a kindred monarchy. In his restless boyhood he had learned or half-learned many subjects, but one lesson that had fixed itself in his mind was the transcendent importance of the monarchical principle. He viewed officials of the French Republic as usurpers, and he could never understand how a legitimate ruler like Tsar Nicholas II trafficked with the heirs of those who murdered Louis XVI. He believed devoutly that those who wore crowns ruled by divine right. On the margin of his ambassador's letter now he scratched:

The situation stands just thus: Cuba has belonged to Spain as a colony for hundreds of years. This is a European state. America wants "by fair means or foul"—apparently the latter—simply to relieve Spain of her colony. . . . Just to suffer this event, is Europe ready to do that . . . ? Shall we other monarchs look on placidly as a brave colleague of ours has her land and probably too—through Cuba's loss—her throne torn from her? Through the insolence of the Yankee, who will be secretly supported by John Bull? I believe it is now high time that we other monarchs . . . agree *jointly* to offer our help to the Queen in case the American-British Society for International Theft and Warmongering looks as if it seriously intends to snatch Cuba from Spain. A common note which all of us Continentals sent to Uncle Sam and John Bull with the statement that we would mutually stand together and not allow Cuba to be stolen from H[er] M[ajesty] could not fail to have . . . effect. . . . Feeling in this connection among the great monarchs should be tested at once and reported upon to me.

In this fit of feeling, the Kaiser was troubled by no qualms about the prudence of helping Spain. America naturally repelled him. Surrounded by courtiers and military aides from the Junker class, he knew of the stress they felt from American competition. He had several times broached to Russian officials the notion of a European economic union against the United States. In his marginal note on the dispatch from Madrid, he commented that a move in behalf of Spain would serve two ends: "For one thing the rascals will see that Europe's kings really stand together and mutually share misfortune and joy and are not prepared to yield before republican money-madness; in the second place, it would be a very excellent device for furthering and establishing the continental union against America planned by myself and the Tsar."

The Kaiser's proposal was at once ill-considered, impulsive, rash, bold, and imaginative.[1] In Berlin it was not given the studious inspection that it may have deserved. Emulating his industrious predecessor, Frederick the Great, Wilhelm wrote far too many marginal notes, and for all his earnestness, occasional brilliance, and famous memory, he failed to keep them all consistent. His officials had learned that he often contradicted himself, forgot, or flitted from one impulse to another. Some regarded the Emperor's marginalia as something like swearing, a means by which an excitable temperament relieved itself. Others frankly thought the monarch insane. The Imperial Chancellor, Prince Hohenlohe, worried about resemblances between Wilhelm and the mad King Ludwig II of Bavaria. So startling a directive as one to plan a *démarche* in support of Spain caused bureaucrats in Berlin to tend to think less about its merits than about ways of circumventing it.

The new Foreign Minister, Bernhard von Bülow, was a master of this art. He could not afford to contradict or even argue with the Kaiser. For all his own self-confidence, he knew his dependence on imperial favor. Whether or not he thought of himself as a second and more polished Bismarck, he had to remember that Wilhelm had gotten rid of Bismarck, and Bülow was not even Chancellor yet. He may have felt at the time what he wrote later in his *Memoirs*—that the Kaiser's interest in the Spanish-American tangle was evanescent. Out of regard for his career, he had to seem to take the Kaiser seriously. The sort of words that he wrote for the Emperor's eyes were typified in a letter of February, 1898, to Wilhelm's closest friend, Philip Eulenburg: "I hang my heart more and more every day on the Emperor. He is so remarkable . . . ! He combines in a manner that I have never before seen the soundest and most original intelligence with the shrewdest good sense. He possesses an imagination that can soar on eagle wings above all trivialities, and with it the soberest perception of what is possible and attainable. . . . What swiftness and sureness of apprehension!"

In his reply to the marginal note, Bülow suggested that, like a metaphysical poet, the Kaiser might have meant either more or less than he said. To the Emperor himself he offered congratulations on pointing out "the danger of American republican land-grabbing and arrogance for the future of monarchical Europe just as emphatically as he demonstrates the necessity for unity among the great powers in the face of this menace to their common interests." He promised "to initiate the necessary steps immediately."

At the same time, he wrote to Eulenburg, who was with the Kaiser at Rominten: "I trust it will comply with the All-Highest's intentions if, in carrying them out, I endeavor to prevent England and France from using a German action in behalf of Spain in order to embroil us in quarrels with America from which they themselves abstain or at our expense secure economic advantages." German trade with the United States, he observed, ran second only to that of England. Under the latest American tariff law, the United States could negotiate discriminatory treaties, and it would be imprudent to abandon this rich commerce to a rival. At the very least, Russia and France should be associated with any move in behalf of Spain. "If England and France abstain," he warned, "not only would the success of the action become doubtful, but this very fact could, from a political as well as an economic standpoint, bring us important disadvantages."

Surely, the Foreign Minister implied, these considerations would present themselves to the Emperor's luminous intelligence.[2]

A sounding from the court soon encouraged Bülow to go farther. A brief message came to him from Eulenburg. In the days before charges of homosexuality drove him to private life, Eulenburg enjoyed the reputation of having great influence with Wilhelm. He prided himself on serving as mediator between Kaiser and government, and he reported to Bülow that he too had taken exception to a German initiative in favor of Spain. He had suggested to the Emperor that Germany stay in the background, get Austria to sound out other courts, and let her take the credit or blame. The Kaiser had found this advice acceptable, saying: "The action is the thing. One must choose the most practical method."

With this report in hand, Bülow could presume to give advice. Since he had already talked with the most powerful member of the Foreign Ministry's permanent staff, Friedrich von Holstein, and found him averse to backing Spain, he could feel safe against rear attack from that sensitive, gifted, and industrious intriguer. In another telegram to Eulenburg, therefore, Bülow went on not only to approve the use of Austria as a front but to suggest that Austria try to use Spain, encouraging the Queen Regent to appeal to France, Russia, and Britain. Germany would thus take the last place in line instead of the leading role that the Kaiser had first proposed. Yet when Eulenburg showed this message to the Emperor, Wilhelm unhesitatingly scribbled some marginal notes adding up to complete concurrence.

Bülow gave the *coup de grâce* to the Kaiser's plan by forwarding an instruction to the German chargé d'affaires in Vienna. If the Cuban question should be brought up again, he directed, the German position should be made clear. Effective action would require unanimity among the powers, with the unqualified adherence of England and France. "Our most gracious master," he declared, "has . . . expressed his decision that Germany cannot for practical reasons anticipate the western powers in taking a positive stand on the Cuban question, though she will be ready to give the most earnest consideration to any appropriate proposals which come to us from London or Paris." The notion of German leadership for a combination against the United States had vanished like the memory of a dream.

By 1898, when Spanish-American relations approached a crisis, Bülow was in even better position to stifle any imperial impulse. He could claim partial credit for the seemingly brilliant coup at Kiaow-chow. More important still, he had steered the navy bill through the Reichstag, as his predecessor had failed to do. His success in winning support from both left and right had more than endeared him to the Emperor. When Spain began openly approaching the powers, Wilhelm still felt a pull on his emotions, but he made no attempt to dictate to Bülow. The Foreign Minister wrote the German ambassador in Madrid on February 15, 1898, "Our Gracious Master decides that we must always be ready to support the monarchical principle wherever it can be done with success, but that a suggestion . . . *by Germany* would not be a suitable method." Any proposals for European action, he said, would have to come from Paris.

When there seemed risk that the French might not refuse, Bülow hastened to take fresh precautions. Such reserve as the French government showed, he wrote to Eulenburg, seemed due to the intimacy between her ally, Russia, and America. "Any French representations in Washington would be merely of an academic character," he remarked, and, in view of the even more restrained attitude of England, "it can be said . . . that the notion of effective action by Europe cannot be realized." After the Queen Regent appealed formally to the Austrian Emperor, Bülow wrote coldly to his ambassador in Madrid: "the only attitude possible for Germany . . . [is] to hold aloof. There is no need to explain in justification that it is Germany's duty to avoid engaging herself further or earlier than France in a question which has aroused the passions of the American people more and more. The second Napoleonic Empire's Mexican adventure is sufficient warning for us." As Orestes Ferrara remarks in *The Last Spanish War,* "Bülow believed that Germany should leave no door open, through which an American question might penetrate to Europe." Whatever chance of success the Kaiser's bold fancy might have had, it was snuffed out by the soft, short fingers of his Foreign Minister.[3]

The Austrian government, unlike the German, did undertake to marshal aid for Spain. Emperor Franz Josef had an affection for monarchy as deeply rooted if not as romantic as that of the German Kaiser. Moreover, he had a remote family tie to the Spanish Queen Regent. She was the niece of his favorite cousin, the Archduke Albert, and the daughter of the Archduke Charles Ferdinand. Franz Josef wished to see her at least keep her throne. But his impulses were totally unlike those of Wilhelm II. During fifty years of rule, he had kept to a fixed schedule and an almost monastic regimen, concentrating single-mindedly on the day-to-day administration of his motley and unstable empire. No such humor as the Kaiser's could even have entered his head. At most, he told his Foreign Minister to do what could be done for Spain so long as it involved no risks or serious commitments for Austria.

The Foreign Minister acted, at any rate, as if these were his instructions. Count Agenor Goluchowski, who held the office, had, if anything, less verve and imagination than his imperial master. Casting up the account, Arthur J. May writes in *The Hapsburg Monarchy,* "Caution, passivity, conservatism, safety first, last, and always were the guiding rules of the Ballplatz during the Goluchowski period." Like all Austro-Hungarian civil officials, Goluchowski was the Emperor's servant. A trim, impassive Galician Pole, he had been elevated suddenly from a provincial administrative post. He knew that he might be dismissed any morning and, like others before him, never see the Emperor again. He himself seemed indifferent to Spain's cause. In 1896, when Tetuán represented Spain as on the brink of collapse, Goluchowski shrugged his shoulders. There was no chance, he remarked to the Italian ambassador, of Europe's even giving platonic support. When the German chargé d'affaires talked with him in 1897, as a result of the instructions from Bülow, Goluchowski said he had no thought of taking an initiative in behalf of Spain.

His subsequent actions can only have resulted from hints or directives given by Franz Josef. In late November, 1897, he suddenly delivered an address to the Committee on Foreign Affairs of the Hungarian diet, warning Europe of the American economic peril. Goluchowski declared:

The disastrous war of competition which we meet with at every step and in every field of human activity, upon the part of countries beyond the seas, a contest which is now going on but which will become greater in the near future, calls for immediate and comprehensive resistance unless the nations of Europe are to be seriously crippled in their most vital interests and are willing to fall victim to a disease which will surely lead to their destruction. They must fight shoulder to shoulder against this common danger, and they must go into this contest armed with every weapon of defense that their resources afford.

This address had its domestic uses. Hungarian liberals had launched an excited campaign for tariff autonomy; separatist feeling had received a boost from a recent speech by the German Kaiser extolling Hungary's accomplishments; these currents had become all the more dangerous because of violent disorders between Czechs and Germans in other parts of the empire. Goluchowski needed to show his concern with Hungary's agricultural interests. But it seems likely that he would not have given precisely this address except at the direction of his Emperor, and it is plausible that Franz Josef suggested it partly as a test of European feeling toward the United States.

Soon afterward, Goluchowski did a virtual about-face on the question of joint European representations in Washington. Talking with diplomats in Vienna, he began to treat the notion seriously. By the end of 1897, the French ambassador was describing him as positively enthusiastic. The change of heart, as the Frenchman noted, came soon after the Emperor had accorded a long interview to the Spanish Minister for Foreign Affairs. Goluchowski claimed to be still unsure whether Austria should take an initiative, in view of the fact that France, Britain, Russia, and Germany were colonial powers while Austria was not, but he did endorse the principle, and it seems a safe guess that he did so because Franz Josef had been pressed into making some indefinite commitment to the Queen Regent.

As Spanish-American relations became more and more tense, the Austrian Minister tried as best he could to persuade some other government to lead a move in Spain's behalf. From diplomats in Vienna, he obtained an impression that France and Italy would join in a collective note to the United States, but only if all the powers co-operated. He already knew this to be the German attitude. In early March, 1898, he told the French ambassador that Russia and Britain were the only two powers about which he had serious doubts. He thus hinted that France had only to beckon to her ally in order to become leader of a continental coalition.

To the German ambassador Goluchowski remarked that Austria lacked strength and that "only a common and energetic naval demonstration would be likely to achieve a result." He suggested, in other words, that if Germany wanted something done, she should do it herself, and, at the same time, he made what appeal he could to the Kaiser's Nelson complex.

When the Queen Regent finally asked Austria to plead her case before the powers, however, the Emperor and his Minister evidently agreed that they could not refrain from taking the lead. Goluchowski telegraphed the Austrian ambassador in Madrid: "His Majesty . . . cannot withhold his support from the Queen Regent in her distress." The Emperor, reported the French ambassador in Vienna, "is very much moved, though he has little hope of inducing the powers to act."

Having given the promise, the Austrian government did its duty. All the powers were invited to join in collective representations to the United States, the form of which was to be determined later. When objections were raised, Goluchowski did what he could to answer them. To the French and British, he stressed the interest of colonial powers in restraining the United States. To the Germans and Russians, he emphasized the monarchical principle. When warned by his ambassador in Berlin that Bülow seemed unlikely to give assent, he called in Germany's representative in Vienna and, in effect, asked him to tell the Kaiser that the Spanish monarchy seemed doomed unless Europe intervened. When the Russian Foreign Minister seemed balky, Goluchowski and Franz Josef discussed a personal appeal by the Austrian Emperor to the Russian Tsar. They decided against it only after learning that the Queen Regent had herself addressed the Russian ruler. The Austrian effort was not halfhearted.[4]

But Austria's best was feeble. Since her trade with America was negligible and she had no colonies, she could hardly set an example.

She was asking others to take risks in which she could not share. Even if Franz Josef and Goluchowski had been less cautious men and even if they had shared the warped prophetic insight of the German Kaiser, they still could not have proposed effective combination by the powers. Austria could only act as broker, as a go-between for nations with more varied interests at stake. Germany, which could have sought a genuine alliance against America, had decided not to do so. The remaining possibilities for real leadership lay in Paris, St. Petersburg, and London.

In the past, the French had shown no enthusiasm for action in behalf of Spain. When Tetuán asked European aid in 1896, France recoiled. Her policies were, in effect, those of her young Foreign Minister, Gabriel Hanotaux. Though Hanotaux endeavored to transact all official business before one o'clock so that he could return to his walk-up apartment and spend afternoons and evenings composing a biography of Richelieu, he had time to keep an autocratic hand over his subordinates and rarely, if ever, did he allow his decisions to be overridden in the cabinet. He recognized his country's economic stake in Spain and admitted to the Spanish ambassador that the French people sympathized with her. His own envoy in Madrid, the shrewd and worldly Marquis de Reverseaux, advised him not to dismiss Spain's appeal lightly. A war, he thought, would be "almost as prejudicial to the interests of Europe as to Spain." Hanotaux was not impressed.

When Russia's ambassador to Spain passed through Paris, the Foreign Minister queried him about Tetuán's proposal. Satisfied that the Russian had no commitment to it, he suggested that the Tsar's government block it. "I said France could not hold out alone," he noted, "but intimated that Russia might and that it would be imprudent for Europe to engage in a *démarche* which might set all America against it." When Hanotaux was informed by the Spanish ambassador that Tetuán's projected memorandum could not be delivered, he expressed sorrow but smiled as he said, *"Enfin, c'est un incident clos."*[5]

During the course of the next year, it is true, the Foreign Minister came to feel less sure that support of Spain would be imprudent. He had long urged the Spanish government to institute reforms in Cuba and when Cánovas and then Sagasta finally did so, he offered congratulations, expressing regret only that Spain had not followed his advice earlier. The reforms seemed to him to put Spain in a stronger position as against the United States. Perhaps more important, they strengthened the case for Spain put forward with increasing fervŏr by right-wing Parisian newspapers. Hanotaux was not blind to feeling against America among French agrarians and against "Americanism" among orthodox Catholics. Coming himself from an agricultural community and revering the great French cardinals, Richelieu and Lavigerie, he sat in a right of center cabinet heavily dependent on rural electors and such clericalists as voted. With the Dreyfus case already bringing public opinion to a boil, Hanotaux may have begun to change his definition of prudence. Certainly, he was impressed by reactions elsewhere in Europe to the McKinley administration's new and higher tariff and by the disquiet which prospective American annexation of Hawaii was said to excite in Berlin and Tokyo. "The United States at this time are making many enemies," he mused on the margin of a dispatch, "—it is something to be watched. We could perhaps render a considerable service to Spain."

In this mood Hanotaux gave some thought to the possibility of leading a diplomatic offensive. Early in October, 1897, soon after Woodford reached Spain, the Foreign Minister brought up the topic of Cuba in a cabinet meeting. There is no evidence of what he said. The archives show only that he carried with him detailed memoranda on French interests in the island and on past Spanish-American negotiations.[6]

Not long after the cabinet session, however, he sent off an inquiry to St. Petersburg. Spain would appeal to France and Russia if the United States made fresh demands, he predicted. What would Russia's attitude be? At the same time, he telegraphed Reverseaux in Madrid, instructing him not to work too hard at discouraging the Spaniards. As a Foreign Ministry official noted in a memorandum, while "it is very important that we not become committed prematurely, we should also be alert to the danger of seeing Spain, convinced that she has nothing to expect from us, knock at other doors." Hanotaux had become more receptive to the notion of a *démarche* by the powers.

He continued to flirt with this thought, even when no encouragement came except from Vienna and Madrid. The Russian government
responded to his suggestion with little warmth, and Reverseaux reported the German ambassador in Madrid as definitely opposed. When
Spain formally asked if she could count on French help in securing
European support, Hanotaux could not answer one way or the other.
Even after consulting the rest of the cabinet, he could only counsel the
Spaniards to think again before appealing to the powers. In a talk
with the Spanish ambassador, he asked rhetorically, "Is it not to be
feared that a *démarche,* which, as Spain herself avows, could have only
a purely platonic character, might wound the pride and arouse the sen-
sibilities of a democracy so little accustomed to diplomatic forms and
thus produce an effect contrary to the one hoped for?" He promised
to inquire again about feeling in St. Petersburg. Not long after, he
jotted on a memo slip, "I am very preoccupied with the increasing
friction between Spain and the United States. Is there really nothing
that can be done? The possibility of a war between the U.S. and Spain
becomes probable and more and more dangerous."[7]

Each day seemed, however, to make the problem more perplexing.
The *Maine* issue brought fresh strain to Spanish-American relations.
The conservative press in Paris devoted more and more space to attacks on the United States. In the Chamber of Deputies, the agrarian
bloc aroused considerable response with a demand for further commercial reprisals against the United States. Since a general election
was likely at any time, Hanotaux must have felt loath to invite criticism
on the score of having failed to help Spain. As one of his ambassadors
let slip later, he feared that war might bring revolution in Spain, that
revolution might inflame feeling in France among monarchists on one
side and radical republicans on the other, and that passions of either
kind would hurt the middle-of-the-road Méline government in its appeal to the electorate. Powerful domestic considerations counseled
action.

The general diplomatic situation, on the other hand, encouraged
inaction. When the de Lôme letter made its sensation in the press,
Hanotaux was struck by a sentence in it accusing England of encouraging war so that "Americans should amuse themselves with [Spain]

... and leave her alone." Hanotaux called these words to the attention of his envoy in Washington. In early March, 1898, he learned of the visit paid to McKinley by Pauncefote, the English ambassador. He did not know, of course, that Pauncefote carried the secret proposal for Anglo-American co-operation in China, but he had reason to suspect something of the sort. France's Russian ally had just seized Port Arthur, and it seemed possible that the English government had asked American backing in China in return for a promise to discourage any European move in support of Spain. Hanotaux urgently asked France's ambassadors everywhere to report any information touching Anglo-American negotiations. There seemed risk that the French government might be damned at home if it failed to support Spain, endangered abroad if it did.

The situation in Asia remained clouded, and Hanotaux strongly advised the Spanish government against appealing to the powers. When Spain disregarded this counsel, the French government faced the necessity of answering. Hanotaux temporized. "France would willingly agree if all others did," he told the Austrian ambassador, "but . . . the *démarche* could work to the disadvantage of Spain if it were rejected and nothing ensued." He recorded his subsequent conversation with the Spanish ambassador, and noted, "I showed him that the abstention of England would lead to certain checkmate; I pointed out to him that Italy followed England, that Russia was very hesitant, and that we ourselves would be placed in the greatest embarrassment in the face of abstention by England." Hanotaux's position was almost as cautious and noncommittal as Bülow's.[8]

Hanotaux soon found that many of his fears were baseless. The British government slowly made plain that it would not fight over Port Arthur. In addition, the chargé d'affaires in London, a young diplomat with excellent connections in English society, reported that Pauncefote had visited McKinley, not to make a pact with America, but to urge that the American government conciliate Spain. In England itself, he said, only "jingo journals" talked of Anglo-American friendship; "serious people" remembered past ill-will and thought that if Cuba fell, Britain's own possessions might become targets. He reported a conversation in which the permanent Under-Secretary of

State for Foreign Affairs, Sir Thomas Sanderson, spoke of Britain's position as exactly parallel to that of France. During a space of two weeks, in the middle of March, 1898, the French Foreign Minister seemed to discover, in the first place, that there was no danger of an Anglo-American alliance in Asia and, in the second place, that Britain might actually join in some pan-European expression of sympathy for Spain.

On March 26 Hanotaux spoke publicly of possible intervention to preserve peace. During an interrogation in the Chamber of Deputies, he declared, "If the two parties, with common accord, seek sure and impartial friends to assist the friendly settlement of so serious a question, they will see every good intention to meet their desire, and ours will not be wanting." The Foreign Minister gave no ostentatious support to Spain. Indeed, he referred to the United States warmly as "a growing republic, sister to our own, full of ardor, confident of its worth, which urgently demands an end to evils which affect her interests and which have already endured for a long time." His speech nevertheless amounted to open encouragement of the *démarche* that Spain and Austria were proposing.

Through diplomatic channels, moreover, he suddenly took up the project with a will. Whereas he had once used Russia to protect France from a Spanish appeal, he now turned about. In his own hand he drew up a telegram to St. Petersburg, asking the Russian Foreign Minister "if he could not consent to join in a *démarche* altogether amicable and in no way wounding to the United States by some or all of the powers." He spoke to the German ambassador in Paris, saying confidently that common action by the powers might actually prevent war. When solicited by the Spanish government, he agreed to approach Britain. The French ambassador to England happened to be in Paris; Hanotaux promised to send him back with orders to press for a favorable British decision; he himself would talk with Salisbury when the Marquis passed through the French capital in the last days of March. Overnight, the French government became sponsor for a European move in behalf of Spain.[9]

But the French proposal had far less substance than the earlier project of the German Kaiser. In his speech, his messages to St.

Petersburg, and even his conversations with the Spanish ambassador, Hanotaux made it perfectly clear that he had no thought of laying demands or threats in Washington. Diplomats and informed newspapermen both reported that McKinley desired to keep the peace. Hanotaux hoped to offer him Europe's moral aid. While sounding out Russia and England, he asked the French ambassador in Washington to speak with Secretary of State Sherman and say that France would not act without American consent.[10] In seeking to maintain peace and to placate pro-Spanish opinion in France, Hanotaux did not intend to bruise American feelings. He had no thought whatever of building an anti-American alliance.

Even for a limited undertaking, however, the French government found it hard to secure Russian co-operation. The thirty-year-old Tsar yielded nothing to Wilhelm II or Franz Josef in his attachment to monarchism and exercised more autocratic power than either, but he had neither the disciplined will of the Austrian Emperor nor the impetuous intuition of the German Kaiser. The parts of Nicholas II's diary that have been published consist almost entirely of long passages on parties, family affairs, and religion, with hardly a word on matters of state. In records kept by men around him, he appears as a vague young man, saying little, endeavoring mainly to avoid offense, only rarely intervening capriciously in the business of his ministries. The result, to be sure, was not cabinet government as in a constitutional monarchy. Regardless of a Council of Ministers which convened from time to time, the Tsar's ministers reported individually to him and negotiated with one another like minor sovereigns. More often than not, the decisions which Nicholas made were those recommended by the last strong man to see him.

His policy with regard to the Spanish-American imbroglio was shaped by his Foreign Minister, Count Mikhail Nikolaevich Muraviev. Plucked from the legation in Copenhagen to succeed a Foreign Minister who died suddenly, Muraviev lacked both training and experience at court. It was even said of him that he could not compose a grammatical dispatch, and few observers failed to contrast his insularity with the cosmopolitanism of such of his colleagues as the Finance Minister, Count Sergei Witte. But Muraviev quickly worked his way into an influential clique. He seemed intuitively to grasp the whims that floated unspoken in the mind of the Tsar. When serious differences arose, he was often able to win a decision over more gifted rivals, and quickly won the power to deal at least with minor affairs much as he wished— and from the Russian standpoint the Spanish question clearly was a minor affair.[11]

Muraviev wanted nothing to do with the Spanish-American quarrel. In 1896, when there had been risk of an appeal from Tetuán, his predecessor had been able to keep silence. Whether or not he was responsible for an editorial in a semiofficial journal warning Spain that no outside aid would come to her, he left the Spanish ambassador guessing that Russia would have answered favorably if all the other powers had. In 1897, however, Muraviev had to declare his views, for it was Russia's ally, France, that was putting the question. He spoke candidly to the French ambassador:

> In spite of our deep sympathies for Spain, the present state of our international relations requires the Imperial Government in this question to maintain the greatest reserve.
> The bonds of friendship which unite Russia to the United States prevent the Imperial Government from taking any action which could have an unfavorable effect on relations between the two countries and be taken amiss by public opinion in the United States.
> This attitude is dictated to the Imperial Government not only by its particular interests but also by considerations of a general order. . . . Intervention by one or two powers in the dispute would have no result except to complicate the situation and give the Cuban question an importance which it is, on the contrary, in the interests of the powers to minimize as much as possible.

It was conceivable, Muraviev remarked, that Russia might join in advising Spain to save face by accepting arbitration, but that was as far as she would go.

Since the French government still did not discourage the Spaniards, Muraviev spelled out for Hanotaux some of the considerations in his mind. On January 5, 1898, the French ambassador in St. Petersburg reported a conversation with the Foreign Minister: "Count Muraviev declared to me unhesitatingly that he would regard as inopportune any *démarche* in the United States by the powers. It seems to him dangerous to intervene in a question raised today by the United States. He would view as seriously disadvantageous the admission of the United States into any version of the concert of powers, for this could later be invoked as a precedent with regard to other questions, such as those in the Far East for example, where the European powers should all, in his opinion, remain united."[12]

Muraviev's reluctance to become embroiled with the United States undoubtedly grew during the crisis that followed the seizure of Port Arthur. This risky venture had been undertaken at his insistence and against the advice of most other ministers. So long as there seemed danger of Britain's opposing this move with force, Muraviev dared not drive any other government into England's arms. He fought with Witte in order to make concessions to Japan in Korea and thus keep Japan neutral. He had been warned by his minister in Washington that the United States was likely to negotiate with Britain a new arbitration treaty which "might involve the United States in conflicts with other powers." It must have seemed obvious to Muraviev that Russia should not precipitate an Anglo-American *rapprochement* by gratuitously reproaching American conduct toward Spain.[13]

He could not be sure, it is true, that this logic would seem so obvious to the Tsar. Newspapers which could be read by Nicholas said that American success against Spain would imperil monarchy and the established world order. Both *Novosti* and *Novoe Vremya* carried such declarations. In any case, Muraviev could not keep the moral issue from the Tsar's attention, for on March 25, 1898, the Spanish Queen appealed to Nicholas directly.

As it happened, this appeal coincided with an easing of tension in the Far East. Only a few days after the Queen Regent's message came, Muraviev received a note from the British government confirming what the press had predicted—that England would acquiesce in Russia's absorption of Port Arthur. This cheerful news did not change the Foreign Minister's mind about the Spanish issue. He remarked to the Austrian ambassador, one of his few foreign friends, "Any purely friendly action would be useless; any minatory action dangerous." The Russian ambassador in Madrid felt that Russia had no reason for interest in Spain's cause, and Muraviev evidently thought the same. On April 2, he told both the French and the Austrians that Russia would go along with a tender of good offices if all the other powers did so. His candid asides to ambassadors made it plain that he agreed without enthusiasm and that he might back out if complications threatened.[14]

The Italian government, for whatever influence it may have had, adopted a position much like the Russian. Except for the British, it was the only one that wanted something from Spain. Anxious to block the expansion of French influence in Africa, it wished to prevent the Spanish government from siding with France. At the time of Tetuán's first appeal to the powers, however, Foreign Minister Emilio Visconti Venosta had said frankly that Europe could not and would not assist Spain. When Spain renewed its appeal in 1898, his mind had not changed. He ultimately agreed to do whatever the others did, remarking to the Austrian ambassador in Rome that no power would challenge the United States if she refused to receive a collective note. The thought of anything beyond a mere gesture did not enter his mind.[15]

Whether there could even be a gesture depended, of course, on the English government. Germany, Austria, France, and Italy had agreed to participate only if Britain did so. Russia expected a British refusal to release her from a similar pledge. And the British government was in the midst of that re-evaluation of her relations with the United States which followed the Venezuelan crisis. The world did not know of the proposed alliance in China, but it could read of speeches by Chamberlain and others on Anglo-American kinship. There seemed little reason to expect that Britain would participate in any action likely to offend the American government.

On the question of whether or not Britain should act at all, opinion among British officials divided. England had reason to desire Spanish good will, for if Spain should co-operate with a continental coalition, the straits of Gibraltar and British communications in the Mediterranean might be imperiled. Sir Henry Drummond Wolff, the ambassador in Madrid, wished his government to support Spain. He had encouraged Tetuán's project. Shortly before the memorandum was to go out, he wrote Salisbury enthusiastically of Spanish dependence on Britain and of Britain's great opportunity to make Spain her debtor by protecting Cuba from the United States. When the idea of a Spanish appeal to the powers was revived in the winter of 1897–1898, he went to the limit of discretion both in encouraging the Spaniards and in counseling his own government to agree.

In London, the Prime Minister sympathized with Spain but saw little practical justification for backing her. Salisbury replied:

It is of course gratifying to us that the Spaniards should think so highly of English moral support as they do: but their preference is open to the interpretation that they want somebody to bell the cat. I am afraid that we ought not to covet the front rank which Spanish opinion gives to us: but rather humbly to seek for leave to take a back seat. . . . [We] have hardly any right, out of devotion to Spain, to increase the friction which now exists between England and America. Cuba does not interest us at all except as a means of keeping the Queen Regent on the throne; and the Continental Powers who are much nearer neighbors than we are, are much more interested to avoid any revolutionary catastrophe. We ought not therefore to offer ourselves as candidates for the post of Archibald Bell-the-Cat.

In October, 1897, when advised that Spain would soon solicit European support, Salisbury instructed Wolff to assure the Spanish government of Britain's sympathy but *not* of her willingness to give moral support. In 1898, when Spain became insistent, he tried to evade her pleas by speaking of American Anglophobia and saying that evidence of British backing would hurt rather than help the Spanish cause.[16] Ill and absent from his desk during much of March and April, he did not have to make a final decision, and he evidently preferred not to do so. He left the question of Britain's participation in a European action up to the men who were acting for him.

In the Foreign Office, the permanent Under-Secretary, Sir Thomas Sanderson, took much the same view as Wolff. It was he who told the French chargé d'affaires that "serious people" distrusted the United States and that Britain's position was parallel to that of France. When the French government became sponsor for the proposed *démarche,* Sanderson privately advised the French chargé to persevere. The cabinet, he thought, could "associate itself" with such a move.

Arthur Balfour, who took Salisbury's place both in the Foreign Office and at the head of the cabinet, adopted the more cautious view. He first informed the Spanish ambassador that Britain could not give advice to the United States. He promised only to instruct the British ambassador in Washington to speak of Spain's desire for peace. When pressed by Austria and France as well as Spain, he then argued that any move would be premature so long as direct Spanish-American negotiations continued. He would promise nothing other than eventually to consult the cabinet.[17]

The final decision resulted at least in part from intervention by Queen Victoria and, oddly enough, the Pope. On March 17 the Queen received María Cristina's personal appeal. "Poor thing," she sighed in her journal, and she wrote Lord Salisbury, "England should not refuse to join with the other Powers if asked."[18] Her will was hardly law, of course, but it did command respect. Quite apart from her station and experience, she possessed a simple Tory conscience which sometimes shamed her clever and cynical ministers into unexpected acts of principle. Balfour received no direct word from Victoria, but he undoubtedly knew her wishes, and they probably had more influence with him than the counsel of Wolff or Sanderson.

During the two days between the summons to the cabinet and its actual sitting came the Pope's appeal to Spain which Spanish sources described as inspired by McKinley. In reality the inspiration came from Berlin. On March 8 a special courier left the German capital for the Vatican. On March 15 Bülow telegraphed Eulenburg that the Kaiser hoped for a papal tender of good offices. On March 27 he directed the German representative at the Vatican to tell the Pope that Spain was ready to give up Cuba and to propose that his Holiness employ some American clergyman to sound out feeling in Washington.

The Austrian ambassador in Berlin believed the whole idea to have been the Kaiser's. Remembering how the German-Spanish Carolines dispute had been settled by the Pope in the 1880's, Wilhelm hoped, he thought, to rescue Spain, improve his own standing with German Catholics, and at the same time undercut French influence at the Vatican. It seems at least equally probable that Bülow saw the likelihood of other powers agreeing to the joint *démarche* and sought, as a matter of pride, to frustrate a project which he had opposed from the outset.

In any event, the German initiative brought the Pope's commission to Archbishop Ireland, Ireland's overoptimistic dispatch from Washington, Merry del Val's imprecise report to Madrid, and the ill-founded announcement by the Spanish government.[19]

The British cabinet convened on April 4 under the impression that McKinley had actually sought papal intervention. McKinley had not yet contradicted the report, and the Foreign Office had received no communication from Pauncefote for several days. In discussion the English ministers evidently agreed that if the American President were so eager for peace, he would not resent a kindly move by the powers. After the meeting, Balfour called in the Austrian ambassador and told him Britain would join the others. His only condition was that the British ambassador in Washington should first talk with the President and make sure that McKinley was willing to receive a joint note.[20]

The Austrian government had already drafted an instruction which all the powers were to send in identical form to their envoys in Washington. With little or no editing, its text received approval in the other capitals. All six Foreign Ministers thus directed their representatives to call on McKinley as soon as Pauncefote had given him advance warning and appeal "to the feelings of humanity and moderation of the President and of the American people in their existing differences with Spain." The result was the little ceremony that took place in the White House on April 6.

Despite all the precautions that preceded this joint *démarche,* it came close to involving the powers in some of the very complications they had foreseen and sought to avoid. McKinley not only omitted to mention the joint note in his message to Congress, but he actually spoke of intervening in Cuba in the name of humanity and civilization. Bellicose members of the House and Senate used similar language even more recklessly. European statesmen felt affronted that their representations had received so little regard. Their pride was engaged.

Though Franz Josef reportedly shrugged his shoulders and said Spain was lost, Goluchowski showed more vexation. He told the Spanish ambassador that Spain now had the active sympathy of all the civilized world. Earlier it had been the Emperor rather than the Foreign Minister whose feelings were stirred.

In Russia the same thing happened. Muraviev, who had previously maintained a cool detachment, spoke harshly of McKinley and condemned the whole American action as a plot by speculators with investments in Cuba. Italian officials were reported beside themselves with anger against the United States. Though a harmless action in itself, the delivery of the collective note led to a rise in the emotional temperature.[21]

Once cautious decisions for joint action had been taken, moreover, governments in Europe were in danger of losing control over events. Their diplomatic representatives had more power to act on their own, and it was by no means certain that their deeds would conform with their governments' intentions. In Madrid the ambassadors met and agreed jointly to urge that Spain grant an armistice. The Austrian said that the Queen Regent had asked them to do so. The Frenchman contended that after the collective move in Washington, it was unnecessary for any of them to ask for further instructions. The Russian showed hesitation until the others persuaded him to join in.[22] A step which did in fact irritate many Spanish politicians was taken without reference to ministers at home.

In Washington the same process started. The Austrian ambassador received a vague message from Vienna instructing him to consult his colleagues about the advisability of a second collective note. On April 11, just after the President's message to Congress, he met with the representatives of the other powers. The German, French, and Russian envoys felt that they should first obtain advice from home. After the meeting broke up, Pauncefote received a message from London which seemed to him adequate and appropriate. Signed by Sanderson, it informed him that Spain wanted the United States advised by the powers to accept the latest Spanish concessions. It ended, "We must leave any action on this request to your discretion."

Pauncefote asked the other ambassadors to come to his home on the afternoon of April 14. There he gave vent to feelings long suppressed. The French representative reported him as having said, "One cannot, without protesting in the name of conscience, allow to be committed the act of brigandage which the United States are preparing at this moment." Laying before his colleagues a draft of a new collective note, he proposed that they ask immediate authorization to present it to the Secretary of State.

The German ambassador had reservations about the wisdom of such a step. He raised the embarrassing question of what would ensue if the second note received no more attention than the first. He also suggested that a note to the Secretary of State was likely, in any case, to seem less important than the previous one, addressed to the President. At his instance, it was agreed that the ambassadors should recommend, instead of a new collective note, an identical note which each government could deliver to the American envoy accredited to it. They combined to frame a dispatch which each could send to his Foreign Minister. The text read:

> The time has come to dispel the erroneous impression which prevails, that armed intervention of the United States in Cuba . . . commands, in the words of the Message, the support and approval of the civilized world. Under these circumstances, Representatives of the Great Powers at Washington consider that their respective Governments might usefully . . . make it known that their approval cannot be given to an armed intervention which does not appear to them to be justified.

Like the original collective note, the proposed identical communications were to contain no threats. Unlike it, however, they were to be plainly critical of the United States.[23] If they had been presented, other and more serious events might have followed.

Most of the ambassadors' governments seemed willing to run this risk. Goluchowski gave his instant approval. Hanotaux said France would go along with any move in which Britain participated, and he urged the English government to agree. Visconti Venosta remarked that he thought the note would serve no purpose but that Italy could not refuse. Muraviev told the Austrian ambassador that he thought it potentially dangerous, but only because it risked involving the United States in European questions in the future. He also made the interesting observation that McKinley had not spoken in the name of the great powers but in that of the civilized world. Nevertheless, he consulted the Tsar and announced that Russia would take part in any action agreed upon by the other powers.[24]

Though the British ambassador in Washington had sponsored the project, the British government gave approval only conditionally. The Queen regarded America's behavior as "monstrous." She later wrote to Salisbury, "The Queen feels very strongly that the Powers ought, at any rate, to unite . . . *recording* their *protest* against such unheard of conduct. If [the Americans] . . . declare Cuba independent really such a precedent *ought* to be *protested* against. They might just as soon declare Ireland independent!" Sanderson, who had been responsible for the instruction to Pauncefote, believed that outbreak of war would seriously threaten Britain's colonial holdings.

Balfour, who still held acting charge of the Foreign Office, felt that he should act at once. As he confessed in letters to both Sanderson and Chamberlain, he found himself in "great perplexity." He doubted that the proposed note would be efficacious. On the other hand, he respected Pauncefote; "he is on the spot, and he is a man of solid judgment." He did not feel that there was time to obtain Chamberlain's opinion, though he probably could have guessed that the Colonial Minister would oppose any association with "the 'Concert of Europe' (*absit omen!*)." In any case, he temporized, writing that Britain would be ready to join in any representations in favor of peace and even "to make it quite clear that we have formed no judgment adverse to Spain," but, as he also wrote, "it seems very doubtful whether we ought to commit ourselves to a judgment adverse to the U.S., and whether in the interests of peace anything will be gained by doing so." Balfour thus suggested that the note should not be so harsh as the ambassadors desired, but he did not impose a veto.[25]

It was the German Kaiser, curiously enough, who put a finish to the project. Bülow had agreed to the first collective note after all his subterfuges failed. Presented with the proposal for a second *démarche,* he took much the attitude of most other foreign ministers. He wrote the Kaiser, "I personally feel fairly indifferent . . . , although I think that a public branding of this wanton attack would be very appropriate."

The Kaiser did not agree. He wrote on the margin: "I think it perfectly mistaken, pointless, and therefore harmful. We should put ourselves in the wrong with the Americans." Wilhelm had become convinced that none of the powers would really act. His ambassador in Washington took the view that Goluchowski had voiced earlier— that only a show of naval force would make any impression on the Americans. And on the margin of another document the Kaiser wrote scornfully, "Ask Hanotaux how many cruisers he would send if the United States rejected a new appeal!"

Bülow consequently informed the Austrians that Germany could not participate. As soon as Hanotaux learned of this, he withdrew his own concurrence, and the entire project collapsed.[26] The display of European unity had begun and ended with the ambassadors' visit to McKinley on April 6.

The Kaiser's original notion of a continental league against both Britain and the United States had vanished. His Foreign Minister was too adroit, too practical, too Europe-centered, too sensitive to ambivalence in public feeling. Spain's cause had been taken up ineffectually by the Austrian and French Foreign Ministers, who insisted from the outset on the principle of unanimity. Preoccupied with intra-European rivalries, Goluchowski, Hanotaux, and other diplomatists decided to postpone a confrontation with America until some later day. They were aware too of divisions in public opinion and of potential losses in trade and investment.

It is true that Spain did not offer Europe a perfect cause. Everyone knew that the Spanish government was corrupt and unstable; no one could doubt that the Cubans had legitimate grievances. The Spanish-American crisis did provide the powers with an opportunity to combine against the United States. Though their rulers were all emotionally on the side of Spain, yet they could not unite purposefully. And no such opportunity was to come again.

XVI · CHALLENGE OR OPPORTUNITY?

In a somewhat foolish letter to Theodore Roosevelt, John Hay wrote of the conflict with Spain as "a splendid little war." His first adjective was ill-chosen. His second was not. Compared to the war for the union, the Franco-Prussian conflict, or even the Seven Weeks' War between Prussia and Austria, it was not much of a struggle. Nevertheless, it engaged the world's attention as much as any occurrence of the decade.

By and large, Europeans expected the United States to win. Americans later liked to cite the few who predicted Spanish victory, as General Karl von Bieberstein had in the *Deutsche Revue* for March, 1896. But most European magazines and newspapers depicted the United States as a bully picking a quarrel with a nation she badly overmatched.

Even so, few Europeans were prepared for the naval battle that took place in Manila Bay barely a week after war had been declared. Six American warships sailed into that close water, engaged a numerically superior Spanish force off Cavite, a hook just southwest of Manila itself, and in seven hours' exchange of fire achieved total triumph. Only a few prescient Europeans had even guessed that the war might extend to Spain's Philippine possessions. The best informed writers had not credited the American navy with such enterprise and efficiency. Nor had anyone expected two hundred thousand men to be mobilized so quickly, old Confederates to take commands alongside former Union officers, Democrats and Republicans to enlist with matching zeal, or northern immigrants and southern Negroes to line up before recruiting booths. Almost nothing bore out the earlier predictions that America's mixed population would prove hard to mobilize for a foreign war.

Six weeks after the Manila engagement came a landing in force near Santiago and victories at Daiquiri, El Caney, and San Juan Hill. Though these successes have since come to appear partly accidental, they seemed notable triumphs at the time. They were climaxed by the utter destruction of the main Spanish fleet in a naval battle off Santiago and by the almost concurrent capture of the city itself. Though the United States had conquered neither Cuba nor the Philippines, European newspaper readers could hardly escape feeling that in America they saw a giant laying about him with frightening and unexpected force.

Newspapers and magazines burst out with wide-eyed exclamations that Europe had now to reckon with a seventh great power. Even in England, where the United States was already viewed as a factor in international politics, the London *Times* carried a long editorial declaring: "This war must in any event effect a profound change in the whole attitude and policy of the United States. In future America will play a part in the general affairs of the world such as she has never played before. When the American people realize this, and they realize novel situations with remarkable promptitude, they will not do things by halves." *Blackwood's* and the *National Review,* Tory journals previously unreconciled to the implications of the Venezuela episode, at last accorded the United States title as a power. The editor of the latter remarked that America might be of use to Britain in the great Anglo-German struggle that he so often prophesied. The battle of Manila Bay opened almost the last of English eyes to the new status of the United States.

Not everyone was pleased. The "Looker-on" in *Blackwood's* and even an anonymous writer in the Liberal *Westminster Review* warned of possible American designs on the British West Indies. Wilfrid Scawen Blunt jotted in his journal, "I hope Spain will be able to hold her own, not that Cuban independence lacks my sympathy, but because between Spain and the United States I am obliged to be on the side of the older and more barbarous country. The Yankees as the coming race of the world would be worse even than ourselves."[1] Aline Gorren, an American writing in *Scribner's* for October, 1898, observed that many who had been idealistically pro-American felt disillusioned because the United States had launched out so jubilantly on paths of conquests. The *Literary Digest* for July 10 reported several Liberal papers as dubious about proposals for an Anglo-American alliance, fearing that the United States might give up isolationism and use an alliance for aggressive purposes.

On the whole, however, the press and people of the British Isles greeted the new evidence of America's growing strength with pleasure and pride. H. W. Wilson published in the *Pall Mall Magazine* for July an article entitled, "The Anglo-Saxon Against the World." England had a stake in American victory, he contended, partly because the other races would measure Anglo-Saxon fighting qualities by America's performance against Latin Spain. Ambassador Hay reported that nonconformist churches and lay groups had sent congratulations and offered prayers of thanks to God. The American consul general in London wrote privately to his cousin, President McKinley, "It is really a pleasure to be over here at this time, on account of the extremely friendly feeling that is manifested on every hand towards the United States. Even those who are engaged in competitive trade speak well of the United States."[2] Liberal dailies in London and Manchester sang America's praises. In December, Sidney Low published in *The Forum* an article on "The Change in English Sentiment toward the United States," saying that any writer who spoke of America as a potential enemy "would be laughed at by the great majority of readers." The notion that America's increasing power was advantageous to Britain had taken deep root.

It is hard to say whether American successes in the war had any influence on the British government. Chamberlain made a sensational speech at Birmingham on May 13 in which he asserted:

I do not know what arrangements may be possible with the United States, but this I know and feel—that the closer, the more cordial, the fuller and the more definite, these arrangements are with the consent of both people, the better it will be for both and for the world. And I even go so far as to say that, terrible as war may be, even war itself would be cheaply purchased if in a great and noble cause the Stars and Stripes and the Union Jack should wave together over an Anglo-Saxon alliance.

But Chamberlain had been talking of Anglo-American solidarity for years. He had carried his colleagues with him in the March overture to Washington for a working agreement on China, and there is no evidence that he placed any new proposals now before the cabinet.

When pressed in the House of Commons on June 10, he confessed, "Nothing in the nature of a cut-and-dried alliance is at the moment proposed. The Americans do not want our alliance at this moment. They do not ask for our assistance, and we do not want theirs." There is no evidence that the Colonial Secretary had spoken at Birmingham for anyone but himself.

On the other hand, the Foreign Office showed even less disposition than before to risk friction with America. Balfour had personal feelings about the importance of American friendship, but as acting Foreign Minister he had gone along with the powers' *démarche* and had almost approved the proposed second note. Salisbury, who had been far less pro-American, stood more firmly than Balfour against any gesture that might irritate the United States, when he regained his health and resumed the foreign secretaryship. Reporting the collapse of the second *démarche* scheme, he remarked to the Queen, "Even the very temperate and guarded note which was addressed by the Powers to the U.S. Government was very much resented by a large portion of the community as an undue interference, and had no other effect than to harden the war feeling."[3] He implied that even that relatively innocent action had been a mistake.

Salisbury would have nothing to do with any scheme that might make Britain seem to oppose American annexation of Spain's Philippine colony. He may have shared Sanderson's view that such an event could endanger the peace of Europe; the Permanent Under-Secretary voiced such an opinion to the French chargé d'affaires without the customary caution that it was individual and private. But Salisbury had concluded that, whatever the Americans said, they would keep the islands. He said so to the German ambassador as early as June 3.

When the Spanish government asked the powers to assume joint control of Manila, the Marquis scarcely waited before replying that crown law officers regarded the scheme as a violation of neutrality and that Britain could not participate. At the first opportunity he told Ambassador Hay all about it. When the Germans subsequently proposed that the powers declare the Philippines neutralized, Salisbury discouraged them from the outset. He told the German ambassador "that England had no special interest in the future disposition of the Philippine Islands. In addition she had had such unhappy experiences in combined action with the powers . . . that the temptation to act in common with the other powers . . . was not great." Under the German scheme the guaranteeing powers would have obtained coaling stations, yet not even the lure of territory could move Salisbury.

Still less could any sentimental impulse induce him to take a risk. When the British ambassador in Madrid reported shortly after the Manila battle that Spain might offer to abandon Cuba, the Queen telegraphed the Prime Minister, "Trust it may be true. Do we mean to help and further this proposal if considered[?] But Cuba should be independent not American." Salisbury must have presented her view to the cabinet, for Chamberlain soon asked Hay informally whether the United States would be willing to halt the war if Spain evacuated the island. Salisbury himself cabled Pauncefote confidentially, "If you should think now or at any future stage in this unhappy war that offers of mediation from the European powers would be welcomed or received favourably by the United States please inform me."

On the other hand, Salisbury also told the Austrian and German ambassadors that he doubted if the Americans wanted peace yet, and he said flatly that Britain would join in no immediate effort to mediate. Only after Hay had come to him with a summary of McKinley's probable demands did Salisbury volunteer any service at all. Then he merely offered to urge that the Austrian Emperor advise Spain "to take advantage of the President's liberal disposition while it is yet possible." Even when it seemed almost certain that the United States and Spain would come to terms, he refused to involve Britain.

Only once, and then well after America and Spain had ceased fighting, was Salisbury tempted to deviate from his policy of complete noninterference. The Spanish government, still ignorant of America's final terms, suggested that if Britain helped to discourage excessive American demands, Spain might cede some land in the neighborhood of Gibraltar. What the Spanish government sought, of course, was backing against American insistence on the cession of the Philippines. After long meditation, the Prime Minister reported to the Queen that he felt some inclination to offer Spain support, but only against a hypothetical and improbable American demand for the Canaries or the Balearics. He finally decided not to act even on this impulse.[4] More than Balfour, Salisbury held to a policy of staying out of America's way.

Though Salisbury was not altogether pleased by the fact, he had come to acknowledge that the United States should be weighed in calculations of the balance of power. At the Lord Mayor's banquet in London on November 9, he spoke of 1898 as:

the first year in which the mighty force of the American republic has been introduced among the nations whose dominion is spent, and whose instruments, to a certain extent, are weakened. I am not implying the slightest blame—far from it—I am not refusing sympathy to the American republic in the difficulties through which they have passed, but no one can deny that their appearance among the factors at all events of Asiatic, and possibly of European diplomacy is not a grave and serious event, which may not conduce to the interests of peace, though I think in any event they are likely to conduce to the interests of Great Britain.

Salisbury instructed Pauncefote to seek a resolution of outstanding issues with the United States, such as the disputed boundary between Alaska and Canada and the proposed American-controlled interoceanic canal. Even though he answered questions from European diplomats by saying that talk of an Anglo-American understanding was idle, he obviously intended to bring about something resembling an entente.

The Venezuela crisis had disposed the British government to avoid trouble with America and led some Englishmen to think of a partnership. After the events of 1898, even the most conservative and realistic statesmen began to visualize an Anglo-American bloc.

For a brief moment, the German government also considered an entente with the new power. The Manila battle and its aftermath made less impression in Germany than elsewhere. Only the *Marine-Politische Korrespondenz* and a few navalist writers voiced the mixed astonishment and alarm that seemed common in England and the rest of continental Europe. Most commentators seemed to reason that armies were more important than navies and that the Spanish war offered only a poor test of America's real fighting strength. Nevertheless, the tone of commentary showed Germans coming gradually to take the United States more seriously.

Shortly after the American naval victory at Santiago, officials in Berlin began to think of an American alliance as a possible means of strengthening Germany in Europe. Ever since the dropping of Bismarck, it had been Germany's policy to keep a free hand. Though tied to Austria-Hungary and Italy by the Triple Alliance, the government had flirted alternately with England and with Russia. In March and April, 1898, conversations with the British government had been carried almost to the point of discussing marriage articles.

After these negotiations collapsed, the Kaiser made one of his boldest overtures to the Tsar. In a letter in English to his young cousin "Nicky," he declared that England had offered an alliance "with the addition of Japan and America, with whom pour-parlers have already been opened!" He went on, "Now as my old and trusted friend I beg you to tell me what you can offer me and will do if I refuse. . . . Before I take my final decision and send my answer in this difficult position, I must be able to . . . judge and weigh in my mind before God . . . what is for the good of the Peace of my Fatherland and of the world."

The Tsar replied, also in English, that the British government had made overtures to him even earlier, that he had turned them down "without thinking twice over it," and that, as for the Americans, they had been on good terms with Russia for a long time and he saw no reason why they "should suddenly turn against old friends—only for the 'beaux yeux' of England." Neither Britain nor Russia seemed to attach as much value to a German alliance as the Germans believed they should.

It was when faced with the unsettling thought that their coquettish behavior might have cost them both suitors that some German statesmen started casting about for new allures.

Bülow had joined the Kaiser's entourage for the summer, leaving his hand-picked deputy, Baron von Richthofen, in charge of the Foreign Ministry. Fumbling with the snarled threads of Anglo-German negotiations, Richthofen came to the conclusion that the English underrated Germany because they felt confident of Japanese and American backing. On July 6 he addressed a secret message to Count Paul Hatzfeldt, the German ambassador in London. In it he charged England with deliberately stirring up anti-German feeling in the United States, hoping that the Americans would become frightened and seek British protection. Richthofen remarked ominously that England did not search out allies until almost ready for war:

Hence we find ourselves facing the situation—*inherently probable*—that England will not allow the opportunity to pass of drawing in her trans-Atlantic cousins as allies in a war of conquest. . . .

For England an alliance with the United States and Japan would be an absolutely ideal situation, for, on the one hand, command of the seas would be assured to this group for years and, on the other hand, the English would receive from the other partners a free hand in Africa. For this reason it would probably be wholly fruitless to seek to persuade English statesmen of their *free will* to give up this aim. . . . In order for us to upset this hope, it is not England but *America* whom we should approach.

We would have the task of promptly showing America's political leaders that the plans which are ascribed to us by English sources grow from England's unfettered imagination; that we are, to be sure, like all other powers with maritime interests, obliged by need for coal to seek the acquisition of naval bases, but . . . the best security which the United States could ask that Germany's extra-European pretensions will remain moderate and relatively modest lies in Germany's continuous need to keep all her forces assembled and ready in Europe against a war for existence. For these reasons an agreement with Germany on bases in the Pacific Ocean would be infinitely more advantageous for the United States than an understanding with England. In the first place, Germany is the less demanding of the two; in the second place—and this is the important point—after obtaining a firm and friendly modus vivendi with Germany, America could tranquilly disarm again, while an accord with England would raise altogether new security considerations for the United States and necessitate permanent readiness for war.

At present, said Richthofen, the United States was protected by Europe's internal rivalries and especially by Germany's neutrality as between Britain and Russia. Once the United States had joined hands with England, Germany would have to change her policy, ally with her continental neighbors, and jointly with them build up her naval strength. America would thus be forced into a costly and dangerous arms race. Political leaders in the United States, Richthofen felt confident, could not fail to see the "absolute logic" [*Folgerichtigkeit*] of this situation. He directed Hatzfeldt to sound out Hay, his American colleague in London.

This extraordinary, impetuous, and imaginative analysis attracted the Kaiser. Indeed, the ideas may well have been his own, for Richthofen rarely thereafter showed an adventurous mind, and Bülow, who was Richthofen's master and idol, did not entirely sympathize with the American alliance scheme. Bülow remarked, at any rate, that it would be imprudent to cease making eyes at England. It was the Kaiser who, while agreeing with Bülow, added: "It is necessary for us, at all events, to reach an understanding *directly with America,*" and who jotted on the margin of a Foreign Office memorandum, "I am disgusted in the extreme by the fashion in which Lord Salisbury treats us. . . . But we must hasten to reach an understanding with the Yankees." The Emperor evidently saw an accord with the new seventh power as a means of strengthening Germany's free hand.

As so often was the case, however, he and his counselors had other, conflicting aims which they were not prepared to give up. When the Manila battle indicated that Spain might lose the Philippines, the Admiralty made up its mind that Germany should have a naval base in the islands. The *Hamburgische Korrespondent,* a newspaper with naval connections, spoke of Germany's interest in the Philippines as early as May 5. The Naval Staff soon presented the Foreign Ministry with a detailed list of its desires, including the island of Mindanao, the Carolines, and the Samoan archipelago.

In his memoirs, Bülow claims that the Kaiser telegraphed him even before the naval battle, "Tirpitz is as firm as a rock in his conviction that we must have Manila and that this would be of enormous advantage to us." Wilhelm himself took the view that the islands should not be allowed to change hands without some advantage accruing to Germany. Significantly, the first dispatch to the German ambassador in Washington hinting at the German-American alliance project began with the declaration, "His Majesty the Emperor considers it the first task of German diplomacy . . . to obtain naval bases in the Far East."

The Kaiser and his ministers pursued this aim even though friction with the United States was probable and was sure to jeopardize any alliance project. The government showed enough awareness of risk to refuse any support to Spain. When Spain suggested occupation of Manila by the powers, Bülow gave the Spanish ambassador an absolutely chilling answer, beginning, "His Majesty cannot be guided by his sympathies but only by his concern for the interests of Germany." On the other hand, the government adopted the wishful assumption that America would be either unwilling or unable to keep the Philippines.

A large German squadron was ordered to Manila, presumably to be on hand in case partition came. When incidents between the German and American commanders became the subject of complaint from the United States, the Emperor bridled. He snapped that the affairs of the squadron were the business of his navy and not fit subject for comment by diplomats or by foreigners. Bülow instructed Richthofen to tell the American ambassador that criticisms of the squadron could not be passed on to the Emperor. "If it became known," he added, "German public opinion . . . might regard it as gratuitous interference with our lawful freedom of action. . . . A friendly understanding with America is of great value to us. But neither among Americans nor elsewhere can we allow the idea to arise that we will permit ourselves to be intimidated by America."

In reflection on a *rapprochement* with the United States, just as in the prolonged and meticulous consideration of a possible English alliance, the German government allowed pride and hope of trifling territorial gain to deflect its attention from more consequential long-term goals.

The grand scheme that Richthofen had sketched was scarcely given a trial. Hatzfeldt answered that Hay, his colleague in London, would not be a suitable go-between; he was too much of an Anglophile. Richthofen turned to the American ambassador in Berlin, Andrew Dickson White, only to find that White could give him no specific encouragement. And the German ambassador in Washington proved pessimistic, reporting that public antagonism toward Germany ran high, that the upper classes were unshakeably Anglophile, and that McKinley was unlikely to chance a bold new orientation in diplomacy.

More important, the likelihood of an immediately profitable arrangement with America disappeared. It came to seem probable that the United States would keep the whole Philippine archipelago. In hopes that something might yet be rescued, Richthofen dropped his earlier idea altogether. He approached the British government with a scheme for joint Anglo-American-German neutralization of the Philippines, an arrangement that would give Germany at least a naval station. He also began hinting that Europe might need eventually to unite against America. The wayward notion of an American alliance had been forgotten.

In November the semiofficial *Kölnische Zeitung* declared, "The European powers must reckon with the fact that the Union has abandoned for good its policy of isolation, and entered upon a course which must bring her in contact with other nations in all parts of the world." The government appeared, however, to have decided that America would be neither partner nor rival. In the winter of 1898, when the Russian Treasury Minister spoke of America as Europe's common enemy, the Kaiser commented that it was far too late for the powers to unite.[5] Germany had given up the idea of treating the United States as a prospective foe and, at the same time, retreated from the notion of making her an ally. She would neither force her nor entice her into European politics.

A similar, somewhat puzzled neutrality characterized France. Press comment immediately after the Manila battle acknowledged America's new status somewhat fearfully. Said the semiofficial *Temps:* "It is apparent that that which gives supreme importance to what passes before our eyes is the appearance on the scene of a new power of the first order." Jean de Lanessan, the widely read foreign affairs commentator for *Rappel,* predicted that the United States would play a larger role in Asian politics than any power except Russia and would soon make its influence felt in Europe. Charles Humbert in

L'Éclair compared America of 1898 to Germany of 1866, at the time of the Austro-Prussian war: "the American nation, henceforward turned toward matters of war and recognizing that the prestige of victory is an indispensable precondition for her industrial and commercial expansion, . . . will intervene in the affairs of Europe."

The government gave little sign that it shared such fears. Hanotaux and his colleagues were unable for the moment to think about the distant future. A general election on May 8 reduced their parliamentary majority to such a slim margin that they could not feel confident of retaining office. And, indeed, barely six weeks passed before an adverse vote in the Chamber decided Premier Méline to resign. By the end of June Hanotaux was out of the Quai d'Orsay. Henri Brisson had taken the premiership, and a dark, energetic, former journalist from the mountains of Ariège, Theophilé Delcassé, occupied the Foreign Ministry.

Uncertain of his tenure, Hanotaux had been able to do little besides keep a wary eye on the United States. At the outset of the war, he took the precaution of strengthening the French squadron in the West Indies and, despite objections from the Admiralty, insisted on France's being well represented among the fleets observing operations in the Philippines.

He himself suspected that the United States probably would not keep the islands. When the French ambassador in Washington predicted that McKinley would be unable to resist public pressure for annexation, Hanotaux underlined that part of the dispatch. The Austrian ambassador in Paris, however, reported him as saying that Protestant America would probably not seek control over Catholic Filipinos.

Nevertheless, Hanotaux would have nothing to do with the Spanish scheme for a joint protectorate by the powers. When the Russian government urged that France step in and seek to bring about peace before the United States could annex the islands, Hanotaux was reported as reacting with anger and resentment. He had obtained from the Consular and Commercial Affairs Division of the Foreign Ministry a memorandum showing how little direct interest France had in the islands. He was not prepared to say to the Spaniards or even

in confidence to his Russian allies that the French government opposed or feared American expansion at the expense of Spain. Indeed,
he refrained from comment on two dispatches from Washington warning that America might seize the Canaries and Balearics. Like Salisbury, Hanotaux evidently felt it the part of wisdom to stay out of
America's way.[6]

Neither he nor his successor, it is true, could pretend complete disinterest in the war. In the first place, the French government had
agreed, jointly with the Austrian, to take custody of Spanish interests
in the United States. In the second place, there was constant pressure
upon the Foreign Ministry from financial interests wanting to save
what they could of their Spanish investments. From the early weeks of
the war, Hanotaux tried to bring the American and Spanish ambassadors together for informal discussions of peace. He passed on whatever information he gathered about the terms which each party had in
mind. Once he possessed a fairly accurate definition of American conditions, he used every open diplomatic channel to press acceptance on
the Spaniards. He sought out the Austrian ambassador, for example,
in order to make despairing comments on Spain's economic plight,
hoping presumably that Franz Josef would be inspired to use his influence with the Queen Regent.

Delcassé simply continued Hanotaux's policy. Learning that neither
side would take an initiative but that either would listen to a statement
from the other, he volunteered to serve as go-between, saying to the
American ambassador "very emphatically that he entirely disapproved
of the idea that any European nations should attempt to intervene
. . . with a view to bringing about peace" but "that if he should ever
be requested by the belligerents to act for them as an intermediary in
his private and unofficial capacity, he would be most happy to put
himself at their disposal and do his best to serve them." He passed on
to Madrid a confidential summary of American conditions that he had
received. At Spain's request, he agreed that the French ambassador
in Washington be empowered to negotiate a truce, and he rejoiced
when the document was finally signed. In seeking to bring peace, however, neither he nor his predecessor ever allowed himself in any way
to risk offending the United States.[7]

Nor did either permit himself to be carried away, as Richthofen seemed to be, by the rumor that an Anglo-American alliance was making. When Chamberlain made his Birmingham speech, the French ambassador to Britain happened to be in Paris. Hanotaux talked with him at length and may have been reassured that Chamberlain spoke for himself alone. He recognized that Britain might seek an alliance in order to get part of the Philippines or possibly the Canaries or Tangier, and watched American public opinion with some care. When the consul general in New York sent in a special report on growing anti-French feeling, Hanotaux thanked him personally and asked for more such information. At one point he suspected, as the Germans did, that English news agencies might be deliberately stirring up American public opinion against Europe. But neither he nor Delcassé jumped to the conclusion that an Anglo-American alliance existed or stood in the offing.

Since both Hanotaux and Delcassé could foresee the crisis with Britain that was to come when Captain Marchand met General Kitchener at Fashoda on the Nile, both had some temptation to revive the earlier idea of a diplomatic revolution—a French rapprochement with Germany. Yet neither gave the slightest evidence of responding favorably to the notion, fairly widely circulated in the press, that France and Germany should bury their differences in order to confront the new Anglo-Saxon alliance. *Le Temps,* which was considered the Foreign Ministry organ, never even conceded that an Anglo-American alliance was likely.

Even at the height of the Spanish war and of publicity about Anglo-American friendship, the French attitude remained one of skeptical watchfulness. When McKinley in his annual message of December 5, 1898, spoke of unsettled issues with Britain and made no mention of English good will, the French press huzzahed. Charles Humbert, who had been one of the gloomiest of prophets after the battle of Manila Bay, published a column in *L'Éclair* saying, in effect, that the United States meant to maintain her comfortable isolation and leave England in uncomfortable isolation.[8]

Earlier, the French government, like the German, might have given consideration to a possible American alliance. More conceivably,

France might have decided to regard the United States as a new enemy. If so, France might have encouraged Russia to make a stand against America in the Far East. As it was, Hanotaux and Delcassé chose to leave the United States alone, and their policy undoubtedly had some influence upon France's Russian ally.

Of all the European powers, Russia was the one that should have been most concerned over the Spanish war. The Russian Foreign Ministry's lack of enthusiasm for the prewar *démarches* had been due in part to fear of America's becoming involved in Near Eastern and especially Far Eastern affairs, although in the past, America's gradual Pacific expansion had seemed advantageous—as Muraviev asserted early in 1898, the establishment of American suzerainty over Hawaii would simply cut out England and Japan. Even before the outbreak of war, however, Muraviev had foreseen that America might conquer the Philippines, and he had been warned by the chargé d'affaires in Washington of the increasing friendliness between the United States and Britain.

Then came the Manila battle and Chamberlain's Birmingham speech. Muraviev feared that America might turn the Philippines over to England. He urged France to intervene, force Spain to make peace, and take the Philippines for herself.

After France refused, Muraviev might have begun to worry lest America take the islands and hold them, but acting with and not against Britain. Cassini warned him, "We could console ourselves with the passing of the Philippines into the hands of our friends, the Americans, whom we love and value. But the transfer of these islands to the United States, friends and possible allies in the future of Great Britain, should give us pause to think things over." The Russian ambassadors in London, Berlin, and Madrid suspected that something was afoot between London and Washington, and the Russian consul general in New York claimed that English news agencies were flooding the United States with anti-Russian propaganda.

Nevertheless, Muraviev seemed untroubled. It may be that, like his colleague, Minister of War A. N. Kuropatkin, he trusted economic rivalry to create antagonism between the United States and Britain as well as between both Anglo-Saxon powers and Germany. It may have been, as the Deputy Foreign Minister later told the French ambassador, that Russia had changed her mind about the Philippines and decided they belonged in Japan's rather than Russia's sphere of influence. If so, Muraviev would presumably have continued to view United States expansion as helpful rather than harmful to Russian interests.

It may have been simply that Muraviev did not begin to think seriously about the problem until it was too late. On August 10, several days after the Spanish-American armistice had been concluded, he told the Japanese ambassador in St. Petersburg that he felt certain the United States would not take the Philippines. Russia was the European state most concerned with the balance of power in Asia; nevertheless the Tsarist government apparently gave little thought during the war either to the possibility of checking the new power or to that of seeking some closer tie wth her.[9]

After the war, the government began to show some vague concern. On August 29, 1898, the Tsar issued his celebrated appeal for an international conference on the reduction of armaments, the appeal that was to result in the Hague Conference of 1899. E. J. Dillon, the very well informed Russian correspondent of the *Daily Telegraph,* asserted in an article in the *Contemporary Review* for November, 1898, that alarm over America's growing strength had been a powerful factor in the Emperor's mind.

Soviet scholars have since unearthed documents showing that the proposal had been made by Kuropatkin and Muraviev well before the Spanish war started. The War Minister had stressed the technical and financial difficulty of matching recent French and German progress in artillery. The Foreign Minister, in a memorandum of April 5, listed various considerations, not one of which specifically involved the United States. On the other hand, Dillon enjoyed a close relationship with Witte, the Finance Minister and the most powerful officer in the cabinet; there was a long delay between the submission of the Kuropatkin and Muraviev memoranda and the Tsar's final decision; and it may be that in his mind the American peril had some importance.

Talking later with the German ambassador in St. Petersburg, Witte put great stress on Europe's need to reduce land armaments so that fleets could be built to match the combined strength of America and Britain. Muraviev employed the same argument in December, 1898, when urging disarmament on officers of the French General Staff. It does seem clear that the disarmament appeal was not conceived as a reaction to the emergence of the United States as a power. It may be, however, that its actual issuance was influenced by this consideration. It is equally possible that the Russian ministers merely believed others to be concerned and thought mention of the American peril might promote acceptance of the Tsar's proposal.[10]

On the whole, the Russian government was surprisingly indifferent to the new power. Russian diplomats abroad appeared far more perturbed than ministers at home. On June 10, Count Osten Sacken, the perceptive and experienced Russian ambassador in Berlin, wrote to Muraviev of the Spanish war, England's evident interest in an American alliance, and the continuing antagonism in Asia between Britain and Russia. "All of this," he wrote, "creates for Europe a new situation urgently demanding serious and reflective consideration by the statesmen at the head of the various cabinets of the Continent." The Tsar, for his part, wrote the Kaiser at the end of 1898 that Britain would like to use the United States against Russia but that he thought an Anglo-American alliance unlikely.[11] If the French had shown more concern, the Russian government might have given more thought to the American question. As it was, Russia did not really reconsider her relations with the United States until after the American Open Door note of 1899.

Perhaps even more surprisingly, the Japanese government showed no marked reaction to the evidence of America's new status and drive. Japan was herself just emerging from weakness and isolation, and her foreign relations, like America's, were in constant flux. Nevertheless, she claimed to be a power, at least in the Far East. Expansionist and imperialist ideologies appeared to have considerable strength within the country. In 1893 and again in 1897, important newspapers had cried out against American annexation of Hawaii. As late as July, 1898, when the United States actually took the islands, *Yomiuri,* the organ of a major political party, declared that Japan could not permit the erection of a naval base at Honolulu because it would upset the balance of power in Asia. The same paper insisted that Japan's destiny lay in southward expansion and called on the government to lay hands on some part of Spain's crumbling empire.[12] It always seemed possible to diplomats and other observers that Japan might oppose American acquisition of the Philippines and perhaps reach for the islands herself.

Still another equally evident possibility was that Japan might seek an American alliance. After the war with China, the government had found itself isolated and unable to resist the Russian-French-German demand for Japanese retrocession of conquered territory. The European seizures of Kiaowchow, Port Arthur, and Wei-hai-wei had enraged some Japanese, especially because Port Arthur was a site which Japan had earlier been required by the powers to relinquish. Opposition parties waged a vigorous campaign, calling on the government to protest the German and Russian actions. A Foreign Affairs League was organized for the specific purpose of maintaining agitation on this issue. At one of its sessions, held a few weeks after Dewey's victory at Manila, Oishi Yamata called for an Anglo-American-Japanese alliance. Oishi became Minister of Agriculture and Commerce in a new cabinet formed in June, 1898. There was at least a remote chance that the policy he had advocated might be adopted by the government.

In fact, neither course was followed. Three premiers succeeded each other in rapid succession, each preoccupied with domestic affairs, for the second of the three governments was the first ever to be based upon political parties rather than clans, and some regarded this change as foreshadowing revolution. Japan was experiencing an economic depression for which almost no one could see a solution, and none of the three cabinets dared take any action that might cause panic among capitalists or discourage foreign investment. From Peking came reports of palace revolutions that might transform China, and the policies of the powers there seemed wholly unpredictable. The successive Japanese governments concluded that they could not afford either to resist the United States or to woo her.

When questioned in the Diet, a spokesman for Premier Marquis Hirobumi Ito refused to make any declaration on possible American annexation of the Philippines; the issue, he said, was hypothetical. *Nichi Nichi,* the organ of the Ito family, declared meanwhile that Japan should welcome American expansion since it would mean enlarged trade.

The second government, headed by Marquis Shigenobu Okuma, came to power in June, 1898. The parties it represented had made repeated jingoistic declarations on Japan's future in Asia. But Okuma, who was both Premier and Foreign Minister, maintained silence not only about the Philippine question but even about Russian ambitions. Through diplomatic channels, he quietly sought information about American intentions and about the attitudes of the powers. He instructed Japanese consuls to report the feelings of Philippine rebels toward Japan. But he finally declared to the American government that he would welcome American annexation of the islands and that he saw dangers and disadvantages in any other course, including a grant of independence. In November, when Okuma's government fell, the new Foreign Minister, Shuzo Aoki, informed Japanese diplomats that the cabinet of Premier Field Marshal Viscount Aritomo Yamagata would maintain precisely the same attitude on the Philippine issue.[13]

Not one of the powers recurred seriously to the thought of uniting against an American peril. The British and German governments considered seeking an American alliance. The French, Russians, and Japanese, whose interests were most seriously affected by America's move into the Philippines, remained silent. Though acknowledging that the United States had forced her way into their exclusive club, the powers chose, in effect, to leave her alone. Had one or more viewed the new power as a serious threat, Americans might have been faced with grave issues of national security. Had any besides England elected to strive for American friendship, the conditions facing American statesmen might also have been quite different. As it was, only the British government volunteered concessions in return for American good will. The others neither menaced the United States nor courted her. The result was to leave decisions with regard to America's future role in the interplay of the powers very much up to the Americans themselves.

Having defied the world's greatest powers—or at the least challenged their supremacy—the United States found itself more respected than before. The fact of power was hard to deny.

PART SIX

END OF A BEGINNING

"The United States is . . . a world power. . . . When a people have commercial interests everywhere, they are called upon to involve themselves in everything. A nation of ninety million souls, which sells wheat to the universe, coal, iron, and cotton, cannot isolate itself. As Boutmy has written, it has a sense of puissance oblige. *Its power creates for it a right. The right turns itself into a pretension. The pretension becomes a duty —to pronounce upon all those questions that hitherto have been arranged by agreement only among European powers. These powers themselves, at critical times, turn toward the United States, anxious to know its opinion. . . . The United States intervenes thus in the affairs of the universe. . . . It is seated at the table where the great game is played, and it cannot leave it."*

André Tardieu, Notes sur les États-Unis (*Paris, 1908*)

The war appeared to change McKinley. He came out for Hawaiian annexation. He resolved to keep some foothold in the Philippines. Eventually he decided to take the whole archipelago, Guam, and Puerto Rico. He seemed to become an imperialist.

In the case of Hawaii, his conversion came at the last moment. Though he had submitted an annexation treaty to the Senate in 1897, he had not pressed it. Indeed, he assured opponents that it would not pass. When annexationists resorted to a joint resolution, needing only majorities in both chambers rather than two-thirds in the Senate, he still gave them no open encouragement. The project appeared hopeless, for Speaker Reed, who opposed annexation, had proved powerful enough in the past to prevent the House's even discussing measures distasteful to him. But the war and especially Dewey's victory persuaded many congressmen that Hawaii was really needed.

The New York *Tribune* declared on April 23 that the islands might have to be seized. Annexationists demonstrated that they could collect the 219 signatures required for a petition to override the Speaker. Paul Dana of the *Sun,* who helped round up signers, wrote to General Wilson, "I think we are dealing with [Reed] as effectively as if we pointed a gun straight at his head." After Reed caved in, it seemed certain that a resolution would pass, and at that stage McKinley took a stand. On June 4, 1898, the New York *Tribune* announced that he wished annexation.[1]

As when he asked for intervention in Cuba, the President appeared to be jumping aboard a vehicle he could not brake. The resolution was to pass the House by a vote of 209–91, the Senate by 42–21. Except for starchy mugwump sheets like the New York *Evening Post* and the Springfield *Republican,* the press acclaimed annexation. Religious and business journals that had drawn back after Cleveland's revelations in 1893 either took the view that five years had erased moral stains or interpreted Dewey's triumph as a sign from Providence. Reed, who had remained in opposition, was pictured by the sympathetic *Nation* as "standing alone, so far as party friends are concerned, and as one of a feeble minority, mostly Democrats." McKinley had certainly taken the more popular position. But, significantly, he had also convinced himself that he was right. In the hearing of one of his private secretaries he declared, "We need Hawaii just as much and a good deal more than we did California. It is manifest destiny."[2]

This does not mean that he had experienced a complete change of mind. Many who spoke for annexing Hawaii said in the same breath that they would oppose other colonies. The *Catholic World* and the Protestant *Independent* did so. Representative Francis Newlands of Nevada, who had introduced the joint resolution, defended it as establishing "scientific boundaries" for America. McKinley could have spoken as he did about Hawaii and still doubted that imperialism offered the best policy for the future. On the other hand, it is certainly worth notice that, despite his stated conviction, he appeared even more circumspect with regard to Hawaii than he was to seem with regard to the Philippines.

There is a faint possibility that from the very outset of the war the President nurtured in his mind the hope of taking from Spain some part of her Pacific empire. He was later to tell his friend, H. H. Kohlsaat, that Dewey's victory had surprised him completely and that he had to search out the Philippines on his office globe: "I could not have told where those darned islands were within 2,000 miles!" Probably, however, the President was stretching the truth, for he had been told as early as September, 1897, that the navy planned to strike Manila. The Secretary of the Navy twice discussed with him the orders to be given Dewey, and McKinley himself approved the directive sent on April 24, reading, "War has commenced. . . . Proceed at once to the Philippine Islands. Commence operations at once, particularly against the Spanish fleet. You must capture vessels or destroy. Use utmost endeavors." On Friday, April 29, two days before the battle, Comptroller Charles G. Dawes wrote in his diary: "An engagement is expected by Sunday in the Pacific between our Asiatic Squadron and the Spanish ships at Manila."[3] The President could not, of course, anticipate a complete triumph. But he did know that Dewey had the Spaniards outgunned; he could expect some kind of victory; and he may have hoped that it would give the United States a claim to territory beyond Hawaii.

After learning of Dewey's victory, McKinley certainly made no move to discourage others from thinking imperialist thoughts. In its resolution for intervention in Cuba, Congress had declared explicitly against taking or keeping Cuba, and the President could have proclaimed that this self-denying ordinance applied to the Philippines as well. Instead, the White House allowed the New York *Tribune* to report on May 4: "it is held by the President and his political and military advisers that it will be time enough to discuss the sale, barter or retention of the islands when Spain has been driven to abandon Cuba and sue for conditions of a general peace."

The thought of retaining the islands occurred to the President as soon as to any imperialist. Even Lodge was slow to grasp that an opportunity existed. He wrote to Henry White on May 5, "The victory at Manila was at first so overwhelming I did not take in all its possibilities." He had needed "a day's reflection" before realizing "that we must on no account let the Islands go. . . . We hold the other side of the Pacific and the value to this country is almost beyond imagination." Despite the excitement created by the naval victory, few voices spoke for conquering and keeping the islands. Lodge did not disclose his views in public. Neither did Chandler or Cullom. Though the New York *Sun* came out for keeping the Stars and Stripes over Manila, few other jingo papers did so. Hearst's San Francisco *Examiner* said the colony had been "a source of corruption and weakness to Spain" and might be so for America. The St. Louis *Republic* reported a straw poll among members of the House and Senate yielding only one vote unequivocally for annexation, that of Representative Joel P. Heatwole of Minnesota who said, "On general principles, I believe we should hold fast to all that we can get." Frye of Maine, a longtime champion of imperialist causes, refused to comment at all. At the time when the New York *Tribune* reported the White House considering possible retention of the islands, there was no evident public movement for such a course, even among avowed imperialists.[4]

Nor was there any such movement when the President authorized an expeditionary force to take Manila. Another of Kohlsaat's recollections was of McKinley's saying, "If old Dewey had just sailed away when he smashed that Spanish fleet, what a lot of trouble he would have saved us." At the time, however, the President showed no misgivings. According to Secretary of War Alger, indeed, he made his decision even before Dewey's victory. Owing to technical disagreements between the commanding general of the army and the officer designated to captain the expedition, the order was not given until May 16. In the meantime, McKinley was warned against committing troops to the islands. Oscar S. Straus wrote him that "nothing but entanglement and embarrassment" could result; "I fear we will not be able afterwards to withdraw our troops without turning over the islands to anarchy and slaughter." But McKinley was not deterred. He let the expedition depart as soon as the two generals reached a compromise.[5] The President seemed untroubled by the prospect of having to decide, not whether to take the islands, but whether to keep them or give them back.

The explanation need not be that McKinley's mind was already teased by imperialist thoughts. Nearly everyone seemed to regard Dewey's victory as putting a finish to Spanish sovereignty. The vehemently anti-imperialist Springfield *Republican* declared on May 5 that the Philippines were in America's hands and that it would be immoral to return them to "a dominion hated, crushed, and unregenerate." The *Republican* urged their transfer to some other power. The Boston *Herald* and the New York *Evening Post* favored granting independence. According to the French ambassador, congressmen talked of nothing but possible sale, partition, or transfer. It seemed to be generally assumed that the islands were America's to dispose of as she would.[6] The President may just have shared this popular belief.

Whatever McKinley may have meditated before the war or just after Dewey's victory, it was not in any case the acquisition of all the Philippines, for at the beginning of June he sketched peace terms that would have given the United States nothing but a naval base in the islands. Ambassador Hay reported a semiofficial inquiry about conditions for an armistice. The Secretary of State replied that the President would ask evacuation of Cuba, surrender of Puerto Rico, cession of a coaling station in the Ladrones, and the "Philippine Islands to be allowed to remain with Spain except a port and necessary appurtenances, to be selected by the United States." Hay was cautioned, "These terms will be acceptable to the President at the present juncture, saving further sacrifice and loss of life. Prolongation of the war may change this materially." But there can be little doubt that the President meant them seriously, for he also stipulated that there should be no indemnity and that the United States would assume payment of American claims in Cuba.[7] Had his intention been to seem conciliatory but to prevent negotiations, he would have included some financial clause that bankrupt Spain could not accept. At this stage, he almost certainly had no aim beyond the acquisition of Manila.

Had Spain accepted his terms at once, he might even have been ready to give up all claim on the Philippines. He may have wanted a naval base and trading station in the Far East, but his mind was busier with immediate preoccupations. As he studied preparations for a campaign in Cuba, he must have remembered how murderous the climate and terrain had proved to Spanish regular troops. He knew the volunteers assembling in American army camps to be enthusiastic but undisciplined and short of artillery, shells, transport, rifles, cartridges, and even uniforms. He must have wanted, if at all possible, to escape sending raw troops against Spanish veterans or against the mosquitoes and miasmata of Cuba. Foreseeing campaigns that could well be long, costly, and bitter, he may have thought of the Philippines merely as a pressure point. He may have hoped that Spain, fearing loss of her richest colony, would agree to a quick settlement. He may have believed that acquisition of Puerto Rico would be ample salve for imperialists.

Abruptly, however, he abandoned such thoughts. When Hay described Salisbury as willing to communicate McKinley's terms to Madrid, the Secretary of State cabled back almost immediately, "The President cannot make proposals for peace. My confidential message to you indicated his state of mind at that time and was only intended to advise you of it. . . . It has seemed to the President that any action on our part at this time would be premature and be liable to misinterpretation. . . . If proposal comes from Spain on the basis of my telegram . . . before situation changes, President will consider it."[8]

One reason for this *volte-face* was undoubtedly increased concern for the Philippine rebels. When first reports came to Washington of an impending conference between Dewey and the rebel leader, Emilio Aguinaldo, the admiral had been cautioned, "It is desirable, as far as possible, and consistent for your success and safety, not to have political alliance with the insurgents or any faction in the islands that would incur liability to maintain their cause in the future." Dewey had nevertheless met with Aguinaldo. While he denied having entered into any alliance, press dispatches reported the rebels preparing arsenals for the American invaders and Aguinaldo calling for a republic under American protectorate. The Secretary of State explained to Hay that the President had drawn back from his original peace proposal because the insurgents had "become an important factor in the situation and must have just consideration in any terms of settlement."[9]

Another, more important reason for the President's swift retreat was mounting evidence of public interest in the Philippines. Among the few newspapers that had begun to call for annexation were the Washington *Silver Knight* and the silverite Denver *Rocky Mountain News*. More important, the news columns of eastern and midwestern newspapers reported annexationism bubbling up among some of the very groups that had clamored for intervention in Cuba. On May 16, for example, the New York *Tribune* described a branch of the Sons of the American Revolution exulting that Dewey had "paralyzed the . . . oppressor's hand, deprived her of her richest colony," while an adjoining column quoted a sermon in Calvary Baptist Church by the Reverend Dr. MacArthur. "The Philippine Islands . . . should be made the garden of the universe," he declared. ". . . We will fill them with school houses and missionaries." On May 21 the Newark *Advertiser* printed a resolution by local Daughters of the American Revolution predicting "that our country at the close of this war will enter upon a new career, grander and more imposing than anything that had distinguished her in the past." This language was vague, but no more so than that of earlier resolutions and sermons on the Cuban problem.

Even weak signals from the groups that had brought on the crises of March and April could cause nerves to flutter. The *Tribune* quoted on May 17 a speech made by Chauncey Depew before the Republican

Club of New York: "in my daily business I have clipped out for me reports in the papers from all over this country. Every morning they are placed before me, so that I may see how things that may have some bearing on the railroad business are going. I can't help seeing what a strong feeling is spreading over the whole land in favor of colonial expansion. The people are infatuated with the idea. . . . This feeling is getting so strong that it will mean the political death of any man to oppose it pretty soon." In Chicago the editor of the Baptist *Standard* wrote on May 21 of a developing "popular craze" for annexations.

The President must have heard similar warnings, and, just after he had sent off his proposed peace terms, he discovered that this incipient movement might have strong leadership. The *North American Review* appeared with two articles, one by Truxtun Beale, contending that the United States should take the Philippines in order to win the trade of China, the other by Senator Morgan, arguing against keeping the islands on account of the Filipinos' racial inferiority and the danger of conflict with other powers. Beale was a California Republican who had held a diplomatic post under President Harrison. Morgan had, of course, been a conspicuous jingo and imperialist.

The litmus-sensitive New York *Tribune* on June 6 published an editorial attacking Morgan and, in effect, endorsing Beale. Other Republican journals followed suit. When debate opened in the House on the Hawaiian question, Republicans from New England, New York, Pennsylvania, Illinois, Iowa, Michigan, and California advanced arguments that would also justify annexing the Philippines. The President could see that there was danger of his own party's taking up the imperialist cause.

McKinley began to feel that the United States might need more than just a harbor or naval base. William M. Laffan, publisher of the New York *Sun,* talked with him on July 13 and wrote Lodge that he had heard the President say, "we will first take the Phillipines [*sic*], the Ladrones, the Carolines and Porto Rico. Then when we have possession, undisputed, we will look them all over at our leisure and do what seems wisest. Personally I am in favor now of keeping Luzon and fortifying Manila. . . . I think the United States possessed of all of Spain's colonies would do well to act with great magnanimity and show European governments the lofty spirit that guides us. Apart from that idea I favor the general principle of holding on to what we get." Lodge himself assured Chandler on July 23 that he had just seen McKinley and that "in the Pacific [he] means to go much farther than anyone I think guesses."[10]

Just how far, the President himself did not seem to know. On the afternoon of July 26, Jules Cambon, the French ambassador, brought to the White House a message from the Spanish Foreign Minister, inviting negotiations for peace. At the moment, though Spain's naval power had been utterly broken, American ground forces occupied only the eastern tip of Cuba, a beachhead on Puerto Rico, and the outskirts of Manila. Of the islands that McKinley had mentioned to Laffan, the United States held a close grasp only on Guam. General Shafter, commanding at Santiago, had just reported cases of fever among the troops mounting at a rate of five hundred a day. General Anderson at Cavite had intimated that all was not going well in relations with the Philippine insurgents, and Dewey was to cable on July 30 that Aguinaldo had "become aggressive and even threatening toward our Army." Though press dispatches described Spain as bankrupt and demoralized, the President could not feel sure that she would accept any terms he imposed. He jotted on a scrap of paper:

> As a condition to entering upon negotiations looking to peace, Spain must withdraw from Cuba and Porto Rico and such adjacent islands as are under her dominion. This requirement will admit of no negotiations.
>
> As to the Philippines, I am of the opinion, that with propriety and advantage they can be the subject of negotiation and whenever the Spanish gov't desire it, I will appoint Commissioners to that end.

For four days he discussed the matter with individual advisers and eventually with his full cabinet. Secretary of State Day took the view that the government ought not to assume responsibility for "eight or nine millions of absolutely ignorant and many degraded people." As the President summarized it, Day wanted to keep only "a hitching-post" in the islands. The Secretary of the Treasury and the Secretary of the Navy agreed, while the Secretary of the Interior and the Attorney General argued for keeping the entire archipelago on account of its prospective commercial value, and the Secretary of Agriculture contended that there was a great opportunity to Christianize the natives. The Naval War Board, which included Captain Mahan, advised retention on strategic grounds. Secretary of War Alger evidently warned that it might be politically unsafe to do anything else.

McKinley held his foggy middle ground. After innumerable drafts of a protocol had been exchanged, discussed, revised, and rewritten, the final terms stipulated that Spain surrender Cuba and Puerto Rico and leave "the control, disposition, and government of the Philippines" to be determined by later negotiations.[11]

When picking the five commissioners to represent him in Paris, McKinley selected three who favored outright annexation. That may have been accident, for his principal object was to make the eventual treaty acceptable to the Senate and the public, and his original slate had been made up of men who were not publicly committed. Only after several refusals did the President end up with Secretary Day and Democratic Senator George Gray of Delaware, both of whom opposed annexation, Senators Davis and Frye, who were known to favor it, and, as a fifth member, Whitelaw Reid, whose New York *Tribune* had come out editorially for taking the islands. But, since Reid and Day could both be counted on to vote as the President asked, McKinley retained the power to make any decision he chose.[12]

By the second week in September, when the commission left for Paris, the President had decided that he must ask for all of Luzon. Otherwise, his parting directions to the commissioners remained delphic. He said:

It is believed that the true glory and the enduring interests of the country will most surely be served if an unselfish duty conscientiously accepted and a signal triumph honorably achieved shall be crowned by such an example of moderation, restraint, and reason in victory as best comports with the traditions and character of our enlightened Republic. . . . It is none the less true, however, that, without any original thought of complete or even partial acquisition, the presence and success of our arms at Manila imposes upon us obligations which we can not disregard. The march of events rules and overrules human action.

As sessions opened in Paris, the President set off on a midwestern speaking tour. When questions came in by cable, he answered that the commissioners should adhere to the armistice protocol and his instructions.

Not until late October did he finally have to make up his mind. The Spanish negotiators tried to tempt the Americans with the thought of keeping Cuba instead of making it independent. Though some of the commissioners and McKinley's new Secretary of State, John Hay, found this notion attractive, the President did not. He cabled tersely, "We must carry out the spirit and letter of the resolution of Congress." But the Spanish proposition had also involved the issue of the Cuban debt, and McKinley had to instruct his commissioners in no circumstances to assume responsibility for any part of it. By taking this stand, he obliged himself to decide the Philippine issue, for, as he was warned, the Spanish commissioners were certain then to ask if Spain would be responsible for the Philippine debt. He could not long defer the precise instructions which his commissioners repeatedly begged.[13]

He sat down and wrote out in pencil a cablegram. Before it could be sent out, he received a message detailing the antiannexationist views of Day and Gray. The Secretary of State drafted a revised cablegram. The President added to it in order to meet some of Day's and Gray's arguments.[14] The final text dispatched on October 26 read:

The information which had come to the President since your departure convinces him that the acceptance of the cession of Luzon alone, leaving the rest of the islands subject to Spanish rule, or to be the subject of future contention, can not be justified on political, commercial, or humanitarian grounds. The cession must be of the whole archipelago or none. The latter is wholly inadmissible, and the former must therefore be required.

In a famous interview with a delegation of Methodist clergymen in 1899, McKinley explained that this conclusion had come to him almost in a flash of revelation:[15]

I walked the floor of the White House night after night until midnight; and I am not ashamed to tell you, gentlemen, that I went down on my knees and prayed Almighty God for light and guidance more than one night. And one night late it came to me this way—I don't know how it was, but it came: (1) That we could not give them back to Spain—that would be cowardly and dishonorable; (2) that we could not turn them over to France or Germany—our commercial rivals in the Orient—that

would be bad business and discreditable; (3) that we could not leave
them to themselves—they were unfit for self-government—and they would
soon have anarchy and misrule over there worse than Spain's was; and
(4) that there was nothing left for us to do but to take them all, and to
educate the Filipinos, and uplift and Christianize them, and by God's
grace do the very best we could by them, as our fellow-men for whom
Christ also died.

There can be little doubt that these thoughts actually did come to
the President. As early as July 27, they came to him through the mail.
His old friend, Spencer Borden, wrote him a letter that merits quota-
tion because of its resemblance to what McKinley said later:[16]

It would be cowardly and pusillanimous for us to turn the islands back to
Spain, giving them the power again to misrule the natives. . . . We would
be equally despicable to ask Great Britain to take and care for them—
which would make a greater row—and we must never permit the three
bullying nations that deprived Japan of the fruits of her victory over
China, to play the same game with us.
    There is only one logical course to pursue. Spain has shown herself
unfit to rule her colonies, and those that have come into our possession as
the result of war, must be held, if we are to fulfill our duties as a nation
. . . , giving them the benefits of a christian civilization which has reached
its highest developement [*sic*] under our republican institutions.

The President must have recognized at a very early date that he
could not simply return to Spain ground that had been occupied by
American troops. No voice in the land had spoken except against such
a course. Lodge commented to Henry White, "I have never seen such
a universal feeling as there is against handing the islands back to
Spain." Nearly all evidence filtering back to the White House pictured
Spanish rule as worse in the Philippines than in Cuba. The American
who had been McKinley's consul in Manila declared every week of his
service to have been "a history of barbarities by Spaniards." Another,
who had represented Cleveland, wrote in *Scribner's* of "Spanish misrule and oppression."[17] Hardly a popular magazine in either the
United States or England failed to print someone's reminiscence or
comment on Spanish iniquity. From the time when he gave up his

initial idea of negotiated peace, McKinley must have known that he could not return the Philippines to Spain.

Nor could he have believed for long that sale or transfer was a feasible alternative. While the war was still in progress, the British and Japanese governments both said that if the United States did not want the islands, they did. The German ambassador in London told Hay of Germany's desire for at least a base or coaling station. The New York *Herald* reported on July 3 a rumor that France and Russia had agreed to support Germany if she sought the whole archipelago. For the United States to offer the islands to any one power would surely bring protests, if nothing worse, from the rest. At home, the Germans and Irish would fight transfer to England, while others would oppose sale to anyone else. Moreover, as McKinley later observed, any such transaction might prove "bad business." The Philippines were reputed not only to offer advantageous bases for trade and navigation but also to possess rich resources, including quantities of gold. Weighing possible trouble with the powers, the likelihood of Senate failure to ratify a bargain, and the danger that the abandoned territory might prove a new California or Transvaal, McKinley could scarcely have given serious consideration to this possibility.[18]

His one real option was to insist on independence for the islands, and he may have postponed final decision partly in order to collect information on the character and disposition of the natives. Early data painted a depressing picture. John Foreman, an Englishman regarded as the foremost expert on the islands, wrote in the July *Contemporary Review*, "The Philippine Islands . . . would not remain one year peaceful under an independent native government. It is an utter impossibility." McKinley saw this article, for he obtained a copy from his private secretary. Though complaining of eyestrain, he may also have read other, similar writings, of which magazines and newspapers were full. At any rate, he saw little to contradict Foreman; hardly anyone claiming firsthand knowledge disputed his conclusions. And before the armistice had been signed McKinley was advised officially by the Japanese Foreign Minister that the Filipinos were incapable of governing themselves.[19]

Yet McKinley did continue to ask for reports on the natives. He requested opinions from Dewey and American generals who had been in the Philippines, and he waited until the commissioners could hear testimony from the admiral, General Merritt, and Foreman himself. When telling the commissioners of his decision, McKinley mentioned information that had reached him after their departure, and he may have been referring to this expert testimony. Perhaps it should have been obvious to him that few authorities would credit the Filipinos with capacity for self-government, yet he may actually have regarded independence as a feasible alternative down to the last moment.

But if doubt lingered in his mind, it was because his thoughts were not really on rational alternatives. His advisers talked of what would be wise, statesmanlike, and in the national interest. He did not.

In his explanation to the French ambassador of why he could not offer precise armistice terms, the President said, "The American people would not accept it if we did not obtain some advantage from our great victories at Manila and from the sacrifices we have made in sending to the Philippines a large body of troops." When Oscar Straus advised him early in August not to take the islands, "he seemed," Straus noted in his diary, "to fear public opinion would not approve such a course." When McKinley first drafted a final directive to his commissioners, he did not mention information newly come or any other such consideration. He wrote simply, "There is a very general feeling that the United States, whatever it might prefer as to the Philippines, is in a situation where it can not let go . . . , and it is my judgment that the well-considered opinion of the majority would be that duty requires we should take the archipelago." The sole concern of the President was with the mood and whim of public opinion.[20]

He had observed how the press gradually swung toward annexation. Shortly after the New York *Tribune* attacked Senator Morgan's *North American Review* article, Cleveland and Bryan came out almost simultaneously against taking the Philippines, and a large part of the Republican press immediately became raucously imperialist. The *Literary Digest* published a survey on July 9, quoting editorials of more or less imperialist tone from the leading Republican dailies of New York, Philadelphia, Baltimore, Chicago, Milwaukee, Minneapolis, Topeka, St. Louis, Louisville, and San Francisco. The *Digest* reported even more significantly that Cleveland had been criticized by conservative Democratic papers and Bryan by silver Democratic organs. On August 4 *Public Opinion* listed twenty-eight major dailies as unreservedly for annexation and many others wavering. By September 10 the *Literary Digest* reported eighty-four papers favoring annexation of the whole archipelago, among them many of the best known and most widely circulated journals in the country.

This evidence suggested that a majority of city and town newspaper editors saw local opinion leaning toward annexation. There were relatively few organization meetings, resolutions, or public rallies to bear this judgment out. From the fastness of the White House, McKinley probably wondered whether the press spoke for the multitude or not.

The President could see that church and business leaders, like newspaper editors, were taking no chance on being ridden down by a mass movement like that which had followed the sinking of the *Maine*. Churchmen may have been caught, of course, by the dream of converting several million Visayas and Tagalogs. McKinley's Presbyterian Secretary of Agriculture was affected by such a fancy, and so, it was said, was the President's invalid wife. But the early and ardent annexationists within the churches were not in the missionary societies, where this motive would have been expected to flourish. Indeed, the Presbyterian, Baptist, and Congregational mission boards held conventions in which the Philippine question was scarcely discussed, and the monthly *Methodist Review of Missions* refrained from any comment at all until after the President reached his decision. Some clergymen and laymen connected with these associations or with the American Bible Society actually joined the Anti-Imperialist League.[21]

Religious periodicals other than those published by mission boards did cite missionary opportunities as one argument for annexation, but few that came out for taking the islands made this the primary justification for their stand. Their tone was rather one of resignation. The widely read nondenominational New York *Outlook,* for example, observed that return of the islands to Spain would "not be tolerated by the American people." As early as May 28 it declared, "The devout man . . . will always seek to ascertain what God's will is, and always endeavor to conform his action to it. The events of the past four months have made that will plain." The *Outlook* was one of those journals that had opposed war and then backed down in fright after seeing the hysteria of the public, and its other editorials laid constant stress on the need for clergymen to "achieve a healthful and needed influence in the time of perilous excitement." Though never saying so publicly, the *Outlook*'s editors evidently believed that would-be leaders who opposed annexation, like those who had opposed war, would simply not be followed.

The Boston *Congregationalist* spoke of "responsibilities which God lays on" and the *Catholic World* of a "logic of events" compelling America to keep the Philippines. Though some of these writers may have been hypocritically masking imperialist convictions, many would seem to have been voicing the feeling that Mr. Dooley put less reverently when he wrote, "We've got the Ph'lippeens, Hinnissy; we've got thim the way Casey got the bulldog—be th' teeth. . . . As Hogan an' McKinley both says: 'Th' natio's in th' hands iv the Lord, an'll give Him what assistance it can spare fr'm its other jooties.' . . . We're a gr-reat civilizein' agent, Hinnissy, an' as Father Kelly says, 'so's th' steam roller.' An' bein' a quiet man, I'd rather be behind thin in fr-ront when th' shtreet has to be improved."

Though some businessmen and business journals took up the cause of annexation joyfully, it may be that many of them were also trying to keep ahead of the steamroller. When thirty prominent men gathered in late August at Saratoga, New York, to debate the Philippine issue, one who spoke for imperialism was Eugene V. Smalley of St. Paul, Minnesota, editor of the *Northwest Magazine* and secretary of the National Sound Money League. He said, "I believe that a nation cannot safely absorb itself in its own affairs. . . . It breeds strange and dangerous disorders. The most wholesome influences upon our home politics will be exerted by getting interested in questions that concern the whole world." Henry Watterson wrote in the Louisville *Courier-Journal,* "We risk Caesarism certainly, but even Caesarism is preferable to anarchism." According to the New York *Journal of Commerce,* most businessmen actually kept a "deathlike silence." James Ford Rhodes, the historian, wrote McKinley that "the higher intelligence and the business interests" and "practically all the preachers and the religious folk" wanted simply to be led by the President.[22]

Many varied considerations undoubtedly entered into the conscious and unconscious thoughts of those who in the name of religion or business advocated imperialism, among them piety, superstition, patriotism, and greed. Teachings from social Darwinists and Mahan had their effect. But the apparent conversion of churchmen and businessmen came so quickly that it is hard to explain in terms of impulses or ideas that had long been present or afloat. Something had shaken these people. While it may have been Dewey's triumph or the sheer sense of being in battle, more likely it was the shocking, terrifying experience of the previous spring, when a nameless, formless, and seemingly leaderless public opinion rode the country into war. Church and business leaders spoke like men determined not to be left behind again.

McKinley could not look to these groups, as he had before April, 1898, to tell him what he should do. Not only was the smell of fear on them, but the very event that had frightened them had proved how impotent they were to subdue and direct the people. The President had to establish his own rapport with the public.

In order to do so, he arranged a speaking tour that would carry him through Indiana, Illinois, and Iowa, three states whose electoral votes had made the difference between victory and defeat in 1896, and through Nebraska and Missouri, where he had lost narrowly to Bryan. Considered either in terms of the contest for the House of Representatives or the approaching 1900 campaign, these were the areas that mattered.

In the course of each speech, McKinley said something that could be interpreted as referring to the Philippines.[23] At Tama, Iowa, on October 11, he asserted, "We want to preserve carefully all the old life of the nation,—the dear old life of the nation and our cherished institutions—"; there was scattered clapping. He went on, "but we do not want to shirk a single responsibility that has been put upon us by the results of the war"; and there was great applause. Yet at Arcola, Illinois, on October 15, he won a similar rousing response with these words: "We have had great glory out of the war, and in its settlements we must be guided only by the demands of right and conscience and duty."

He tried imperialism out at Ames, Iowa, from whence had come innumerable petitions to Congress in favor of pacifist causes. He experimented with anti-imperialism in Denison, the home of the state's war-hawk governor, Leslie M. Shaw. On each occasion, a stenographer made careful notes on the intensity and duration of applause. McKinley's own ears presumably registered the more subtle sounds.

By the time he had circled to Omaha, Nebraska, and started back through Iowa, the President had found his answer. At the Trans-Mississippi Exposition in Omaha, he asked, "Shall we deny to ourselves what the rest of the world so freely and so justly accords to us?" From the audience came a loud cry of "No!" He went on amid great applause to speak of "a peace whose great gain to civilization is yet unknown and unwritten" and to declare, "The war was not more invited by us than were the questions which are laid at our door by its results. Now as then we will do our duty."

After the reception given these words, he virtually ceased to sound the cautious note. At Chariton, Iowa, on the return trip, he said, "Territory sometimes comes to us when we go to war in a holy cause, and whenever it does the banner of liberty will float over it and bring, I trust, blessings and benefits to all the people." [Great applause.] At Columbus, Ohio, he proclaimed, "We know what our country is now in its territory, but we do not know what it may be in the near future. [Applause.] But whatever it is, whatever obligation shall justly come from this strife for humanity, we must take up and perform and as free, strong, brave people, accept the trust which civilization puts upon us." [Enthusiastic cheers and applause.]

The President had heard the voice of the people.

There can be no doubt that this was what he had waited for. He may have wanted it so, or he may have spoken the truth when he later told John G. Schurman, "I didn't want the Philippine Islands . . . and . . . I left myself free not to take them; but in the end there was no alternative."[24] In any case, he took little account of his own wishes. Earlier, when dealing with the Cuban issue, he had sought to escape public clamor and pursue safe, cautious courses defined by himself and conservative statesmen and businessmen around him. After the crisis that brought on the war, he wanted only to hear the people's wishes and obey.

His decision remained to be ratified by the Senate. Though three senators had served on the peace commission, two had been avowed imperialists, and Gray, the conservative, had protested Philippine annexation. It was obvious that others in the Senate would sympathize with his view rather than with Frye's or Davis's.

All the while that public opinion had seemed to crystallize in favor of annexation, an opposition had gathered strength. Cleveland and Bryan together rallied some of what had once been the Democratic coalition. Eastern mugwumps, like the editors of the New York *Evening Post* and the Boston *Herald,* had joined them, as had Carl Schurz and German-Americans who followed him. Some Irish Democrats found reason to become anti-imperialist; they thought of imperialism as something English. Labor leaders found even more cause in the danger of Philippine coolie competition. Others, including both conservative and silverite southerners and westerners, saw in annexation a threat to the Constitution, the American race, or the cause of domestic reform.

From the beginning there was no doubt that such opinions would influence only a minority of the Senate. The majority consisted of exultant imperialists like Lodge, Chandler, and Frye, orthodox Republicans willing to follow McKinley anywhere, and Senators impressed, as the President was, by the apparent drift of popular feeling. Platt of Connecticut believed, for example, that nine-tenths of the people in his state favored annexation.[25] But the minority openly in opposition included such diverse specimens as conservative Democrats—Gorman of Maryland, White of California, Caffery of Louisiana, silverites—Vest of Missouri, Jones of Nevada, Teller of Colorado —and such contrasting Republicans as Hoar, the priggish intellectual from Massachusetts, and Mason, a bucolic demagogue from Illinois. When the President sent the treaty to the Senate immediately after the new year opened, no one could calculate with certainty just how many votes this minority commanded.

There was much difference of opinion as to where the decisive votes lay. Speaker Reed, who opposed taking the Philippines just as he had opposed taking Hawaii, believed the crucial senators were those who could be swayed by union labor. He worried over the fact that so few labor leaders entered heartily into anti-imperialist agitation. Andrew Carnegie, who became inexplicably passionate in the anti-imperialist cause, thought that Bryan held control. The young Democratic leader had come out against imperialism but had refused to call for defeat of the treaty. As he explained to Carnegie, he wanted the war formally ended so that troops could be demobilized; he felt moral scruples against encouraging a minority to defeat the will of a majority; and he thought imperialism might usefully become the Presidential election issue in 1900. Carnegie and many others believed that Bryan's voice could have rallied additional votes against the treaty.[26]

The truly decisive figures, however, were the conservative leaders in the Senate. Gray was one of them; Gorman was a member of their inner directorate. The others, Aldrich, Allison, Elkins, Fairbanks, Spooner, and Hanna, had shown no enthusiasm for taking Hawaii, had resisted war with Spain almost to the bitter end, and had grave doubts about the wisdom of keeping the Philippines. Despite business journals and chambers of commerce that spoke for annexation, these Senators undoubtedly heard, as the President did, of apathy and unspoken opposition among "conservative men." In any case, the policy represented by the treaty was radical enough in itself to unsettle them.

But these senators eventually decided to support the administration. Aldrich, Hanna, and others threw themselves into cloakroom conferences that, according to well-substantiated rumor, involved promises of federal judgeships and even money. Spooner delivered an oration on the constitutionality of annexation. Hanna subsequently wrote McKinley that the fight could not have been won without Elkins. And it was won, on February 6, 1899, by a vote of 57–27—with one vote to spare.[27]

In this battle the Senate leadership had consented to take direction from the White House. McKinley, who spent hour after hour conferring with individuals and delegations from Capitol Hill, appeared to be the real manager, Aldrich, Allison, Elkins, and the rest merely his allies or lieutenants. During the struggle over intervention in Cuba, this had not been the case. Chandler had written contemptuously, "when the column moves the President who is now in the rear will go to the front. He shivers a little but he will go."[28] In the annexation of Hawaii, McKinley had played an inconspicuous role. But the taking of the Philippines seemed his act. Whatever credit or blame it merited was his. The executive branch rather than the Congress had become the source of decision in foreign affairs. As a result, not just McKinley himself, but the United States as a nation, seemed to have chosen imperialism as its policy.

XVIII · THE SEVENTH POWER

Had the President and the Senate acted otherwise, foreign observers might have been bewildered. As it was, they saw the United States behaving as a great power was expected to—taking what it could and keeping it.

The result was that Europeans kept their new conception of America. The continental press did find it mildly amusing that Aguinaldo and his cohorts rejected annexation, declared a war for independence, and kept the American army busy for nearly three years in intermittent guerrilla warfare. Apropos of American press attacks on Germany, the *Berliner Volkszeitung* snapped in 1899 that the Yankees would do well to "beat the Filipinos first." Then in 1902 when the United States belatedly granted independence to Cuba, Europeans interpreted the act less as the honoring of a promise than as an effort to avoid repetition of the Philippine experience. Nevertheless, neither the long-drawn-out contest with Aguinaldo nor the nominal surrender of Cuba diminished by much the reputation which the United States had acquired.

After 1899 writings on the "American peril" used the present, not the future tense. Octave Noël warned readers of the Paris *Correspondant* in March, 1899, that the threat from America was as real and immediate as that from Germany. Ugo Ojetti declared in the Milan *Corriere della Sera* that while Italy could probably defend herself against "victorious America," her colonies might well go the way of Spain's. The editors of *Russkoe Bogatstvo* advised Russians to regard English and American imperialisms as twin phenomena, equally dangerous for their own country. In Germany, Max Goldberger, Wilhelm Polenz, and Otto, Count Moltke, published books in effect declaring that America was working day and night to achieve dominion over the world.[1] To many such students of international politics and trade, the "American menace" had become, not a prospect, but a reality.

Though these writers were significant, they were not altogether representative; the chronicles and periodic commentaries in major

263

newspapers and journals actually touched upon the subject infrequently. Indeed, after Cuban and Philippine affairs passed off the front pages, references to the United States appeared only a little more often than before 1898.

The real change was not in the amount of attention given America but in the attitude which journalists and diplomats now tended to adopt. In the summer of 1900 the periodicals of Europe were full of writings about navies. The German Reichstag was debating the government's thirty-eight-battleship budget, and analysts everywhere were examining its possible impact on the balance of power. The best statistics available indicated that the American fleet ranked just ahead of Germany's and just behind Russia's and France's. This had been its relative standing for some time. Earlier, however, commentators tended to leave it out when computing the potential strength of conceivable combinations. Now, they almost invariably included it.

The idea of the United States as a factor in the balance of power cropped up frequently. A. Maurice Low predicted flatly in the *National Review* for October, 1899, "If the United States is not an ally of England, then most assuredly she will be of Russia. It is a very simple proposition." A writer in *Questions diplomatiques et coloniales* interpreted the re-election of McKinley in 1900 as foreshadowing a bid for alliance with one bloc or another. A French socialist asserted that the great task for Europe was to build a makeweight against the Anglo-Saxon bloc, and an editorialist in the thoroughly antisocialist *Novoe Vremya* declared: "The Americans have discarded the Monroe doctrine and have allied themselves with their traditional enemy and with Japan. A counterpoise to American power is needed."[2]

In the spring of 1899 the St. Petersburg *Vedomosti* suddenly came out editorially for a Russo-American alliance. Prince Ukhtomskii, who was the *Vedomosti*'s editor, made a similar proposal through the columns of an American magazine. He and his newspaper were among the leading advocates of Russian expansion in the Far East. The reason for their unexpected declarations was undoubtedly the fact that negotiations were in progress with Britain for a Chinese railway agreement. The English seemed to be stalling. Ukhtomskii and his collaborators hoped that the threat of a Russian deal with America would make them more businesslike. Perhaps it did, for the agreement was promptly signed, and Ukhtomskii and the *Vedomosti* dropped their American alliance campaign. Nevertheless, it was significant that they had even momentarily broached such a project, for their words not only indicated that they thought a pact conceivable but that they would evaluate it as the equivalent of one with Great Britain.

It was also significant that right-wing German newspapers read importance into Ukhtomskii's suggestion. The agrarian *Kreuzzeitung* copied the *Vedomosti* editorial and published a long commentary on it. Misinterpreting it as evidence that Russia feared an Anglo-American alliance, this thoroughly conservative journal remarked that the interests of England and the United States were actually dissimilar. Germany itself, said the *Kreuzzeitung,* might do well to seek closer relations with the Americans. And this thought was then echoed in the almost equally conservative *Grenzboten.*

In the past such journals as the *Petersburgskaya Vedomosti* and the *Kreuzzeitung* had, like English Tory organs before 1895, viewed the United States at worst as a symbol of liberalism. Their bias was unchanged. They continued to condemn things American. At the same time, however, they began to speak of possible combinations with or against the American republic just as coldly as of possible combinations with or against England or any other power.

When Chamberlain spoke at Leicester in November, 1899, suggesting an Anglo-American-German alliance, many commentators thought his project unlikely to materialize; none thought it impossible. Newspapers speculated from time to time on whether there actually did exist a secret compact between Britain, the United States, and Japan. Like the editorial writer for *Novoe Vremya,* some Russian statesmen believed that it did. And Bülow, Holstein, and Muraviev all at one time or another committed to paper speculations on possible international combinations including the United States.[3]

In no European capital, including London, were such thoughts more than fitful. Dealing chiefly with issues in Europe, Africa, and the Near East, diplomats still concerned themselves mainly with other

European states. Even when confronted with crises in the Far East, they did not always take the United States into account. When they did, however, it was as a major power rather than as a minor one.

Perhaps the cartoons in continental humor magazines were in this case worth several thousand words. Some writers speculated on the possibility that there were two classes of great powers. "Diplomaticus" in the *Fortnightly Review,* for example, observed that there were only three "world powers"—Britain, Russia, and the United States. A Swiss political scientist asked if Europe in its old sense could even be said to exist any more. *Kladderadatsch* expressed this uncertainty by picturing the street of the great powers, with quaint national dwellings for the Europeans and a towering skyscraper for America.[4]

On the other hand, *Kladderadatsch* still at times represented the powers as five or six figures in European costumes. In August, 1899, it was inspired, as other journals were, to comment on the beginnings of the Boxer disturbances in China. It portrayed figures dashing from a burning pagoda. The Vienna *Floh* showed hands and long spoons dipping into a soup bowl labelled "China." In both pictures Uncle Sam was missing. He was also absent from a group pictured in the *Humoristicke Listy* of Prague. But he appeared in comparable cartoons in the Berlin *Ulk,* the Paris *Silhouette,* and the Turin *Fischietto.*[5] Like statesmen, caricaturists did not always think of the United States in connection with the states of Europe. When they did, however, they thought of it as one of the great powers.

This changed conception of America rested in part on misunderstanding. Many Europeans believed that the United States had deliberately chosen to throw itself into competition for colonies, economic concessions, and the other current gauges and emblems of international status. Not everyone was deceived. The *Journal des Débats* remarked astutely on July 3, 1899, "Let us remember how McKinley, who has no will of his own, came to annex the Philippines. Public opinion demanded it, and he was about as much master of the situation as a log drifting downstream." On the other hand, when McKinley was re-elected, nearly every major journal in Europe including the *Journal des Débats* interpreted the event as affirmation of an imperialist policy.

Europeans were impressed, to be sure, with America's population, navy, and industrial output. Especially was this so when figures for 1900 showed America leading in coal, iron, and steel. At about the same moment, it was revealed that the British and German governments had both gone to New York banks to borrow money. Data of this kind had been in evidence for years. The loans were not necessarily more significant than the first sales of American steel in European markets. The difference was that in the meantime Europeans had also been impressed by America's apparent resoluteness and combativeness in foreign relations. They thought they saw in Washington a government not only commanding great resources but also having the will to use them.

This was, of course, a delusion. The American government had rarely displayed any purposefulness whatever. When Hawaii offered itself for annexation in 1893, the Harrison administration moved to accept the gift only when persuaded that the public wanted it. Cleveland reversed the decision and refused the islands. So far as the evidence shows, he did so not from conviction that annexation was against the national interest but merely because the transaction seemed tainted. He thought it *morally* obligatory to make restoration.

Cleveland's demands upon Britain in 1895 were bolder. In them there was some element of national self-assertion. But the President probably would not have acted had he not been under heavy pressure from the Republican opposition and from dissident elements in his own party. And he almost certainly would not have moved had he not seen in the frivolous Venezuelan-Guianan dispute a grave *moral* issue.

The virtual ultimatum that Cleveland presented to Lord Salisbury's government had far-reaching effects. It excited a hostile reaction at home that virtually broke politicians of their habit of electioneering by appealing to hatred for Britain. In England it shocked statesmen and opinion leaders into realization that the United States was a power with whom Britain should come to terms. In effect, Cleveland and Olney startled England and the United States into one another's arms. It cannot be said, however, that they had any such expectation at the time. Even with all the evidence in, indeed, it is hard to divine just what they did have in mind.

In dealing with Cuba, Cleveland and McKinley had a purpose in view. It was to avoid any international complications that might upset business. They wanted the Cuban problem to go away.

When it would not do so, McKinley found himself faced with a terrible choice. He could embark on a war he did not want or defy public opinion, make himself unpopular, and risk at least the unseating of the Republican party if not the overthrow of what he conceived to be sound constitutional government. He was influenced, as Cleveland had been, by moral revulsion against cruelties in Cuba. He was also affected by indications of approaching trouble in Asia and possibly in the Western Hemisphere. But he was occupied most by domestic considerations. When public emotion reached the point of hysteria, he succumbed.

Neither the President nor the public had any aim beyond war itself. The nation was in a state of upset. Until recently its people had been largely Protestant and English; its economy predominantly rural and agricultural. Men in their forties could remember it that way. Now, however, the country was industrialized and urbanized. Catholics were numerous and increasing. People of older stock found themselves no longer economically or even socially superior to members of immigrant groups or to others without family, background, or education who had won success in business or industry. The panic of 1893 made this new condition even more visible by depressing agricultural prices, rents, investment income, professional fees, and white-collar salaries. Movement into and within cities had cut ties with families and churches. Young men and women were thrown together more than they had been, yet economic conditions forced them into later and later marriages. The young also heard old men talking on and on of the great war between the states and of the great men, great deeds, and great ideals that had been. In some irrational way, all these influences and anxieties translated themselves into concern for suffering Cuba. For the people as for the government, war with monarchical, Catholic, Latin Spain had no purpose except to relieve emotion.

The taking of Hawaii and the Philippines was more deliberate. There is even evidence that President McKinley thought Hawaii's annexation desirable. But his preoccupation was still with domestic public opinion. In contemplating the Philippine problem, he evidently considered little else. The conservative senators who served as his lieutenants in the treaty fight showed no more conviction than he that the policy they advocated was necessarily the right one. They and their kind had simply been scared by the public's earlier convulsion. Like the President, they wanted to do whatever seemed necessary to prevent its recurring.

From first to last, the makers of American policy and the presumed leaders of American opinion concerned themselves either with abstract morality or with conditions inside the United States. They scarcely thought of proclaiming to the world that America was a power. They were at most only incidentally concerned about real or imagined interests abroad. They gave no sign that they meant the United States to become a factor in the international balance.

In 1899 and later the government was to proclaim an "Open Door" policy for Asia, stake out a security zone in the Caribbean, and even assist in ending a war in the Far East and resolving a European crisis over Morocco. In initiating these steps, McKinley may still have been thinking mainly about the domestic danger of seeming to be insufficiently aggressive toward foreigners. The same thought may have oppressed even Theodore Roosevelt. A certain number of journalists and business, professional, and church leaders may have endorsed the later policies of the government, as they endorsed the annexation of the Philippines, because it seemed the safest rather than the wisest course. Spaniards were to speak in retrospect of a disillusioned "generation of ninety-eight." Perhaps Americans also had a generation of ninety-eight—a generation of public leaders so frightened by the outbursts of mass emotion they had witnessed that their thoughts were dominated by dread of witnessing it again. But that is a question for some other book.

In the 1890's the United States had not sought a new role in world affairs. Issues in Hawaii, China, Turkey, Venezuela, and Cuba had intruded almost of their own accord. Statesmen and politicians dealt with them according to their judgment of domestic, not foreign, conditions. Cleveland and McKinley had showed more intense preoccupation with matters at home than even the most isolationist advocate of national solipsism in the 1920's and 1930's. Unconcernedly and almost unthinkingly, these statesmen ran the risk of precipitating Europe into a coalition against America. Yet their actions had the paradoxical effect of convincing people abroad that the United States possessed not only the might but also the will to be a force among nations. Some nations achieve greatness; the United States had greatness thrust upon it.

NOTES · ACKNOWLEDGMENTS · INDEX

The following abbreviations are used throughout the notes:
(Aus.) Archives of the Foreign Ministry of the Austro-Hungarian Empire, Haus- Hof- und Staatsarchiv, Vienna.
(Br.)   Archives of the Foreign Office, Public Record Office, London.
(Fr.)   Archives of the Ministry of Foreign Affairs, Paris.
(Jap.) Archiveˢ of the Ministry of Foreign Affairs, Japan: Military Tribunal microfilms, Captured Documents Section, Library of Congress, Washington.
(Sp.)   Archives of the Ministry of Foreign Affairs, Madrid.
(U.S.) Archives of the Department of State, Foreign Affairs Division, National Archives, Washington.
Vagts   Alfred Vagts, *Deutschland und die Vereinigten Staaten in der Weltpolitik* [1889–1906] (2 vols.; New York, 1935).

CHAPTER I · NATION ASTIR

1 *Democracy in America* (Bowen ed.: 2 vols., New York, 1898), I, 599; Julius Fröbel, *Amerika, Europa und die politischen Gesichtspunkte der Gegenwart* (Berlin, 1859), 209; Henri Martin, *La Russie et l'Europe* (Paris, 1866), 316; see Erwin Hölzle, *Russland und Amerika: Aufbruch und Begegnung zweier Weltmächte* (Munich, 1953), 219–221.

2 Paul Knaplund and Carloyn M. Clewes (eds.), "Private Letters from the British Embassy in Washington . . . 1880–1885," *Annual Report of the American Historical Association for the Year 1941*, 94, 157–158; Kurd von Schlözer, *Amerikanische Briefe* (Berlin, 1927), 143–144.

3 S. B. Okun, *The Russian-American Company* (English translation: Cambridge, Mass., 1951), chapter 11; Max M. Laserson, *The American Impact on Russia 1784–1917* (New York, 1950), chapters 9–10; Count Otto zu Stolberg-Wernigerode, *Germany and the United States of America during the Era of Bismarck* (English translation: Philadelphia, 1937), 69–85, 91–92; R. M. Veit Valentin, *Bismarcks Reichsgründung im Urteil englischer Diplomaten* (Amsterdam, 1937), 396; Goldwin Smith, *The Treaty of Washington, 1871* (Ithaca, New York, 1941).

4 Vagts, I, 345, 353–356, 365–367; "Dnevnik A. N. Kuropatkina," *Krasnyi Arkhiv*, II (1922), 93.

5 (London, 1901), 396; Hauser, *Impérialisme américain* (Paris, 1905), 108.

6 *Broad Arrow*, quoted in C. Joseph Bernardo and Eugene H. Bacon, *Ameri-*

can Military Policy since 1775 (Harrisburg, 1955), 260; cf. Stolberg-Wernigerode, *Germany and the United States,* 73–74.

7 Fiske, *American Political Ideals* (New York, 1885), 9–10, 101–152; Strong, *Our Country* (New York, 1885), 159–179; Charles Carlisle Taylor, *The Life of Admiral Mahan* (New York, 1920), 40–53, 130–143.

8 XLIX (Oct. 12, 1889), 455–456, (Nov. 16, 1889), 631–633. See Ralph W. and Muriel E. Hidy, *History of the Standard Oil Company (New Jersey): Pioneering in Big Business, 1882–1911* (New York, 1955), chapter 5; William B. Gates, Jr., *Michigan Copper and Boston Dollars* (Cambridge, Mass., 1951), chapter 3; J. Stephen Jeans (ed.), *American Industrial Conditions and Competition: Reports of the Commissioners appointed by the British Iron Trade Association* (London, 1902), 278–282; and the special volume in the *Proceedings* of the British Iron and Steel Institute: *The Iron and Steel Institute in America in 1890* (London, n.d.).

9 52 Cong., 1 sess., *Congressional Record,* 1439; Vagts, I, 656–658.

10 Shoup in New York *Times,* Jan. 27, 1892; see Alice F. Tyler, *The Foreign Policy of James G. Blaine* (Minneapolis, 1927), 128–164; London *Times,* Aug. 25, 1888; see Charles C. Tansill, *Canadian-American Relations, 1875–1911* (New Haven, 1943), 77–86; 52 Cong., 1 sess., *Congressional Record,* 3399–3400; Vagts, I, 656–662. On the general question of when the United States became a great power, see Thomas A. Bailey's provocative "America's Emergence as a World Power: The Myth and the Verity," *Pacific Historical Review,* XXX (Feb., 1961), 1–16.

CHAPTER II • TO GROW OR NOT TO GROW

1 Benjamin C. Wright, *San Francisco's Ocean Trade, Past and Future* (San Francisco, 1911), 95; Lorrin A. Thurston, *Memoirs of the Hawaiian Revolution* (Honolulu, 1936), 81–90.

2 See John P. Young, *San Francisco* (2 vols.; San Francisco, n.d.), II, 653–654; Stuart Daggett, *Chapters on the History of the Southern Pacific* (New York, 1922), 293–316; and George E. Mowry, *The California Progressives* (Berkeley and Los Angeles, 1951), 18–19.

3 Austin Adams, *The Man John D. Spreckels* (San Diego, 1924), 159–207. There are numerous reports of discussions in business organizations and of sermons in the San Francisco *Chronicle,* Los Angeles *Times,* Portland *Oregonian,* Seattle *Times,* and *Oregon State Journal,* for Feb. 2–13, 1893.

4 *Public Opinion,* XIV (Feb. 4, 1893), 415–417, and (Feb. 11, 1893), 439–441; Schurz in *Harper's Weekly,* XLIII (Feb. 25, 1893), 170; New York *Staatszeitung,* Feb. 2, 7, 8, 26, 28, 1893; New York *Herald,* Feb. 3–March 11, 1893; Thurston, *Memoirs of the Hawaiian Revolution,* 293–294.

5 Albert T. Volwiler (ed.), *The Correspondence between Benjamin Harrison and James G. Blaine* (Philadelphia, 1940), 174. See Julius W. Pratt, *Ex-*

pansionists of 1898 (Baltimore, 1936), 22–26; and William Adams Russ, Jr., *The Hawaiian Revolution (1893–94)* (Selinsgrove, Pa., 1959), 37–48.

6 *Harrison-Blaine Correspondence,* 190, 206, 223.

7 Pratt, *Expansionists of 1898,* 69–73.

8 Thurston to Dole, Feb. 9, 1893, *ibid.,* 117–118.

9 Morgan to Henry Watterson, March 6, 1902, Private Papers of John T. Morgan, Library of Congress. Stockholders in the Canal Company included A. S. Crowninshield, R. D. Evans, and H. C. Taylor: 51 Cong., 2 sess., *Senate Report No. 2234,* 3–5. See August C. Radke, "Senator Morgan and the Nicaragua Canal," *The Alabama Review,* XII (Jan., 1959), 5–34.

10 *Independent,* XLV (April 20, 1893), p. 536; Frederick Bancroft (ed.), *Speeches, Correspondence and Papers of Carl Schurz* (6 vols.; New York, 1913), V, 133–134; Washington *Post,* April 14, 1893.

11 Blount's report is published as Appendix II in United States Department of State, *Foreign Relations of the United States, 1894;* Matilda Gresham, *Life of Walter Q. Gresham* (2 vols.; Chicago, 1919), II, 740–768; see Charles Callan Tansill, *The Foreign Policy of Thomas F. Bayard* (New York, 1940), 404–407.

12 Henry James, *Richard Olney and His Public Service* (Boston, 1923), 83–90, 212–221. See Russ, *Hawaiian Revolution,* 227–229; and Pratt, *Expansionists of 1898,* 138–139.

13 Gresham to Bayard, Feb. 22, 1894, Private Papers of Thomas F. Bayard, Library of Congress; *Public Opinion,* XVI (March 2, 1894), 545.

CHAPTER III · THE HEATHEN'S KEEPER

1 *Annual Report of the American Board of Commissioners for Foreign Missions, 1895,* p. 95; New York *Times,* Oct. 23, 1895.

2 John W. Foster to James H. Wilson, Nov. 4, 1895, July 19, Aug. 9, Sept. 21, 1896, Private Papers of James H. Wilson, Library of Congress; Denby to Gresham, May 10, 12, 1895, *China: Dispatches,* XCVIII (U.S.); Chicago *Tribune,* Sept. 25, 1895; Boston *Herald,* Nov. 23, 1895; *Literary Digest,* XIII (Aug. 29, 1896), 580; New York *Journal of Commerce,* Nov. 2, 1896. See Charles S. Campbell, *Special Business Interests and the Open Door* (New Haven, 1951); and A. A. Fursenko, *Bor'ba za razdel Kitaya i amerikanskaya doktrina otkrytykh dverei, 1895–1900* (Moscow, 1956), especially 35–53 and 176–182.

3 *Literary Digest,* XII (Nov. 2, 1895), 1–2, (Nov. 9, 1895), 32–33; cf. *ibid.,* X (Dec. 1, 1894), 5–6, and Boston *Herald,* Nov. 11, 1895.

4 53 Cong., 3 sess., *Congressional Record,* 232, 233, 551, 577, 691, 1606; 54 Cong., 1 sess., *ibid.,* 31, 32. On the Armenian organizations in the United

States, see Armenian Historical Society, *Armenians in Massachusetts* (Boston, 1937), 46 ff.; and M. K. Jismedjian, *Badmoutin Amerigahai Kaghakagan Gousagtstoutiantz, 1890–1925* [History of American-Armenian Political Parties] (Fresno, 1930), 1–33. On events in Armenia and the resulting international complications, by far the best work is William L. Langer, *The Diplomacy of Imperialism* (Revised edition; New York, 1951), chapters 5, 7, and 10.

5 Laura E. Richards and Maud Howe Elliott, *Julia Ward Howe, 1819–1910* (2 vols.; Boston, 1916), II, 190–191; Hagop Bogigian, *In Quest of the Soul of Civilization* (Washington, D.C., 1925), 156–164; Boston *Herald,* July 28, Oct. 8, 1895; Chicago *Tribune,* March 11, 1896; 54 Cong., 1 sess., *Congressional Record,* 130, 140, 163, 187, 188, 222, 223, 251, 331, 332, 408, 446, 447, 481, 482, 485, 515, 545, 642, 643, 684, 685, 687, 722, 723, 757, 812, 813, 852, 854, 893, 955, 1023, 1024, 1028, 1551, 1570, 1634.

6 *Minutes of the National Council of the Congregational Churches of the United States . . . held in Syracuse, N.Y., October 9–14, 1895* (Boston, 1896), 29, 33; Boston *Herald,* Oct. 14–15, 1895; A.B.C.F.M. *Annual Report, 1896,* viii, xvi–xvii.

7 New York *Herald,* Nov. 20–21, 26, 1895; Boston *Herald,* Oct. 21, Nov. 23, 1895; Chicago *Tribune,* Jan. 6, 1896; Cleveland *Plain-Dealer,* Nov. 19, 1895; New York *Tribune,* Nov. 26, 1896.

8 *Literary Digest,* XII (Feb. 8, 1896), 428–429, (Feb. 22, 1896), 498, XIII (May 9, 1896), 51–52, (Sept. 19, 1896), 660; Boston *Herald,* Oct. 2, 20–21, Nov. 23, 27, Dec. 4, 1895; Richards and Elliott, *Julia Ward Howe,* II, 217; New York *Herald,* Jan. 25, 1896.

CHAPTER IV · CLEVELAND'S CHALLENGE

1 Boston *Herald,* Oct. 20, Nov. 3, 1895; Albany *Evening Journal,* May 1, 1895; *Literary Digest,* XI (Oct. 1, 1895), 664–665.

2 George P. Ikirt to Olney, Oct. 25, 1895, Private Papers of Richard Olney, Library of Congress; T. M. Paschal to Olney, Oct. 23, *ibid.;* see Nelson M. Blake, "The Background of Cleveland's Venezuelan Policy," *American Historical Review,* XLVII (1942), 259–277.

3 *Harrison-Blaine Correspondence,* 243; *Foreign Relations, 1895,* 696–697.

4 Gresham to Bayard, April 23, 1895, Bayard Papers; *Literary Digest,* XI (May 25, 1895), 112–113, (Aug. 3, 1895), 391–392.

5 Adee to Olney, July 10, 1895, Olney Papers. See Merle E. Curti, *Peace or War: The American Struggle, 1636–1936* (New York, 1936), 75–158.

6 Allan Nevins (ed.), *The Letters of Grover Cleveland* (Boston, 1933), 381. On Cleveland, see Nevins, *Grover Cleveland, A Study in Courage* (New York, 1932); Robert McElroy, *Grover Cleveland: The Man and the States-*

man (2 vols.; New York, 1923); and Horace S. Merrill, *Bourbon Leader: Grover Cleveland and the Democratic Party* (Boston, 1957).

7 See T. D. Jervey, "William Lindsay Scruggs: A Forgotten Diplomat," *South Atlantic Quarterly*, XXVII (Oct., 1928), 292–309. On Venezuela, see J. M. Siso Martinez, *Historia de Venezuela* (Mexico, D.F., 1954); R. A. Rondon Marquez, *Guzmán Blanco, 'El Autócrato Civilizador'* (2 vols.; Caracas, 1944); Leon Lameda and Manuel Rosales, *Historia militar y política del General Joaquín Crespo* (Caracas, n.d.); and Romulo Betancourt, *Venezuela: Política y Petróleo* (Mexico, D.F., 1956).

8 Bayard to Phelps, Feb. 17, 1888, 50 Cong., 1 sess., *Senate Executive Document No. 226.*

9 Matilda Gresham, *Walter Q. Gresham*, II, 794–797; Tansill, *Foreign Policy of Bayard*, 708, footnote 190; see Nevins, *Cleveland*, 630–631.

10 Gresham to Bayard, March 31, April 23, 1895, Bayard Papers.

11 Nevins, *Cleveland*, 631–632; Washington *Post*, May 11, 1895.

12 Nevins, *Cleveland*, 512–513, 559–560; James, *Olney*, 19.

13 Olney to Miss Straw, June 23, 1895, Olney Papers; Cleveland to Olney, July 7, 1895, *ibid.* The note appears in *Foreign Relations, 1895*, 545–562.

14 Cleveland to Dickinson, July 31, 1895, Nevins, *Cleveland Letters*, 402; Olney to Bayard, Nov. 20, 1895, James, *Olney*, 226; Cleveland to Olney, Dec. 3, 1895, Nevins, *Cleveland Letters*, 416.

15 See Nevins, *Cleveland*, 639; and James, *Olney*, 118–119.

CHAPTER V · DISMAY IN LONDON

1 Bayard to Olney, Aug. 9, 1895, James, *Olney*, 222–226; Salisbury to Chamberlain, Aug. 14, 29, 1895, to Law Officers, Sept. 20, 1895, Bertie to Salisbury, Aug. 30, 1895 (with marginal notes by Salisbury), F.O. 80/362 (Br.). Communications concerning possible use of force against the Venezuelans are under date of Oct. 12, 1894, in F.O. 80/358 (Br.), Dec. 10, 1894, Feb. 13 and March 24, 1895, in F.O. 80/361 (Br.), and May 7, 16, and July 30, 1895 in F.O. 80/362 (Br.).

2 Chamberlain to Salisbury, Aug. 30, Sept. 11, 1895, *ibid.;* Chamberlain to Governor General, British Guiana, Sept. 7, 1895, F.O. 80/367 (Br.); Chamberlain to Salisbury, Sept. 14, 1895, Victoria to Salisbury, Dec. 19, 1895, Private Papers of the Marquis of Salisbury, Christ Church library, Oxford.

3 Chamberlain to Salisbury, Dec. 8, 1895, *ibid.;* Courcel to Hanotaux, Dec. 20, 1895, *Angleterre*, CMX (Fr.).

4 Bertie to Salisbury, Aug. 30, 1895 (quoting Cartwright of the Colonial Office), F.O. 80/362 (Br.); Pauncefote to Salisbury, Oct. 25, 1895, Salisbury Papers. See *Blackwood's* CLI (March, 1892), 617–637, Marlborough

in *New Review,* VI (Jan., 1892), 31–47, Meath in *Nineteenth Century,* XXXIII (March, 1893), 493–514, William Clarke to Henry Demarest Lloyd in Henry Pelling, *America and the British Left* (London, 1951), 59, and, in addition to Pelling's perceptive account, G. D. Lillibridge, *Beacon of Freedom: The Impact of Democracy upon Great Britain, 1830–1870* (Philadelphia, 1955).

5 J. L. Garvin and Julian Amery, *The Life of Joseph Chamberlain* (4 vols.; London, 1932–1951), III, 66. Innumerable editorials from the British press were clipped by Bayard and are filed with his reports in the State Department Archives.

6 Salisbury to Hicks-Beach, Jan. 2, 1896, Salisbury to Victoria, Dec. 19, 1895, memorandum by Hewitt, Dec. 19, 1895, Pauncefote to Salisbury, Jan. 3, 1896, Salisbury Papers; Arthur D. Elliott, *The Life of George Joachim Goschen* (2 vols.; London, 1911), II, 204; Garvin, *Chamberlain,* III, 72; George Earle Buckle (ed.), *The Letters of Queen Victoria, 1886–1901 (Third Series)* (3 vols.; New York, 1931), II, 581–582, III, 13–14.

7 London *Times,* Jan. 12, 1896; Garvin, *Chamberlain,* III, 160; Balfour to Salisbury, Jan. 27, 1896, Salisbury Papers. These petitions and letters are all filed in F.O. 80/364 (Br.).

8 *Letters of Queen Victoria, Third Series,* III, 14–16; M.I.D. to Salisbury, Jan. 3, 1896, F.O. 5/2302 (Br.).

9 Garvin, *Chamberlain,* III, 161–162; Salisbury to Sanderson, Jan. 9, 1896, Sanderson Papers, Foreign Office Library, London.

10 Buckle to Salisbury, Jan. 10, 24, 1896, Salisbury to Pauncefote, Feb. 7, 1896, Salisbury Papers; Smalley to Olney, Jan. 25, 27, 31, 1896, Olney Papers; J. S. Kennedy to Cleveland, Jan. 13, 1896, Cleveland Papers; R. Barry O'Brien, *The Life of Lord Russell of Killowen* (London, 1901), 309. The negotiations are described in detail in Garvin, *Chamberlain,* III, 159–168; W. Reid, *Memoirs and Correspondence of Lord Playfair* (London, 1899), 416–426; and Tansill, *Foreign Policy of Bayard,* 740–781.

11 Gwendolen Cecil, *Life of Robert, Marquis of Salisbury* (4 vols.; London, 1921–1932), I, 161; the documents relating to this negotiation may be found in James, *Olney,* 254–289. See Nelson M. Blake, "The Olney-Pauncefote Treaty of 1897," *American Historical Review,* L (1945), 228–243.

12 Chamberlain to Salisbury, Dec. 24, 31, 1895, Salisbury Papers; Salisbury to Chamberlain, Jan. 6, 1896, Garvin, *Chamberlain,* III, 69; Chamberlain to Salisbury, Jan. 6, 1896, *ibid.,* 96; London *Chronicle,* Jan. 8, 12, 1896; Chamberlain to Salisbury, Sept. 17, 1896, Garvin, *Chamberlain,* III, 164.

13 Chamberlain to Balfour, Jan. 3, 1898, *ibid.,* 251; Blanche E. C. Dugdale, *Arthur James Balfour* (2 vols.; London, 1937), I, 184; Salisbury to Victoria, Feb. 23, 1898, Salisbury Papers; Balfour to Pauncefote, March 7, 1898, F.O. 5/2364 (Br.).

14 "A Biological View of Our Foreign Policy," *Saturday Review,* LXXXI (Feb. 1, 1896), 118–120; Münster to Marschall, Dec. 25, 1895 (quoting Dufferin), Johannes Lepsius, Albrecht Mendelssohn Bartholdy, and Fried-

rich Thimme (eds.), *Die Grosse Politik der europäischen Kabinette, 1871–1914* (52 vols.; Berlin, 1922–1927), XIII, No. 2368.

CHAPTER VI · RAPPROCHEMENT

1 Edward W. McCook to Lamont, Dec. 24, 1895, Private Papers of Daniel S. Lamont, Library of Congress.

2 Kansas City *Journal*, Dec. 19–20, 1895; New York *Herald*, Dec. 21, 1895; Chicago *Tribune*, Dec. 18, 1895; William H. Grace to Olney, Jan. 17, 1896, Olney Papers.

3 Reid to John Hay, Dec. 31, 1895, Private Papers of Whitelaw Reid, Library of Congress; see *Literary Digest*, XII (Jan. 4, 1896), 271–273, 277–279, (Jan. 18, 1896), 339–340.

4 John Laurie to Salisbury, Jan. 3, 1896, F.O. 80/367 (Br.); Boston *Herald*, July 12, 15, 1895.

5 Peter B. Olney to Olney, Dec. 20, 1895, Olney Papers; George F. Peabody to Cleveland, Jan. 21, 1896, Cleveland Papers; see Walter LaFeber, "The American Business Community and Cleveland's Venezuelan Message," *Business History Review*, XXXIV (Winter, 1960), 393–402.

6 J. C. Reiff to Chandler, Dec. 23, 26, 1895, Chandler Papers; Lodge to Anna Lodge, Dec. 18, 1895, Garraty, *Lodge*, 161; Roosevelt to Lodge, Dec. 20, 1895, *Letters of Theodore Roosevelt*, I, 500; Henry Adams to Olney, n.d., Olney Papers; Whitney to Lamont, Jan. 2, 1896, Lamont Papers; memo by Abram S. Hewitt, Salisbury Papers.

7 Nevins, *Cleveland Letters*, 429–430; Stafford Northcote to Salisbury, March 13, 1896, Salisbury Papers; Cleveland, *Presidential Problems* (New York, 1904), 173–281.

8 Garvin, *Chamberlain*, III, 167; Terrell to Olney, Oct. 27, 1895, Adee to Olney, Aug. 2, 1895, Olney Papers; Cleveland to Olney, Sept. 24, 1896, Nevins, *Cleveland Letters*, 459–460.

9 Olney to G. F. Edmunds, Jan. 18, 1897, to G. Gray, Feb. 1, 4, 1897, to J. Sherman, Feb. 3, 1897, Olney Papers; Nevins, *Cleveland Letters*, 468; New York *Times*, Jan. 14, 15, 20, 23, 1897; Olney, "International Isolation of the United States," *Atlantic Monthly*, LXXXI (May, 1898), 577–588.

10 Feb. 14, 1896, Salisbury Papers; marked text of British draft, Cleveland Papers.

11 Curti, *Peace or War*, 145–158; *Literary Digest*, XII (Feb. 8, 1896), 426–427 (Feb. 28, 1896), 511–512 (April 11, 1896), 692–693; New York *Herald*, Jan. 2, 1896; New York *Staatszeitung*, Jan. 3, 1896; Boston *Herald*, Feb. 23, 1896; Portland *Oregonian*, Feb. 26, 1896; Washington *Post*, April 5, 1896; San Francisco *Chronicle*, July 10, 12, 1896; J. J. McCook to Olney, Jan. 18, 1897, Olney Papers. Other letters from individual busi-

nessmen, clergymen, and educators are scattered through the Olney and Cleveland Papers.

12 H. Norman in *Cosmopolis,* III (July, 1896), 93–106; Albany *Evening Journal,* Feb. 24, 27, 1896.

13 New York *Times,* Jan. 13, 17, 1897; Washington *Post,* Jan. 26, 30, 1897; letters and petitions in Cleveland and Olney Papers under dates of Jan. 12–28, 30, 1897; McCook to Olney, Jan. 20, 1897, Butler to Olney, Jan. 30, Feb. 7, 1897, Olney Papers; Chicago *Tribune,* Jan. 19, 1897.

14 Albany *Evening Journal,* Feb. 16, 1897; Chicago *Tribune,* Jan. 27, 1897; New York *Sun,* Feb. 3, 4, March 19, 1897.

15 Boston *Herald,* Feb. 7, 1897; Indianapolis *Journal,* Feb. 10, 1897; New York *Times,* March 11, 12, 1897; see W. Stull Holt, *Treaties Defeated by the Senate;* and Blake, "The Olney-Pauncefote Treaty."

CHAPTER VII · AMERICA'S ARMENIA

1 Austin Corbin to Chandler, March 16, 1895, Chandler Papers; Quesada to Palma, April 21, 1896, *Correspondencia diplomática de la delegación cubana en Nueva York durante la guerra de independencia de 1895 a 1898* (Publicaciones del Archivo Nacional de Cuba: Havana, 1943—), vol. V, p. 60.

2 See Biblioteca Historica Cubana, *La Revolución del 95 segun la correspondencia de la delegación cubana en Nueva York* (5 vols.; Havana, 1932–1937), I, 7–11; and G. W. Auxier, "The Propaganda Activities of the Cuban *Junta* in Precipitating the Spanish-American War, 1895–1898," *Hispanic American Historical Review,* XIX (April, 1939), 286–305.

3 The monthly *Cigar Makers Official Journal* has information on the Cuban organizations. See also Chicago *Tribune,* Oct. 11, 1895; Philadelphia *North American,* Oct. 14, 1895; and New York *Tribune,* Nov. 27, 1895.

4 *Revolución del 95,* I, 156–158; *Correspondencia diplomática de la delegación cubana,* V, 60.

5 56 Cong., 1 sess., *Senate Document No. 50,* "Hearings . . . on . . . the Nicaragua Canal Company," 153–165; see *Correspondencia diplomática de la delegación cubana,* IV, 224; *Rand McNally Bankers' Monthly,* XIV (Jan., 1897), 389–390.

6 *Biographical Directory of Representative Men of Chicago* (Chicago, 1892), 137–139; Alice Katharine Fallows, *Everybody's Bishop: The Life and Times of the Right Reverend Samuel Fallows* (New York, 1927).

7 New York *Sun,* Oct. 1, Nov. 27, 1895; Philadelphia *North American,* Oct. 14, Nov. 2–3, 22, 1895; Cleveland *Plain-Dealer,* Nov. 22, 1895; Jan. 3, 5, 1896; Kansas City *Journal,* Nov. 30, Dec. 2, 1895; *Revolución del 95,* II, 258–264, 286, 338, III, 19, V, 29, 40.

8 54 Cong., 1 sess., *Congressional Record,* 29, 31–32, 38, 103–104, 130–131,

140, 162–164, 187–188, 222, 276, 291, 409, 430, 447, 482, 516, 601–603, 684–685, 722, 757, 782, 813, 852–853, 894, 953–955, 1023–1024, 1063, 1195, 1199.

9 *Correspondencia diplomática de la delegación cubana,* I, 96, V, 83; Gonzalo de Quesada y Miranda, *Archivo de Gonzalo de Quesada* (2 vols.; Havana, 1948), I, 60.

10 Chicago *Tribune,* Sept. 30, 1895; Atlanta *Constitution,* Oct. 6, 1895; 54th Cong., 1 sess., *Congressional Record,* 25, 37, 42–44, 1065–1068, 2208–2212. See Richard Hofstadter, "Manifest Destiny and the Philippines," in Daniel Aaron (ed.), *America in Crisis* (New York, 1952).

11 Chicago *Tribune,* Oct. 14, 1895; *Correspondencia diplomática de la delegación cubana,* I, 31; Lee to Olney, July 22, 1896, Olney Papers.

12 New York *Tribune,* Sept. 28, 1895; 54 Cong., 1 sess., *Congressional Record,* 1065–1068.

13 The following details are taken from the New York *Sun* and *Tribune,* Philadelphia *North American* and *Public Ledger,* Buffalo *Courier,* Newark *Advertiser,* Cincinnati *Enquirer,* Chicago *Tribune,* Omaha *World Herald,* St. Louis *Republic,* Dallas *News,* Denver *Rocky Mountain News,* and Los Angeles *Times* for Dec. 14–21, 1896.

14 54 Cong., 2 sess., *Congressional Record,* 324, 449, 483, 522, 609, 778; Chicago *Tribune,* Dec. 19–20, 1896; Omaha *World Herald,* Jan. 12–13, 1897; New York *Tribune,* Dec. 22, 1896.

15 *Cigar Makers Official Journal,* XXII (Jan., 1897), 5–7; 54 Cong., 2 sess., *Congressional Record,* 130, 322, 323, 484, 522, 1088, 1419, 1638.

CHAPTER VIII · CLEVELAND

1 *Foreign Relations, 1895,* 1177–1184; *Literary Digest,* X (March 23, 1895), 604–5, (April 6, 1895), 661–3; New York *Herald,* March 22, 1895; Hengelmüller to Goluchowski, April 16, 1895, *Vereinigten Staaten,* XXXV (Aus.).

2 *Foreign Relations, 1896,* 711–745; Olney to de Lôme, May 8, 1896, enclosed in de Lôme to Tetuán, May 9, 1896, Legajo 2414 (Sp.); Rockhill to Taylor, Sept. 11, 1896, *Spain: Dispatches,* CXXX (U.S.).

3 H. Taylor to Olney, Aug. 11, 1896, Olney Papers; Tetuán to Cánovas, Aug. 11, 1896, Legajo 2416 (Sp.). See Orestes Ferrara, *The Last Spanish War* (New York, 1937), 14–78.

4 New York *World,* Oct. 26, 1895.

5 See French E. Chadwick, *The Relations of the United States and Spain: Diplomacy* (New York, 1909), chapters 20, 22–23.

6 Olney to Cleveland, Sept. 25, 1895, Cleveland Papers.

7 *Ibid.;* Himely to Olney, Nov. 18, 1895, Olney Papers.

8 Nevins, *Cleveland Letters,* 410–412; Olney to Cleveland, Oct. 8, 1895, April 9, 1896, Cleveland Papers; Cleveland to Olney, April 7, 9, 1896,

Olney Papers; de Lôme to Tetuán, March 20, 1896, Legajo 2416 (Sp.); Festus Summers (ed.), *The Cabinet Diary of William L. Wilson* (Chapel Hill, 1957), 35–36, 37; Boston *Herald,* April 14, 1896; New York *Evening Post,* April 15, 1896; Olney to Lee, June 29, 1896, *Consular Letters: Habana* (U.S.); Nevins, *Cleveland Letters,* 448; Lee to Olney, July 22, 1896, Olney Papers.

9 Akers to Olney, May 5, 13, 1896, *ibid.;* Olney to Cleveland, May 11, 1896, Cleveland Papers; *Foreign Relations, 1896,* xxix–xxxiv, lxx–lxxvi.

10 Adee to Olney, July 10, 1895, Olney Papers; memorandum on United States recognition policy, n.d. [1895?], *ibid.;* Olney to Miss Straw, Dec. 24, 1896, *ibid.;* Chicago *Tribune,* Nov. 9, 10, 1896; Washington *Post,* Dec. 19, 20, 1896; Olney to Breckenridge, Jan. 25, 1897, Olney Papers.

11 *Correspondencia diplomática de la delegación cubana,* V, 31–32; Cleveland to Olney, July 16, 1896, Nevins, *Cleveland Letters,* 448–449; Nevins, *Cleveland,* 717.

12 *Foreign Relations, 1896,* xxxii; *Cleveland Letters,* 448–449.

13 Legajo 2416 (Sp.); *Foreign Relations, 1897,* 540–548.

14 Olney to Lee, Jan. 18, 1897, Olney Papers; Lee to Olney, Jan. 30, Feb. 10, 1897, *ibid.;* de Lôme to Tetuán, Feb. 12, 1897, Legajo 2416 (Sp.).

CHAPTER IX · CÁNOVAS

1 See Ramiro Guerra y Sanchez *et al., Historia de la Nación Cubana* (10 vols.; Havana, 1952), especially vol. VI, books 1–3 and Ramon Infiesta, *Historia constitucional de Cuba* (2d. ed.; Havana, 1951).

2 The best biography of Martí is Jorge Mañach, *Martí, Apostle of Freedom* (English translation; New York, 1950).

3 Sagasta is quoted in Fernando Soldevilla's annual publication, *El Año Político,* Feb. 25, 1895. References to statements in the Cortes are to *Diario de las sesiones del Congreso de los Diputados.*

4 *Año Político,* March 25, 1895; Madrid *Liberal,* March 25, 1895; Gabriel Maura Gamazo, *Historia crítica del reinado de Don Alfonso XIII durante su menoridad bajo la regencia de su madre Doña María Christina de Austria* (2 vols.; Barcelona, n.d.), II, 211–212.

5 Antonio Ramos-Oliveira, *Politics, Economics and Men of Modern Spain* (London, 1946), 109–110; Francisco de Reynoso, *The Reminiscences of a Spanish Diplomat* (London, 1933), 46–47. By far the best work on Cánovas is Melchor Fernández Almagro, *Cánovas, su vida y su política* (Madrid, 1951), but see also Charles Benoist, *Cánovas del Castillo: La restauration rénovatrice* (Paris, 1930); Marqués de Lema, *Cánovas, el hombre de estado* (Madrid, 1931); Leonor Meléndez Meléndez, *Cánovas y la política exterior española* (Madrid, 1944); Conde de Vallellano, *Antonio Cánovas del Cas-*

tillo (Madrid, 1946); and José M. García Escudero, *De Cánovas a la República* (Madrid, 1951), 77–133.

6 Martínez Campos to Cánovas, July 25, 1895, Carlos O'Donnell y Abreu, duque de Tetuán, *Apuntes del ex-Ministro de Estado* (2 vols.; Madrid, 1902), II, 114.

7 Dubsky to Goluchowski, Feb. 19, 1896, *Spanien,* LV (Aus.).

8 *Año Político,* June 15, 1895, Jan. 28, 1896; Valeriano Weyler, *Mi mando en Cuba* (5 vols.; Madrid, 1910), contains all Weyler's decrees and many of his reports.

9 Fernández Almagro, *Cánovas,* 566–569; see Antonio María de Cascajares y Azara, *La organización de los católicos españoles* (Valladolid, 1898).

10 Madrid *El Tiempo,* March 6, April 4, 1896; *Año Político,* March 27, 1896; Taylor to Olney, April 6, 1896, Olney Papers; Tetuán to de Lôme, April 11, 1896, Legajo 2417 (Sp.).

11 Madrid *Imparcial,* Nov. 24, 1896; Wolff to Salisbury, Dec. 3, 1896, F.O. 72/2006 (Br.); Reverseaux to Hanotaux, Jan. 3, April 28, 1897, *Espagne: Cuba,* II (Fr.).

12 Hanotaux to Reverseaux, Feb. 3, 1897, *ibid.; Año Político,* Oct. 19, 1896, Jan. 13, March 27, 1897. See Gaston Routier, *L'Espagne en 1897* (Paris, 1897), 103–110.

13 Dubsky to Goluchowski, May 27, 1896, *Spanien,* LV (Aus.); Wolff to Salisbury, Feb. 28, 1896, F.O. 72/2024 (Br.); Reverseaux to Hanotaux, March 6, 1896, *Espagne: Cuba,* III (Fr.); Castelar to Adolfo Calzado, March 19, 1896, *Correspondencia de Emilio Castelar, 1868–1898* (Madrid, 1908), 335–336; María Cristina to Princess Louis Ferdinand of Bavaria, March 17, 1897, Adalbert von Bayern, *Vier Revolutionen und einiges dazwischen* (Munich, 1932), 197–198.

14 Renzis to Caetani, April 24, April 29, May 2, 1896, Italy, Ministry of Foreign Affairs, Commission for the Publication of Diplomatic Documents, *I Documenti Diplomatici Italiani, Terza Serie, 1896–1907* (in progress; Rome, 1953—), I, Nos. 85, 90, 93; Nigra to Caetani, May 21, 1896, *ibid.,* No. 100; Wolff to Salisbury, April 20, June 18, June 20, 1896, F.O. 72/2006 (Br.); Mandas to Tetuán, May 19, 1896, Legajo 2416 (Sp.). See Jerónimo Becker, *Historia de las relaciones exteriores de España* (3 vols.; Madrid, 1924–1926), III, 691–704, Hans Hallmann, *Spanien und die französisch-englische Mittelmeer-Rivalität, 1898–1907* (Stuttgart, 1937), 1–5, and F. G. Bruguera, *Histoire contemporaine de l'Espagne* (Paris, 1953), 304–305.

15 Wolff to Salisbury, March 2, 1896, F.O. 72/2024 (Br.); Reverseaux to Hanotaux, March 6, 1896, *Espagne: Cuba,* III (Fr.); Hanotaux to Montebello, July 24, 1896 (reporting a conversation with Schevich, the Russian minister to Spain), *ibid.;* Tetuán to Villagonzalo, July 28, 1896, Villagonzalo to Tetuán, July 30, 1896, Tetuán to Cánovas, Aug. 11, 1896, Benomar to Tetuán, Aug. 16, 1896 (two dispatches), Hoyos to Tetuán, Aug. 17, 1896, Villagonzalo to Tetuán, Aug. 17, 1896, Rascón to Tetuán,

Aug. 17, 1896, Tetuán to ministers in London, Paris, Berlin, Rome, Vienna, St. Petersburg, and Washington, Oct. 10, 1896, Legajo 2416 (Sp.); Taylor to Olney, Aug. 11, 1896, Olney Papers. See Tetuán, *Apuntes,* I, 296–297; and Ferrara, *Last Spanish War,* 14–78.

16 Madrid *Heraldo,* May 21, 1897; Castelar to Adolfo Calzado, May 25, 1897, Castelar, *Correspondencia,* 352; Fernández Almagro, *Cánovas,* 249–250, 615–617, 708–709; Marqués de Lema, *Mis recuerdos (1880– 1901)* (Madrid, 1930), 206, 208; Antonio M. Fabié, *Mi gestión ministerial respecto a . . . Cuba* (Madrid, 1898), 353.

CHAPTER X • McKINLEY

1 Julia B. Foraker, *I Would Live It Again* (New York, 1932), 259. See extracts from Cortelyou's diary in Charles S. Olcott, *William McKinley* (2 vols.; Boston, 1916), especially II, 52–56, and in Margaret Leech, *In the Days of McKinley* (New York, 1959); see also Charles G. Dawes, *A Journal of the McKinley Years* (Chicago, 1950). Miss Leech's volume gives by far the best and most sympathetic account of McKinley's life.

2 Olcott, *McKinley,* I, 289.

3 See Gage, *Reminiscences* (New York, 1930); John D. Long, *The New American Navy* (2 vols.; New York, 1903); Bernard Mayo, *America of Yesterday As Reflected in the Journal of John Davis Long* (Boston, 1923); Margaret Long (ed.), *The Journal of John D. Long* (Rindge, New Hampshire, 1956); and Gardner Weld Allen (ed.), *Papers of John Davis Long* (Boston, 1939).

4 Vagts, II, 1259–1260; Nevins, *Cleveland,* 577–578; Nathaniel W. Stephenson, *Nelson W. Aldrich* (New York, 1930), 111–120; Stephen Gwynn (ed.), *The Letters and Friendships of Sir Cecil Spring-Rice* (2 vols.; New York, 1929), I, 156.

5 New York *Herald,* Jan. 6, 1897; Grosvenor to Chandler, Feb. 14, 1897, Chandler Papers.

6 See 55 Cong., 2 sess., *House Document No. 405,* "Condition of Affairs in Cuba."

7 Lodge to Theodore Roosevelt, Dec. 2, 1896, *Lodge-Roosevelt Correspondence,* I, 240; F. B. Loomis to Reid, Dec. 8, 1896, Reid Papers.

8 Memo by J. J. McCook, n.d. [Dec., 1896?], J. H. Wilson Papers.

9 London *Times,* Jan. 7, 1897; New York *Tribune,* Jan. 9, 1897; *Novoe Vremya,* quoted in London *Morning Post,* June 24, 1897; see *Literary Digest,* XV (July 24, 1897), 381.

10 New York *Herald,* March 17, May 21, 1897; Quesada to Palma, Jan. 14, July 19, 1897, *Correspondencia diplomática de la delegación cubana,* V, 88, 119.

11 New York *Tribune,* May 22, 1897.

12 De Lôme to Tetuán, June 8, 1897, Legajo 2416 (Sp.); Sherman to Taylor, June 26, 1897, *Foreign Relations, 1897,* 507–508; New York *Tribune,* July 15, 1897.

13 Garraty, *Lodge,* 177–179; Tyler Dennett, *John Hay: From Poetry to Politics* (New York, 1933), 179; Allan Nevins, *Henry White* (New York, 1930), 120; Joseph L. Bristow, *Fraud and Politics at the Turn of the Century* (New York, 1952), 64–65.

14 Pauncefote to Salisbury, March 19, 1897, Salisbury Papers.

15 See Pratt, *Expansionists of 1898,* 215–222, and Thomas A. Bailey, "Japan's Protest Against the Annexation of Hawaii," *Journal of Modern History,* III (Jan., 1931), 46–61; *Letters of Theodore Roosevelt,* I, 638.

16 Palma to Samuel L. Janney, June 5, 1897, *Correspondencia diplomática de la delegación cubana,* I, 122; memo by Armand Ruiz, Sept. 12, 1897, *Espagne: Cuba,* III (Fr.).

17 Lee to Sherman, April 20, 1897, *Consular Letters: Habana* (U.S.).

18 New York *Tribune,* May 4, June 4, 18, 1897; Philip C. Jessup, *Elihu Root* (2 vols.; New York, 1938), I, 196.

19 *Foreign Relations, 1898,* pp. 558–561; Woodford to McKinley, Aug. 19, Sept. 3, 6, 22, 24, Oct. 3, 17, 1897, *Spain: Dispatches,* CXXXIA (U.S.); Woodford to Sherman, Oct. 4, 5, 1897, *Foreign Relations, 1898,* 573–579.

20 Walter Millis, *The Martial Spirit* (New York, 1931), 76–77. But the Spanish Governor General himself estimated deaths at around 400,000, which was the figure popularly credited in the United States. See Conde de Romanones, *Sagasta o El Político* (Bilbao, 1930), 117–119.

21 Vagts, II, 1708–1724.

22 Chicago *Tribune,* July 14, 1897.

CHAPTER XI • HYSTERIA

1 55 Cong., 1 sess., *Congressional Record,* 615, 645, 656–662, 684–694, 762–763, 881–882, 946–949, 995–999, 1089–1101, 1130–1139, 1148–1154, 1178–1186.

2 Chicago *Tribune,* July 6, Aug. 19, 1897; Philadelphia *North American,* July 13, Aug. 11, 1897; New York *Herald,* Dec. 3, 4, 6, 1897.

3 Quesada to Palma, Jan. 16, 1898, *Correspondencia diplomática de la delegación cubana,* V, 120, 122–123, 192–198.

4 New York *Herald,* Dec. 24, 25, 1897; Jan. 5, 1898; *Foreign Relations, 1898,* 656.

5 55 Cong., 2 sess., *House Document No. 405,* 19–20; de Lôme to Gullón, Jan. 16, 1898, Legajo 2416 (Sp.).

6 Quesada to Palma, Jan. 21, 1898, *Correspondencia diplomática de la delegación cubana,* V, 122.

7 Day to Lee, June 9, Dec. 2, 1897, Jan. 14, 24, 1898, *Consular Instructions* (U.S.); Mayo, *America of Yesterday,* 153–155; de Lôme to Gullón,

Jan. 24, 1898, Legajo 2416 (Sp.); New York *Staatszeitung,* Jan. 14, 1898; New York *Evening Post,* Jan. 15, 1898.

8 *Foreign Relations, 1898,* 1007–1022.

9 Lodge to White, Jan. 31, 1898, Private Papers of Henry White, Library of Congress; Albert Leavens to Long, Feb. 12, 1898, Private Papers of John D. Long, Massachusetts Historical Society; New York *Herald,* Feb. 13, 1898.

10 Cleveland *Plain Dealer,* Feb. 12, 1898.

11 John E. Weems, *The Fate of the Maine* (New York, 1958), is the most recent account.

12 Reid to Seckendorff, Feb. 17, 1898, Reid Papers; Herrick to McKinley, Feb. 28, 1898, Manderson to McKinley, Feb. 28, 1898, McKinley Papers. Except as otherwise noted, the details in these pages come from the Boston *Herald* and *Evening Transcript,* New York *Herald, Journal of Commerce, Staatszeitung,* and *Tribune,* Brooklyn *Eagle, Wall Street Journal,* Philadelphia *North American* and *Times,* Newark *Advertiser,* Cleveland *Plain-Dealer,* Washington *Post,* Chicago *Standard, Times-Herald,* and *Tribune,* Omaha *World Herald,* St. Louis *Republic,* Atlanta *Constitution,* Mobile *Register,* New Orleans *Times-Democrat,* Denver *Rocky Mountain News,* Los Angeles *Times,* San Francisco *Examiner,* and Portland *Morning Tribune,* for Feb. 16–April 2, 1898, and from the *Literary Digest,* XVI (March 5, 1898), 277–278, (March 26, 1898), 361–363, the *Religious Review of Reviews,* I (April, 1898), 155–162, 183, 204, and *The Converted Catholic,* XV (March, 1898), 68, 72.

13 Cambon to Hanotaux, March 1, 1898, *Espagne: Cuba,* V (Fr.).

14 Hurst to McKinley, March 25, 1898, McKinley Papers.

15 March 2, 4, Long Papers.

16 William Allen Swain to Chandler, March 31, 1898, Chandler Papers; Cambon to Hanotaux, April 1, 1898, *Espagne: Cuba,* VI (Fr.).

17 March 8, 1898, Reid Papers.

18 Lodge to McKinley, March 21, 1898, McKinley Papers; Spooner to Herbert B. Turner, April 2, 1898, Spooner Papers.

CHAPTER XII • ULTIMATA

1 Olcott, *McKinley,* II, 12–13; Mayo, *America of Yesterday,* 216.

2 Polo de Bernabé to Gullón, March 3, 1898, Legajo 2417 (Sp.).

3 L. White Busbey, *Uncle Joe Cannon: The Story of a Pioneer American* (New York, 1927), 186–187; New York *World,* March 11, 1898; Boston *Evening Transcript,* March 8, 1898; *Journal of John D. Long,* 172.

4 H. N. Howland to J. R. Young, Feb. 22, 1898, McKinley Papers; Herrick to McKinley, Feb. 28, 1898, *ibid.;* Washington *Post,* March 7, 1898; Reid to McKinley, March 8, 1898, McKinley Papers; Boston *Evening Tran-*

script, March 10, 12, 1898; Cambon to Hanotaux, March 11, 15, 1898, *Espagne: Cuba*, V (Fr.); New York *Herald*, March 12, 1898; Woodford to McKinley, March 19, 1898, *Foreign Relations, 1898*, 693; Gage, *Memoirs*, 126.

5 Straus to McKinley, March 12, 1898, McKinley Papers; Straus diary, March 19, 1898, Private Papers of Oscar S. Straus, Library of Congress; *Correspondencia diplomática de la delegación cubana*, V, 194–196.

6 McKinley to Day, April 26, 1898, McKinley Papers; McCook to J. H. Wilson, March 26, 1898, J. H. Wilson Papers.

7 Chandler Papers.

8 *Foreign Relations, 1898*, 721.

9 W. C. Reick to J. R. Young, March 25, 1898, McKinley Papers; Reid to Nicholson, March 30, 1898, Reid Papers; Root to T. Roosevelt, Roosevelt Papers, Library of Congress.

10 April 5, 1898, Chandler Papers; cf. Elkins to Reid, April 22, 1898, Reid Papers.

11 Memorandum dated April 11, 1898, Chandler Papers; *Foreign Relations, 1898*, 711–712.

12 *Ibid.*, 704, 713, 733.

13 Lee to Day, April 4, 1898, McKinley Papers; Chandler to Dana, April 7, 1898, Chandler Papers; Olcott, *McKinley*, II, 29.

14 *Foreign Relations, 1898*, 732–733; James H. Moynihan, *The Life of Archbishop Ireland* (New York, 1953), 164.

15 Deym to Goluchowski, April 5, 1898, *Spanien*, LXVIII (Aus.); Hengelmüller to Goluchowski, March 31, April 1, 5, 6, 1898, *ibid.*

16 Cambon to Hanotaux, April 4, 1898, *Espagne: Cuba*, VI (Fr.); Pauncefote to Salisbury, April 8, 1898, F.O. 5/2517 (Br.).

17 *Foreign Relations, 1898*, 740–741.

18 *Ibid.*, 744–747.

19 Cambon to Hanotaux, April 10, 1898, *Espagne: Cuba*, VI (Fr.); Patenôtre to Hanotaux, March 26, 1898, *ibid.*, V; Gullón to Merry del Val, April 3, 1898, Legajo 2417 (Sp.); Polo to Gullón, April 12, 1898, *ibid.*; *Foreign Relations, 1898*, 747–749.

20 Cambon to Hanotaux, April 11, 12, 1898, *Espagne: Cuba*, VI (Fr.).

21 *Ibid.*; Chandler to Dana, April 13, 1898, Chandler Papers.

22 *Foreign Relations, 1898*, 761–763; Cambon to Hanotaux, April 14, 15, 1898, *Espagne: Cuba*, VI (Fr.).

23 Olcott, *McKinley*, II, 52.

CHAPTER XIII · SPAIN ACCEPTS WAR

1 Madrid *Liberal*, Aug. 9, 17–18, 29–30, Oct. 1–3, 1896; Alvaro Figueroa y Torres, Conde de Romanones, *Sagasta o El Político* (Bilbao, 1930), 115;

Reverseaux to Hanotaux, Oct. 12, 1897, *Espagne: Cuba,* III (Fr.); Reverseaux to Hanotaux, Oct. 13, 1897, *ibid.* On Sagasta, besides Romanones's sensitive and literate portrait, see Juan del Nido y Segalvera, *Historia política y parlamentaria del . . . Sr. D. Práxedes Mateo Sagasta* (Madrid, 1915), which is a compilation of speeches, and Natalio Rivas, *Sagasta* (Madrid, 1946). On other Liberal leaders see Luis Antón del Olmet and Arturo Garcia Carraffa, *Moret* (Madrid, 1913); Antonio González Casada, *Segismundo Moret* (Madrid, 1947); Antonio de Goiocoechia, *Maura* (Madrid, 1948); Diego Sevilla Andrés, *Maura: la revolución desde arriba* (Barcelona, 1953) and *Canalejas* (Barcelona, 1956); José Francos Rodríguez, *La vida de Canalejas* (Madrid, 1918); and Romanones, *Notas de una vida* (Madrid, 1928).

2 Gullón to de Lôme, Oct. 17, Nov. 6, 30, Dec. 8, 1897, Legajo 2417 (Sp.); de Lôme to Gullón, Dec. 6, 1897 (text of McKinley's message with marginal notations), *ibid.;* Gullón to León y Castillo, Dec. 7, 1897, *ibid.;* Madrid *Liberal,* Dec. 6, 1897.

3 Woodford to Sherman, Nov. 13, 1897, *Foreign Relations, 1898,* 600–602; Woodford to Sherman, Jan. 24, Feb. 3, Feb. 15, 1898, *Spain: Dispatches,* CXXXIII (U.S.); Woodford to McKinley, Feb. 15, 1898, *ibid.,* CXXXIA.

4 Woodford to McKinley, Jan. 17, 1898, *Spain: Dispatches,* CXXXIA (U.S.).

5 Romanones, *Sagasta,* 117–119.

6 *Año Político,* Oct. 26, 1895; Reverseaux to Hanotaux, Nov. 9, 1897, *Espagne: Cuba,* III (Fr.).

7 Dubsky to Goluchowski, Dec. 2, 1897, *Spanien,* LV (Aus.).

8 Pascual Cervera y Topete, *The Spanish-American War* (Washington, D.C., 1899), 26–27. This is a translation of *Guerra Hispano-Americana: Colección de documentos referentes a la escaudra de operaciones de las Antillas* (Madrid, 1899).

9 Reverseaux to Hanotaux, Oct. 9, 10, 13, Dec. 6, 23, 24, 1897, *Espagne: Cuba,* III (Fr.); Patenôtre to Hanotaux, Dec. 23, 1897, *ibid.;* memoranda by Hanotaux on conversations with León y Castillo, Dec. 17, 1897, Jan. 5, 1898, *ibid.;* Wolff to Salisbury, Oct. 11, 21, 1897, F.O. 72/2056 (Br.); Moret to Wolff, Nov. 28, 1897, Salisbury Papers; Dubsky to Goluchowski, Dec. 2, 1897, *Spanien,* LV (Aus.).

10 Woodford to McKinley, March 9, 1898, *Spain: Dispatches,* CXXXIA (U.S.); *Año Político,* Feb. 26, March 5, April 1, 1898; Patenôtre to Hanotaux, March 6, 1898, *Espagne: Cuba,* IV (Fr.).

11 Patenôtre to Hanotaux, March 16, 28, 1898, *ibid.;* Woodford to McKinley, March 17, 18, 1898, *Spain: Dispatches,* CXXXIA (U.S.); Lema, *Mis recuerdos,* 240.

12 Polo de Bernabé to Gullón, March 3, 1898, Legajo 2417 (Sp.); Woodford to McKinley, March 19, 1898, *Foreign Relations, 1898,* 693.

13 Woodford to McKinley, March 2, 17, 1898, *Spain: Dispatches,* CXXXIA (U.S.); Woodford to McKinley, March 18, 24, 1898, *Foreign Relations, 1898,* 688–694, 695; Woodford to Sherman, March 25, 1898, *ibid.,* 698–701.

14 Woodford to McKinley, March 29, 31, 1898, ibid., 718–721, 727.

15 Madrid *Heraldo*, March 31, April 1, 1898; Dubsky to Goluchowski, *Spanien*, LXVIII (Aus.); Patenôtre to Hanotaux, March 30, 1898, *Espagne: Cuba*, IV (Fr.).

16 Reverseaux to Hanotaux, Dec. 6, 1897, *ibid.*, III.

17 León y Castillo, *Mis tiempos* (2 vols.; Madrid, 1921), II, 103–105; Dubsky to Goluchowski, March 11, 16, 25, 1898, *Spanien*, LXVIII (Aus.).

18 Memorandum by Hanotaux, March 15, 1898, *Espagne: Cuba*, IV (Fr.); Radowitz to Bülow, March 19, 1898, Vagts, II, 1291; Gullón to León y Castillo, March 24, 1898, Legajo 2417 (Sp.); León y Castillo to Gullón, March 25, 1898, *ibid.;* Villagonzalo to Gullón, March 27, 1898 (two dispatches), *ibid.*

19 León y Castillo to Gullón, March 15, 19, 25, 30, 1898, *ibid.;* María Cristina to Victoria, March 17, 1898, *Letters of Queen Victoria: Third Series,* III, 236.

20 Gullón to Rascón, April 1, 1898, Legajo 2417 (Sp.); Mendez Vigo to Gullón, March 28, 29 (four dispatches), 1898, *ibid.;* Gullón to Mendez Vigo, March 24, 1898, *ibid.*

21 Merry del Val to Gullón, March 25, April 2, 1898, *ibid.;* see below chapter 16. See also Josef Schmidlin, *Papstgeschichte der neuesten Zeit*, vol. II (Munich, 1934), 441–448.

22 Gullón to León y Castillo, March 30, 1898, Legajo 2417 (Sp.); Dubsky to Goluchowski, April 2, 3, 1898, *Spanien*, LXVIII (Aus.); *Año Político*, April 4, 1898; Madrid *Nacional*, April 4, 1898.

23 Madrid *Imparcial*, April 6, 1898; *Correspondencia Militar*, March 17, 26, 1898; *Correo Militar*, March 26, 1898, quoting *Ejército Español.*

24 Radowitz to Bülow, quoted in Bülow to Otto von Bülow, March 27, 1898, *Grosse Politik*, XV, No. 4128; Dubsky to Goluchowski, March 30, April 2, 3, 4, 1898, *Spanien*, LXVIII (Aus.); Gullón to Merry del Val, April 4, 1898, Legajo 2417 (Sp.); Cervera, *Letters*, 33–42, and see Victor María Concas y Palau, *La escaudra del almirante Cervera* (Madrid, 1899); Madrid *Nacional*, April 4, 1898.

25 Merry del Val to Gullón, April 4, 6, 1898, Legajo 2417 (Sp.); Dubsky to Goluchowski, April 5, 1898, *Spanien*, LXIX (Aus.); see Moynihan, *Ireland*, 166–167.

26 Woodford to Day, April 6, 1898, *Foreign Relations, 1898,* 743; Gullón to Polo, April 7, 1898, Legajo 2417 (Sp.).

27 Madrid *Heraldo*, April 7, 1898; Dubsky to Goluchowski, April 9, 1898, *Spanien*, LXIX (Aus.); Patenôtre to Hanotaux, April 9, 1898, *Espagne: Cuba*, V (Fr.).

28 Polo to Gullón, April 7, 1898 (two dispatches), Legajo 2417 (Sp.); Merry del Val to Gullón, April 8, 9, 1898, *ibid.*

29 Rascón to Gullón, April 9, 1898, *ibid.;* Mendez Vigo to Gullón, April 5, 1898, *ibid.;* memorandum by Bülow, April 5, 1898; *Grosse Politik*, XV, No. 4136.

30 Madrid *El Día,* April 12, 1898; Dubsky to Goluchowski, April 15, 1898, *Spanien,* LXIX (Aus.); Madrid *Liberal,* April 12, 17, 1898.

31 *Correspondencia Militar,* April 12, 16, 1898; *Correo Militar,* April 12, 1898; Madrid *El Día,* April 12, 1898; Madrid *Nacional,* April 13, 14, 1898; Madrid *Heraldo,* April 13, 14, 1898; Madrid *Tiempo,* April 13, 1898; Madrid *Progreso,* April 16, 1898; Madrid *Liberal,* April 18, 1898.

32 Polo to Gullón, April 10 (three dispatches), 11, 12, 15, 1898, Legajo 2417 (Sp.); Gullón circular, April 21, 1898, *ibid.*

33 Moret to Blanco, April 20, 1898, Legajo 2423 (Sp.); Dubsky to Goluchowski, April 21, 1898, *Spanien,* LXIX (Aus.).

CHAPTER XIV • THE VIEW FROM EUROPE

1 Jane Louise Mesick, *The English Traveller in America, 1785–1835* (New York, 1922); Max Berger, *The British Traveller in America, 1836–1860* (New York, 1943); Philip Motley Palmer, *German Works on America, 1492–1800,* in University of California *Publications in Modern Philology,* vol. 36, No. 10 (Berkeley, 1952); Hildegard Meyer, *Nord-Amerika im Urteil des deutschen Schrifttums bis zur Mitte des 19. Jahrhunderts* (Hamburg, 1929); Frank Monaghan, *French Travellers in the United States, 1765–1932: A Bibliography* (New York, 1933). See also Avrahm Yarmolinsky, *Russian Americana, Sixteenth to Eighteenth Centuries* (New York, 1943).

2 Alexander von Matlekovits, *Die Zollpolitik der österreichisch-ungarischen Monarchie und des deutschen Reiches seit 1868* (Leipzig, 1891), 48–49, 83–85, 530–536, 818; Vagts, I, 1–425; A. von Totis, *Die wirtschaftlichen Verhältnisse der Vereinigten Staaten in ihrer Rückwirkung auf diejenigen Europas* (Berlin, 1881), 40.

3 André Churillon, "Les États-Unis et la vie américain," *Revue des deux mondes,* CX (April 1, 1892), 554–585; Paul de Rousiers, *American Life* (English translation: New York, 1892); Léon Vacher, *Le homestead aux États-Unis* (Paris, 1895); Louis Paul-Dubois, *Les chemins de fer aux États-Unis* (Paris, 1895) and "Les monopoles industriels aux États-Unis," *Revue des deux mondes,* CXXXIX (Feb. 1, 1897), 634–658; Count d'Haussonville, "Le travail des femmes aux États-Unis et en Angleterre," *ibid.,* CXII (July 1, 1892), 64–88; Isidore Finance, *Les syndicats ouvriers aux États-Unis* (Paris, 1895); Pierre de Coubertin, *Universités transatlantiques* (Paris, 1890); O. Laurent, *Les universités des deux mondes* (Paris, 1896).

4 Émile Levasseur, *L'agriculture aux États-Unis* (Paris, 1894), *The American Workman* (English translation; Baltimore, 1900), and *The Concentration of Industry and Machinery in the United States* (English translation; Philadelphia, 1897); Paul Leroy-Beaulieu, "The Conditions for American Commercial and Financial Supremacy," *Forum,* XX (Dec., 1895), 385–400.

On the sudden increase in the teaching of American subjects in French universities, see Sigmund Skard, *American Studies in Europe* (2 vols.; Philadelphia, 1958), I, 143–150

5 Francesco Carega de Murice, *Saggio di economia rurale americana applicata all' Italia* (Florence, 1873); Carlo Gardini, *Gli Stati Uniti* (2 vols.; Bologna, 1887); Dario Papa and Ferdinando Fontana, *New-York* (Milan, 1884); Egisto Rossi, *Gli Stati Uniti e la concurrenza americana* (Florence, 1884), 751. See also Giuseppe Dassi, *Philadelphia and Rome* (Milan, 1876), Giuseppe Sormani, *Eco d'America* (Milan, 1888), Guglielmo Godio, *L'America nei suoi primi fattori* (Florence, 1893), Ugo Rabbeno, *Protezionismo americano* (Milan, 1893), and Andrew J. Torrielli, *Italian Opinion on America as Revealed by Italian Travellers, 1850–1900* (Cambridge, Mass., 1941). For the earlier period, see Joseph Rossi, *The Image of America in Mazzini's Writings* (Madison, Wis., 1954).

6 Viscomte de Meaux, *L'Eglise Catholique et la liberté aux États-Unis* (2 vols.; Paris, 1893); Paul Bourget, *Outre-mer* (Paris, 1894); Max Leclerc, *Choses d'Amérique: les crises économiques et religieuse aux États-Unis* (Paris, 1895); Klein, *L'Eglise et le siècle* (Paris, 1894) and (ed.) *Vie de père Hecker* (Paris, 1897). See Albert Houtin, *L'Américanisme* (Paris, 1904); Moynihan, *Ireland*, chapter 6; and especially Thomas T. McAvoy, *The Great Crisis in American Catholic History, 1895–1900* (Chicago, 1957).

7 McAvoy, *The Great Crisis,* 189; see Colman J. Barry, *The Catholic Church and the German-Americans* (Milwaukee, 1953).

8 Eckart Kehr, *Schlachtflottenbau-und Parteipolitik, 1894–1901* (Berlin, 1930); Gustav Oldenhage, *Die deutsche Flottenvorlage und die öffentliche Meinung* (Gutersloh, 1935); Dietrich Schäfer, *Deutschland zur See: eine historisch-politische Betrachtung* (Jena, 1897), 45; Ernst von Halle, *Die Bedeutung des Seeverkehrs für Deutschland* (Leipzig, 1898); see Vagts, II, 1714 ff.; *Literary Digest,* XII (Jan. 4, 1896), 292–293, XIV (Feb, 27, 1897), 531–532, XV (Aug. 21, 1897), 487–488, (Dec. 24, 1897), 1042–1043; *Das Echo,* XV (March 12, 1896), 434, XXXIII (Jan. 6, 1898), 9–10; Vienna *Neue Freie Presse,* July 8, 23, Sept. 15, Nov. 3, 4, 1897.

9 LVII (1898), No. 18, 251–254.

10 Louis Perlman, *Russian Literature and the Business Man* (New York, 1937), 114–150.

11 *Russkii Vestnik',* CCXLII (Jan., 1896), 322–325.

12 See David Hecht, *Russian Radicals Look to America, 1825–1894* (Cambridge, Mass., 1947), and Max M. Laserson, *The American Impact on Russia, 1784–1917* (New York, 1950); *Russkii Vestnik',* CCLII (Dec., 1897), 451–458; *Novoe Vremya* quoted in London *Morning Post,* June 25, 1897. For an example of such comment as did appear in liberal journals, see *Russkaya Mysl',* XVII (1896), No. 3, 201, which dismisses the Cuban agitation as a passing fit of chauvinism from which the United States will recover as soon as it has added another star to the Stars and Stripes.

13 Merle Curti, "The Reputation of America Overseas, 1776–1860," in *Prob-*

ing Our Past (New York, 1955), 193; Michael Pupin, *From Immigrant to Inventor* (New York, 1922), 9–10, 15; Baron Rosen, *Forty Years of Diplomacy* (2 vols.; London, 1922), I, 67; "Jetzt wohin?" from *Romanzero* in the translation by Edgar Alfred Bowring, *The Poems of Heine* (London, 1887), 450–451.

14 Demolins (2nd ed.; Paris, 1897); Auguste Carlier, *La république américaine* (4 vols.; Paris, 1890); Henri Gaullier, *Études américaines* (Paris, 1891); Adolphe de Chambrun, *Le pouvoir exécutif aux États-Unis* (Paris, 1896); Émile de Laveleye, *Le gouvernement dans la démocratie* (2 vols.; Paris, 1896); Raoul de la Grasserie, *L'état federatif* (Paris, 1897); Federigo Garlanda, *La nuova democrazia americana* (Rome, 1891); Francesco Racioppi, *Nuovi limiti e freni nelle istituzione politiche americane* (Milan, 1894); Stepan Fortunatov, *Politicheskaya Ucheniya v Soedinionnykh Shtatakh* (Moscow, 1879); Boris Chicherin', *Kurs' gosudarstvennoi nauki* (Moscow, 1894), *O narodom' predstavitel'stvoe* (2nd ed.; Moscow, 1899), and *Politicheskie mysliteli drevnyago i novago mira* (2 vols.; Moscow, 1897). See Laserson, *American Impact on Russia,* 372–387.

15 Coubertin, *Universités transatlantiques,* 210; Lavisse, "Brevets et jeunes filles," *Revue de Paris,* VI (Nov., 1895), 218; Blouet, *A Frenchman in America* (New York, 1891), 93; cf. Adolf Schaffmeyer, "Die Amerikanerin," *Westermanns Illustrierte Monatshefte,* LXXII (May, 1892), 194–200.

16 Harold Jantz, "Amerika im deutschen Dichten und Denken," in Wolfgang Stammler (ed.), *Deutsche Phiiologie im Aufriss,* No. 25 (revised edition: Berlin, 1960), 310–371; cf. Heinrich Spiero, *Geschichte des deutschen Romans* (Berlin, 1950), 366–377; Spielhagen, *Ein neuer Pharao* (Leipzig, 1892), especially 330–332. See Lida von Krokow, "American Characters in German Novels," *Atlantic Monthly,* LXVIII (Dec., 1891), 824–837; Julius Goebel, "Amerika in der deutschen Dichtung," in Wilhelm Braune *et al., Forschungen zur deutschen Philologie: Festgabe für Rudolf Hildebrand* (Leipzig, 1894), 102–127; H. H. Boyesen, "America in European Literature," in *Literary and Social Silhouettes* (New York, 1894), 117–130; Andrew de Ternant, "English and Americans in French Fiction," *Gentleman's Magazine,* LVII (Sept., 1896), 287–303; Constantin Breffka, *Amerika in der deutschen Literatur* (Cologne, 1917); Lawrence Marsden Price, *English-German Literary Influences,* in University of California *Publications in Modern Philology,* vol. 9 (Berkeley, 1920), pp. 555–576, and *The Reception of English Literature in Germany* (Berkeley, 1932), 423–435; Hildegard Meyer, *Nordamerika im Urteil des deutschen Schrifttums bis zur Mitte des 19. Jahrhunderts* (Hamburg, 1929); Carl Wittke, "The American Theme in Continental Literatures," *Mississippi Valley Historical Review,* XXVIII (June, 1941), 3–26; Cyrille Arnavon, *Les lettres américains devant la critique française, 1887–1917* (Paris, 1951); Pierre Jourda, *L'exotisme dans la littérature française depuis Chateaubriand* (2 vols.; Paris, 1956), II, 159–184; Durand Echevarria, *Mirage in the*

West: *A History of the French Image of America to 1815* (Princeton, 1957); and Eckart G. Franz, *Das Amerikabild der deutschen Revolution von 1848/49* (Heidelberg, 1958).

17 Raphaël Georges Levy, "La fortune mobilière de France à l'étranger," *Revue des deux mondes,* CXL (March 15, 1897), 415–445; Bülow to Eulenburg, Sept. 29, 1897, *Grosse Politik,* XV, No. 4118; Arthur J. May, *The Hapsburg Monarchy* (Cambridge, Mass., 1951), 240–246, 371.

18 Lenau, quoted in Price, *Reception of English Literature in Germany,* 430. (The phrase is "himmelanstinkende Krämerseelen"); "Theodore Laer" (Ladenburger), *Forty Years . . . ; The Evolution of a German Immigrant into an American Citizen* (New York, 1936), 120.

19 V. I. Gurko, *Features and Figures of the Past* (English translation; Stanford, 1939), 89; Pupin, *From Immigrant to Inventor,* 189.

CHAPTER XV • THE POWERS AND SPAIN

1 Marginal comments on Radowitz's reports of Sept. 21, 28, 1897, Vagts, II, 1278. On the Kaiser see especially Erich Eyck, *Das persönliche Regiment Wilhelms II* (Zürich, 1948), and Joachim von Kürenberg, *The Kaiser* (English translation: London, 1954).

2 *Memoirs of Prince von Bülow* (English translation: 4 vols.; Boston, 1931–1935), I, 161, 170; Johannes Haller, *Philip Eulenburg: The Kaiser's Friend* (English translation: 2 vols.; New York, 1930), II, 36; Bülow to the Kaiser, Sept. 28, 1897, Vagts, II, 1279.

3 *Grosse Politik,* XV, Nos. 4119, 4120, 4121, 4123, 4125; Vagts, II, 1279; Ferrara, *The Last Spanish War,* 95.

4 *I Documenti Diplomatici Italiani: Terza Serie,* I, No. 97; *Grosse Politik,* XV, Nos. 4122, 4124; Arthur J. May, *The Hapsburg Monarchy,* 304; Goluchowski's speech in Tower to Sherman, Nov. 22, 1897, *Austria: Dispatches,* XLIII (U.S.). See also May, 235–255; and Alois, Freiherr von Czedik, *Zur Geschichte der k. u. k. österreichischen Ministerien, 1861–1916* (3 vols.; Vienna, 1917), II, 98–101; Reverseaux to Hanotaux, Dec. 23, 24, 1897, March 2, 18, 27, 1898, *Espagne: Cuba,* III , V (Fr.); Goluchowski to Deym, March 13, 1898, Szögeny to Goluchowski, March 14, 1898, *Spanien,* LXVIII (Aus.); Eulenburg to Ausw. Amt, March 16, 1898, Vagts, II, 1288.

5 Mandas to Tetuán, May 19, Aug. 19, 1896, Legajo 2416 (Sp.); Reverseaux to Hanotaux, March 6, 1896, Hanotaux to Reverseaux and Montebello, July 24, 1896, *Espagne: Cuba,* III (Fr.); Ferrara, *Last Spanish War,* 69–70.

6 Hanotaux to Reverseaux, Feb. 3, 1897, marginal notes by Hanotaux on Patenôtre to Hanotaux, May 23, 1897, Reverseaux to Hanotaux, July 24,

1897, *Espagne: Cuba,* III (Fr.); *Journal des Débats,* April 15, Aug. 3, 1897. On Hanotaux see Louis Gillet, *Gabriel Hanotaux* (Paris, 1933).

7 Memorandum of Oct. 8, 1897, Hanotaux to Montebello, Oct. 21, 1897, to Reverseaux, Oct. 26, 1897, memorandum by Hanotaux, Oct. 28, 1897, Montebello to Hanotaux, Nov. 11, 1897, Reverseaux to Hanotaux, Dec. 6. 1897, memorandum by Hanotaux, Jan. 26, 1898, *Espagne: Cuba,* IV (Fr.).

8 Louis M. Sears, "French Opinion of the Spanish-American War," *Hispanic American Historical Review,* VII (July, 1927), 25 ff.; *Journal des Débats,* Feb. 19, 1898; *Le Temps,* Feb. 20, 1898; Liechtenstein to Goluchowski, April 20, 1898, *Spanien,* LXIX (Aus.); Hanotaux to Cambon, Feb. 12, 1898, to ambassadors in St. Petersburg, Berlin, Madrid, and London, March 12, 1898, to Patenôtre, Feb. 18, 1898, to Reverseaux, March 15, 1898, memorandum by Hanotaux on a conversation with León y Castillo, March 15, 1898, *Espagne: Cuba,* IV (Fr.); León y Castillo to Gullón, March 15, 1898, Legajo 2417 (Sp.).

9 Geoffray to Hanotaux, March 16, 1898, Hanotaux to Vauvineux, March 26, 1898, *Espagne: Cuba,* V (Fr.); Wolkenstein to Goluchowski, March 19, 1898 (reporting a conversation with Count Münster), *Spanien,* LXVIII (Aus.); León y Castillo to Gullón, March 26, 1898, Legajo 2416 (Sp.).

10 Hanotaux to Cambon, March 29, 1898, *Espagne: Cuba,* V (Fr.).

11 "Iz dnevnika A. A. Polovsteva," *Krasnyi Arkhiv,* XLVI (1931), 120 ff.; Yurii Solov'ev, *25 let moei diplomaticheskoi sluzhby, 1893–1918* (Moscow, 1928), 92–93; see also Eugene de Schelking's untrustworthy *Recollections of a Russian Diplomat* (New York, 1918), 161.

12 Moscow *Vedomosti,* quoted in Madrid *Liberal,* July 2, 1896; Casa Valencia to Tetuán, July 30, 1896, Legajo 2416 (Sp.); Montebello to Hanotaux, Nov. 11, 1897, Vauvineux to Hanotaux, Jan. 5, 1898, *Espagne: Cuba,* IV (Fr.).

13 E. H. Zabriskie, *American-Russian Rivalry in the Far East* (Philadelphia, 1946), 125–142. See also Andrew Malozemoff, *Russian Far Eastern Policy, 1881–1904* (Berkeley, 1958), 69–123.

14 Liechtenstein to Goluchowski, March 28, 1898, *Spanien,* LXVIII (Aus.); Schevich to Muraviev, May 16, 1898, *Krasnyi Arkhiv,* LX (1933), 9–10; Vauvineux to Hanotaux, April 2, 1898, *Espagne: Cuba,* V (Fr.). On the Far Eastern issue at this time, see Langer, *Diplomacy of Imperialism,* 445–536.

15 Caetani to Nigra, May 1, 1896, *Documenti Diplomatici Italiani: Terza Serie,* I, No. 91; Benomar to Tetuán, Aug. 16, 1896, Legajo 2416 (Sp.); Pasetti to Goluchowski, *Spanien,* LXVIII (Aus.). See Francesco Cataluccio, *La politica estera di E. Visconti Venosta* (Florence, 1940), 85–88.

16 Wolff to Salisbury, June 20, July 28, 1896, Salisbury to Wolff, June 24, 1896, Salisbury Papers; Dubsky to Goluchowski, Oct. 21, 1897, Deym to Goluchowski, March 28, 1898, *Spanien,* LXVIII (Aus.); Wolff to Salisbury, Nov. 9, 1897 (two dispatches), F.O. 72/2057 (Br.); Salisbury to Wolff, Oct. 19, 1897, F.O. 72/2036 (Br.).

17 Geoffray to Hanotaux, March 28, 29, 1898, *Espagne: Cuba*, V (Fr.); Rascon to Gullón, March 23, 1898, Legajo 2417 (Sp.); Deym to Goluchowski, March 30, 1898, *Spanien*, LXVIII (Aus.).

18 *Letters of Queen Victoria: Third Series*, III, 240; Victoria to Salisbury, April 1, 1898, Salisbury Papers.

19 *Grosse Politik*, XV, Nos. 4125, 4128; Szögeny to Goluchowski, April 9, 1898, *Spanien*, LXVIII (Aus.).

20 Deym to Goluchowski, April 4, 1898, *ibid.;* Balfour to Pauncefote, April 4, 1898, F.O. 5/2364 (Br.).

21 Hoyos to Gullón, April 13, 1898, Legajo 2417 (Sp.); Reverseaux to Hanotaux, April 14, 1898, *Espagne: Cuba*, VII (Fr.); Vauvineux to Hanotaux, April 14, 1898, *ibid.; Journal des Débats*, April 15, 1898.

22 Dubsky to Goluchowski, April 9, 1898 (two dispatches), *Spanien*, LXVIII (Aus.); Patenôtre to Hanotaux, April 10, 1898, *Espagne: Cuba*, VI (Fr.).

23 Hengelmüller to Goluchowski, April 11, 14, 1898, *Spanien*, LXIX (Aus.); Cambon to Hanotaux, April 11, 15, 1898, *Espagne: Cuba*, VII (Fr.); Pauncefote to Salisbury, April 11, 12, 14, 1898, F.O. 5/2517 (Br.); Sanderson to Pauncefote, April 11, 1898, F.O. 5/2364 (Br.); see Vagts, II, 1397–1410, Ferrara, *The Last Spanish War*, 139–150, and R. G. Neale, "British-American Relations during the Spanish-American War: Some Problems," *Historical Studies—Australia-New Zealand*, VI (Jan., 1953), 1–17.

24 Goluchowski to Hengelmüller, April 16, 1898, Liechtenstein to Goluchowski, April 16, 1898, *Spanien*, LXIX (Aus.); Barrère to Hanotaux, April 16, 1898, memorandum by Hanotaux, April 17, 1898, *Espagne: Cuba*, VII (Fr.); Radolin to Bülow, April 16, 1898, Vagts, II, 1304.

25 Victoria to Salisbury, April 22, 1898, Salisbury Papers; Geoffray to Hanotaux, April 12, 1898, *Espagne: Cuba*, VII (Fr.); Vagts, II, 1305; Dugdale, *Balfour*, I, 192–193; Deym to Goluchowski, April 15, 1898, *Spanien*, LXIX (Aus.).

26 *Grosse Politik*, XV, No. 4140; Vagts, II, 1305; Szögeny to Goluchowski, April 19, 1898, *Spanien*, LXIX (Aus.).

CHAPTER XVI • CHALLENGE OR OPPORTUNITY?

1 Wilfrid Scawen Blunt, *My Diaries . . . 1888–1914* (2 vols.; London, 1919), I, 358; London *Times*, May 12, 1898; *Blackwood's*, CLXIII (May, 1898), 702–703, (June, 1898), 861–862; *National Review*, CLI (July, 1898), 635–637; *Westminster Review*, CL (Aug., 1898), 171–173.

2 Hay to Day, May 4, 1898, *Britain: Dispatches*, CXCII (U.S.); W. M. Osborne to McKinley, May 17, 1898, McKinley Papers.

3 *Letters of Queen Victoria: Third Series*, III, 244.

4 Geoffray to Delcassé, July 13, 1898, *Espagne: Cuba*, XI (Fr.); *Grosse Politik*, XIV, No. 3801, XV, No. 4166; Almodovar to Rascón, June 10,

1898, Rascón to Almodovar, June 12, 1898, Legajo 2423 (Sp.); Victoria to Salisbury, May 6, 1898, Salisbury Papers; Hay to Day, May 8, 9, 10, June 15, 1898, *Britain: Dispatches*, CXCII (U.S.); Salisbury to Pauncefote, May 10, 1898, F.O. 5/2364 (Br.); Deym to Goluchowski, May 12, 1898, *Spanien*, LXX (Aus.); Hay to Day, June 5, 1898, McKinley Papers; Wolff to Salisbury, Aug. 23, 1898, F.O. 72/2067 (Br.); Salisbury to Victoria, Sept. 13, 1898, Salisbury Papers.

5 Isaac Don Levine, *The Kaiser's Letters to the Tsar* (London, n.d.), 50–55; *Grosse Politik*, XIV, Nos. 3530, 3808, 3823, 3839, XV, 4151, 4160, 4161, 4162, 4165, 4232; Vagts, II, 1323, 1350, 1363; Bülow, *Memoirs*, I, 256; Mendez Vigo to Almodovar, June 24, 1898, Legajo 2423 (Sp.).

6 *Questions diplomatiques et coloniales*, IV (May 15, 1898), 106–109; memorandum by Hanotaux, April 20, 1898, *Espagne: Cuba*, VII (Fr.); Cambon to Hanotaux, May 13, 1898, *ibid.*, IX; Wolkenstein to Goluchowski, May 14, 1898, *Spanien*, LXX (Aus.); memorandum by Commercial Affairs Division [May, 1898?], *Espagne: Philippines*, III (Fr.); Hanotaux to Montebello, Aug. 12, 1898, *ibid.*, IV; Cambon to Hanotaux, May 20, 1898, *Espagne: Cuba*, X (Fr.); Cambon to Hanotaux, June 24, 1898, *Espagne: Philippines*, IV (Fr.).

7 Porter to Day, May 4, May 24, June 7, July 21, 1898, *France: Dispatches*, CXVI (U.S.); Hanotaux to Patenôtre, May 13, 1898, to Cambon, June 9, 1898, memorandum by Hanotaux, June 9, 1898, *Espagne: Cuba*, IX (Fr.); Wolkenstein to Goluchowski, June 11, 1898, *Spanien*, LXX (Aus.); memorandum by Delcassé, July 19, 1898, *Espagne: Cuba*, XII (Fr.); see *Foreign Relations, 1898*, 785–786, 819–830.

8 Geoffray to Hanotaux, with marginal notes by Hanotaux, May 14, 1898, memorandum by Hanotaux, May 18, 1898, *Grande Bretagne* (*politique extérieure*): *dossier général, 1897–1898* (Fr.); Charpentier to Hanotaux, May 6, 1898, *Espagne: Cuba*, IX (Fr.); Wolkenstein to Goluchowski, June 3, 1898, *Spanien*, LXX (Aus.); *Questions diplomatiques et coloniales*, V (Dec. 15, 1898), 474.

9 Zabriskie, *American-Russian Rivalry*, 198–199, 200–205; Liechtenstein to Goluchowski, April 16, 1898, *Spanien*, LXIX (Aus.), Montebello to Hanotaux, May 11, 1898, *Espagne: Cuba*, IX (Fr.); Peter von Meyendorff, *Correspondance diplomatique de M. de Staal* (2 vols.; Paris, 1929), II, 384; Reverseaux to Hanotaux, June 1, 1898 (reporting attitude of Count Kapnist), *Espagne: Cuba*, XI (Fr.); Osten Sacken to Muraviev, June 10, 1898, *Krasnyi Arkhiv*, LVI (1933), 68; Schevich to Muraviev, June 12, 1898, *ibid.*, LX (1933), 17; Kuropatkin diary, Sept. 23, 1898, *ibid.*, LIV (1932), 59; Vauvineux to Delcassé, Nov. 11, 1898 (reporting Lamsdorff's view), *Espagne: Philippines*, VI (Fr.); Hayashi to Okuma, Aug. 10, 1898, M.T. 470 (Jap.).

10 L. Teleshev, "K istorii pervoi Gaagskoi konferentsii 1899 g.," *Krasnyi Arkhiv*, L–LI (1932), 64–96, and "Novye materialy o Gaagskoi mirnoi konferentsii 1899 g.," *ibid.*, LIV–LV (1932), 49–79 (Muraviev's memo-

randum is in the former, pp. 73–77); *Grosse Politik*, XIV, No. 3530, XV, No. 4232; memorandum by Muraviev, Oct. 30, 1898, *Krasnyi Arkhiv*, LIV–LV (1932), 67–79.

11 *Ibid.*, LVI (1933), 67–68; *Grosse Politik*, XIII, No. 3529; see James K. Eyre, Jr., "Russia and the American Annexation of the Philippines," *Mississippi Valley Historical Review*, XXVIII (March, 1942), 539–562.

12 Kobe *Weekly Chronicle*, July 9, 1898. See Shigenoba Okuma (ed.), *Fifty Years of New Japan* (2 vols.; London, 1909), I, 133–193.

13 Kobe *Weekly Chronicle*, May 14, July 9, 1898; see Kenzi Hamade, *Prince Ito* (Tokyo, 1936); Okuma to Kato, July 27, 1898, M.T. 470 (Jap.); Okuma to Ueno Risaburo, Aug. 2, 1898, *ibid.*; Okuma to Nakagawa, Sept. 1, 9, 1898, M.T. 471 (Jap.); Aoki to Hayashi *et al.*, Nov. 24, 1898, *ibid.*; see James K. Eyre, Jr., "Japan and the American Annexation of the Philippines," *Pacific Historical Review*, XI (March, 1942), 55–71.

CHAPTER XVII • AMERICA'S IMPERIALISM

1 Dana to Wilson, June 3, 1898, J. H. Wilson Papers; see Pratt, *Expansionists of 1898*, 317–326.

2 Olcott, *McKinley*, I, 379; William A. Robinson, *Thomas B. Reed: Parliamentarian* (New York, 1930), 363–365.

3 Kohlsaat, *From McKinley to Harding* (2 vols.; New York, 1923), I, 68; *Letters of Theodore Roosevelt*, I, 685–686; Long, *New American Navy*, I, 182; U. S. Navy Department, Appendix to the Report of the Chief of the Bureau of Navigation for 1898: *The Spanish-American War*, 67; Dawes, *Journal of the McKinley Years*, 157.

4 Lodge to Henry White, White Papers; see *Literary Digest*, XVI (May 14, 1898), 571–573, (May 28, 1898), 636.

5 Kohlsatt, *From McKinley to Harding*, I, 68; Alger, *The Spanish-American War* (New York, 1901), 326; U.S. War Department, *Correspondence relating to the War with Spain* (2 vols.; Washington, D.C., 1902), II, 635; Straus to McKinley, May 12, 1898, McKinley Papers; Chandler to Dana, May 8, 1898, Chandler Papers.

6 Boston *Herald*, May 5, 1898; New York *Evening Post*, May 8, 1898; Cambon to Hanotaux, May 4, 1898, *Espagne: Philippines*, III (Fr.).

7 Day to Hay, June 3, 1898, *Great Britain: Dispatches*, CXCII (U.S.).

8 Hay to Day, June 5, 1898, McKinley Papers; Day to Hay, June 7, 1898, Private Papers of John Hay, Library of Congress.

9 Day to Hay, June 14, 1898, *Great Britain: Instructions*, XXXII (U.S.); 55 Cong., 3 sess., *Senate Document No. 62*, part III: "Correspondence of the Department of the State with Consuls in the Orient," 341 ff. See Garel E. Grunder and William E. Livesey, *The Philippines and the United States* (Norman, Oklahoma, 1951), 18 ff., and Emilio Aguinaldo and

Vicente Albano Pacis, *A Second Look at America* (New York, 1957), chapters 3–6.

10 Laffan to Lodge, July 13, 1898, Lodge Papers; Lodge to Chandler, July 23, 1898, Chandler Papers.

11 Olcott, *McKinley*, II, 61–75; Leech, *In the Days of McKinley*, 278–291; William R. Braisted, *The United States Navy in the Pacific* (Austin, Tex., 1959), 52–53; Mahan to Chandler, July 5, 1898, Chandler Papers. On Alger see J. A. Porter to Alger, Aug. 5, 1898, McKinley Papers; and Nakagawa to Okuma, July 30, 1898, M.T. 471 (Jap.).

12 Fuller to McKinley, Aug. 19, 1898, McKinley Papers; Chandler to McKinley, Aug. 17, 1898, *ibid.;* Straus diary, Aug. 26, 1898, Straus Papers; Hengelmüller to Goluchowski, Aug. 24, 1898, *Spanien,* LXX (Aus.).

13 *Foreign Relations, 1898,* 904–914, 927–928, 932.

14 McKinley to Hay, Oct. 26, 1898, McKinley Papers; draft instructions to commissioners [Oct. 25, 1898?], *ibid.;* Hay to McKinley, Oct. 27, 1898, *ibid.; Foreign Relations, 1898,* 935.

15 Olcott, *McKinley*, II, 110–111.

16 McKinley Papers.

17 Lodge to White, Sept. 23, 1898, White Papers; War Department, *Correspondence,* II, 718 ff.; Isaac M. Elliott, "Manila and the Philippines," *Scribner's,* XXIV (July, 1898), 12–22; *Religious Review of Reviews,* III (Aug., 1898), 469–470.

18 Hay to Day, July 14, 1898, *Great Britain: Dispatches,* CXCII (U.S.); Hay to Day, July 28, 1898, McKinley Papers; Buck to Day, July 6, Aug. 13, 1898, *Japan: Dispatches,* LXXI (U.S.); Nakagawa to Okuma, July 30, 1898, M.T. 471 (Jap.).

19 Okuma to Nakagawa, Sept. 1, 1898, *ibid.;* Leech, *In the Days of McKinley,* 328.

20 Cambon to Delcassé, Aug. 1, 1898, *Espagne: Cuba,* XIII (Fr.); Straus diary, Aug. 9, 1898, Straus Papers.

21 Arthur Judson Brown, *One Hundred Years: A History of the Foreign Mission Work of the Presbyterian Church of the U.S.A.* (New York, 1936), 861–863; *Baptist Union,* VIII (July 30, 1898), 553; Boston *Herald,* Sept. 30, 1898; see Fred H. Harrington, "The Anti-Imperialist Movement in the United States, 1898–1900," *Mississippi Valley Historical Review,* XXII (April, 1935), 211–230.

22 Rhodes to McKinley, Sept. 28, 1898, McKinley Papers; see Pratt, *Expansionists of 1898,* chapter 7.

23 See *Speeches and Addresses of William McKinley* (New York, 1900), 84–155.

24 Jacob G. Schurman, *Philippine Affairs* (New York, 1904), 1–3.

25 Coolidge, *Platt,* 287–288.

26 Bryan to Carnegie, Jan. 13, 30, 1899, Private Papers of Andrew Carnegie, Library of Congress; see Paolo E. Coletta, "Bryan, McKinley, and the Treaty of Paris," *Pacific Historical Review,* XXVI (May, 1957), 131–146.

27 Hoar to Storey, Jan. 10, 1899, Private Papers of Moorfield Storey, Library
   of Congress; Carnegie to Bryan, Jan. 10, 1899, Carnegie Papers; Mason to
   Carnegie, Feb. 8, 1899, *ibid.;* A. P. Gorman to Carnegie, Feb. 9, 1899,
   ibid.; John C. Cowen to McKinley, Jan. 25, 1899, McKinley Papers;
   Hanna to McKinley, Feb. 7, 1899, *ibid.;* C. K. Davis to McKinley, Feb. 9,
   1899, *ibid.*
28 Chandler to Dana, March 29, 1898, Chandler Papers.

CHAPTER XVIII • THE SEVENTH POWER

1 Octave Noël, "Péril américain," *Le Correspondant,* CXCIV (March 25,
   1899), 1083–1104, CXCV (April 10, 1899), 116–144; Ugo Ojetti, *L'Amer-
   ica vittoriosa* (Milan, 1899); *Russkoe Bogatstvo* (Nov., 1900), 151–154;
   Max Goldberger, *Das Land der unbegrenzten Möglichkeiten* (Berlin, 1903);
   Wilhelm Polenz, *Das Land der Zukunft* (Berlin, 1903); Otto, Graf Moltke,
   Nord-Amerika: Beiträge zum Verständnis seiner Wirtschaft und Politik
   (Berlin, 1903)..
2 Louis Paul, "L'impérialisme Anglo-Saxon," *Revue socialiste,* XXIX
   (March, 1899), 257–274; *Novoe Vremya* quoted in *Literary Digest,*
   XVIII (March 11, 1899), 289.
3 On reactions to Chamberlain's speech, see *Questions diplomatiques et
   coloniales,* VIII (Dec. 15, 1899), 504–505; *Grosse Politik,* XIII, No. 3566,
   XIV, Nos. 3778, 3941, 4035; *Documents diplomatiques français, première
   série,* XIV, Nos. 528, 578. See also A. Dobrov, *Dal'nevostochnaya politika
   S.Sh.A. v period russko-yaponskoi voiny* (Moscow, 1952), 237; and my commentary on Dobrov in the *American Historical Review,* LXII (Jan., 1957),
   345–351; *Das Echo,* XVIII (April 13, 1899), 566; *North American Review,*
   CLXIX (July, 1899), 6–7.
4 *Fortnightly Review,* LXXII (Sept., 1899), 545; Marc Debrit quoted in
   Public Opinion, XXIX (Nov. 15, 1900), 619; *Kladderadatsch,* LI (Feb. 5,
   1899).
5 *Ibid.,* LII (Aug. 5, 1900); others in *Questions diplomatiques et coloniales,*
   XXXIV (Aug. 1, 1900), 340, (Aug. 15, 1900), 450–451, (Sept. 15, 1900),
   674–675.

ACKNOWLEDGMENTS

My debts are, first of all, to three institutions: the John Simon Guggenheim Foundation for a fellowship in 1958–1959, the Social Science Research Council for a Faculty Research Fellowship through 1959–1961, and Harvard University for allowing me the time to make use of these grants.

Then, like any scholar, I have mountainous obligations to libraries, librarians, archivists, and keepers of collections, specifically in the Archives du ministère des affaires étrangères in Paris, the Archivo del ministerio de asuntos exteriores in Madrid, the Haus- Hof- und Staatsarchiv in Vienna, the Public Record Office in London, and the National Archives in Washington; the Christ Church Library at Oxford, the Houghton Library at Harvard, the Illinois State Historical Society, the Manuscripts Division of the Library of Congress, and the Massachusetts Historical Society; the Biblioteca Nacional in Madrid, the Bibliothèque Nationale in Paris, the Staats-Bibliothek in Vienna, the British Museum, the Library of Congress, and the New York Public Library. Partly because the Harvard College Library has been home base but partly too because of its almost unrivaled richness in modern historical materials, I am especially indebted to it and its staff.

For permission to use certain manuscript materials I wish to express thanks to Mr. George Cabot Lodge, Mr. George White, and the Marquis of Salisbury.

From certain authors I have obtained a great deal more than footnote acknowledgments can indicate. Julius W. Pratt's *Expansionists of 1898* is an irreplaceable study of the imperialist movement in America. Dexter Perkins's *Monroe Doctrine, 1867–1907* contains an account of the Venezuelan boundary crisis which mine supplements but by no means supplants. William L. Langer's *Diplomacy of Imperialism* was my guide through the tangle of intra-European relations, as were Herminio Portell Vilá's *Historia de Cuba* and Melchor Fernández Almagro's *Cánovas* and *Historia política de la España contemporanea* in the mazes of Cuban and Spanish politics. Paul Lazarsfeld's studies in public opinion, especially *Personal Influence,* which he wrote with Elihu Katz, were enormously valuable in helping me to understand what I was finding.

Frank Freidel, Oscar Handlin, William L. Langer, and Juan Marichal made suggestions or read portions of the manuscript. I am grateful to all of them, to Ann Allison, Anne Hoover, and Eve Altmann for their efforts to create neat typescript for me, and to John and LaRee Caughey and my wife, Nancy, for so many things that I can't begin to number them.

E. R. M.

Lexington, Massachusetts